World Economic Situation and Prospects 2013

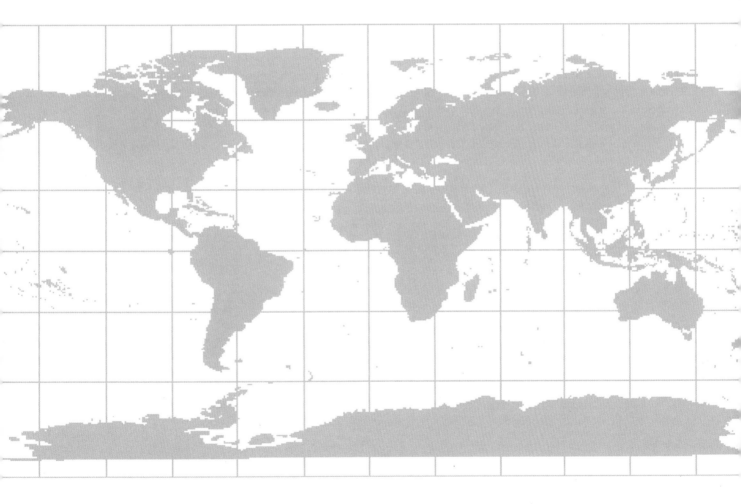

United Nations
New York, 2013

...product of the United Nations Department of Economic and Social Affairs (UN/DESA), the ...nference on Trade and Development (UNCTAD) and the five United Nations regional commis-...c Commission for Africa (ECA), Economic Commission for Europe (ECE), Economic Commission for ...rica and the Caribbean (ECLAC), Economic and Social Commission for Asia and the Pacific (ESCAP) and ...omic and Social Commission for Western Asia (ESCWA)).

For the preparation of the global outlook, inputs were received from the national centres of Project LINK and from the participants at the annual LINK meeting held in New York from 22 to 24 October 2012. The cooperation and support received through Project LINK are gratefully acknowledged.

The United Nations World Tourism Organization (UNWTO) contributed to the section on international tourism.

The report has been prepared by a team coordinated by Rob Vos and comprising staff from all collaborating agencies, including Grigor Agabekian, Abdallah Al Dardari, Clive Altshuler, Shuvojit Banerjee, Sudip Ranjan Basu, Hassiba Benamara, Alfredo Calcagno, Jeronim Capaldo, Jaromir Cekota, Ann D'Lima, Cameron Daneshvar, Adam Elhiraika, Pilar Fajarnes, Heiner Flassbeck, Juan Alberto Fuentes, Marco Fugazza, Masataka Fujita, Samuel Gayi, Andrea Goldstein, Cordelia Gow, Aynul Hasan, Jan Hoffmann, Pingfan Hong, Michel Julian, Alex Izurieta, Felipe Jimenez, Cornelia Kaldewei, Matthias Kempf, John Kester, Pierre Kohler, Nagesh Kumar, Alexandra Laurent, Hung-Yi Li, Muhammad Hussain Malik, Sandra Manuelito, Joerg Mayer, Nicolas Maystre, Elvis Mtonga, Alessandro Nicita, Victor Ognivtsev, Oliver Paddison, José Palacin, Mariangela Parra-Lancourt, Ingo Pitterle, Daniel Platz, Li Qiang, Kazi Rahman, Benu Schneider, Krishnan Sharma, Robert Shelburne, Vatcharin Sirimaneetham, Samiti Siv, Shari Spiegel, Astrit Sulstarova, Amos Taporaie, Aimable Uwizeye-Mapendano, Sebastian Vergara, John Winkel, Yasuhisa Yamamoto, Frida Youssef and Yan Zhang. Katherine McHenry provided administrative assistance.

Shamshad Akhtar, Assistant Secretary-General for Economic Development at UN/DESA, provided comments and guidance.

For further information, see http://www.un.org/en/development/desa/policy/wesp/index.shtml, or contact:

DESA:

Mr. Wu Hongbo, Under-Secretary-General, Department of Economic and Social Affairs; Room S-2922, United Nations, New York, NY 10017, USA; telephone: +1-212-9635958; email: wuh@un.org

UNCTAD:

Dr. Supachai Panitchpakdi, Secretary-General, United Nations Conference on Trade and Development; Room E-9042, Palais de Nations, 1211, Geneva 10, Switzerland; telephone +41-22-9175806; email: sgo@unctad.org

ECA:

Dr. Carlos Lopes, Executive Secretary, United Nations Economic Commission for Africa; P.O. Box 3005, Addis Ababa, Ethiopia; telephone: +251-11-5511231; email: ecainfo@uneca.org

ECE:

Mr. Sven Alkalaj, Executive Secretary, United Nations Economic Commission for Europe; Palais des Nations, CH-1211, Geneva 10, Switzerland; telephone: +41-22-9174444; email: info.ece@unece.org

ECLAC:

Ms. Alicia Bárcena, Executive Secretary, Economic Commission for Latin America and the Caribbean; Av. Dag Hammarskjöld 3477, Vitacura, Santiago, Chile; telephone: +56-2-2102000; email: secepal@cepal.org

ESCAP:

Ms. Noeleen Heyzer, Executive Secretary, Economic and Social Commission for Asia and the Pacific, United Nations Building, Rajadamnern Nok Avenue, Bangkok 10200, Thailand; telephone: +66-2-2881234; email: unescap@unescap.org

ESCWA:

Ms. Rima Khalaf, Executive Secretary, Economic and Social Commission for Western Asia, P.O. Box 11-8575, Riad el-Solh Square, Beirut, Lebanon; telephone: +961-1-978800; email at: http://www.escwa.un.org/main/contact.asp

Executive Summary

Prospects for global economic growth and sustainable development

The world economy is on the brink of another major downturn

As foreseen in last year's issue of this report, the world economy weakened considerably in 2012. A growing number of developed economies, especially in Europe, have already fallen into a double-dip recession, while those facing sovereign debt distress moved even deeper into recession. Many developed economies are caught in downward spiralling dynamics from high unemployment, weak aggregate demand compounded by fiscal austerity, high public debt burdens, and financial fragility.

The economic woes of the developed countries are spilling over to developing countries and economies in transition through weaker demand for their exports and heightened volatility in capital flows and commodity prices. The larger developing economies also face home-grown problems, however, with some (including China) facing much weakened investment demand because of financing constraints in some sectors of the economy and excess production capacity elsewhere. Most low-income countries have held up relatively well so far, but are now also facing intensified adverse spillover effects from the slowdown in both developed and major middle-income countries. The prospects for the next two years continue to be challenging, fraught with major uncertainties and risks slanted towards the downside.

Growth of world gross product (WGP) is expected to reach 2.2 per cent in 2012 and is forecast to remain well below potential at 2.4 per cent in 2013 and 3.2 per cent in 2014 (figure O.1). At this moderate pace, many economies will be unable to recover the severe job losses of the Great Recession.

Figure O.1
Weakening and highly uncertain outlook for the world economy

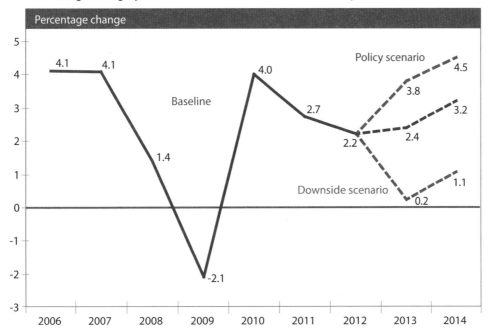

Source: UN/DESA.

a Growth rate for 2012 is partially estimated. Estimates for 2013 and 2014 are forecasts. See "Uncertainties and risks" section for a discussion of the downside scenario and box I.3 for a discussion of the policy scenario.

The global jobs crisis continues

Global unemployment remains very high, particularly among developed economies, with the situation in Europe being the most challenging. The unemployment rate continued to climb, reaching a record high of nearly 12 per cent in the euro area during 2012, an increase of more than one percentage point from one year ago. Conditions are worse in Greece and Spain where more than a quarter of the working population is without a job. Only a few economies in the region, such as Austria, Germany, Luxembourg and the Netherlands, register low unemployment rates of about 5 per cent. Unemployment rates in Central and Eastern Europe edged up slightly in 2012, partly resulting from fiscal austerity. Japan's unemployment rate retreated to below 5 per cent. In the United States, the unemployment rate stayed above 8 per cent for the most part of 2012, but dropped to just below that level from September onwards.

At the same time, long-term unemployment (over one year) in developed economies stood at more than 35 per cent by July 2012, affecting about 17 million workers. Such a prolonged duration of unemployment tends to have significant, long-lasting detrimental impacts on both the individuals who have lost their jobs and on the economy as a whole.

In the outlook, greater and more sustainable job creation should be a key policy priority in developed economies. If economic growth stays as anaemic in developed countries as projected in the baseline forecast, employment rates will not return to pre-crisis levels until far beyond 2016 (figure O.2).

Figure O.2
Jobs crisis continues in Europe and the United States and recovery will be protracted

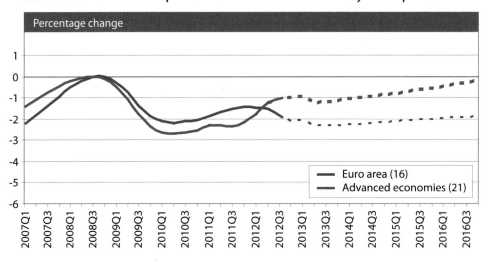

Source: UN/DESA, based on data from ILO and IMF.
Note: The chart shows percentage changes of total employment (as a moving average) with respect to pre-recession peaks. Projections (dashed lines) are based on estimates of the output elasticity of employment (Okun's law), following a similar methodology to that of ILO, *World of Work Report 2011* (Geneva).

The employment situation varies significantly across developing countries. Unemployment rates in most economies in East Asia and Latin America have already retreated to, or dropped below, levels seen prior to the global financial crisis. The growth moderation in late 2011 and 2012 has so far not led to a discernable rise in the unemployment rate in these two regions—a positive sign, with the caveat that a rise in the unemployment rate would usually lag in an economic downturn. If the growth slowdown continues, the unemployment rate could increase significantly. In Africa, despite relatively strong GDP growth, the employment situation remains a major problem across the region, both in terms of the level of employment and the quality of jobs that are generated. The latter remains a common challenge for developing countries. The shares of working poor remain high and most workers tend to be employed in vulnerable jobs in still expanding informal sectors. Furthermore, youth unemployment and gender disparities in employment remain key social and economic concerns in many developing countries.

Poverty reduction and progress towards other MDGs may slow

The global slowdown and increased risks to the employment situation in developing countries will imply a much slower pace of poverty reduction and a narrowing of fiscal space for investments in education, health, basic sanitation and other critical areas needed for accelerating the progress towards achieving the Millennium Development Goals (MDGs). This holds true in particular for the least developed countries (LDCs); they remain highly vulnerable to commodity price shocks and are receiving less external financing as official development assistance (ODA) declines in the face of greater fiscal austerity in donor countries.

Global trends in greenhouse gas emissions remain alarming

Helped by weaker global economic growth, greenhouse gases (GHGs) emitted by the Annex I countries to the Kyoto Protocol are estimated to have fallen by about 2 per cent per year during 2011-2012. This reverses the 3 per cent increase in GHG emissions by these countries in 2010. Emissions fell by 6 per cent in 2009 with the fallout in gross domestic product (GDP) growth caused by the Great Recession. With the more recent decline, GHG emission reductions are back on the long-run downward trend. Given the further moderation in global economic growth, emissions by Annex I countries are expected to decline further during 2013-2014. As a group, Annex I countries have already achieved the target of the Kyoto Protocol to reduce emissions by at least 5 per cent from 1990 levels during the 2008-2012 commitment period.

At the same time, however, GHG emissions in many developing countries are increasing at a rapid pace, and, in all, the world is far from being on track to reduce emissions to the extent considered necessary for keeping carbon dioxide (CO_2) equivalent concentrations to less than 450 parts per million (consistent with the target of stabilizing global warming at a temperature increase of 2°C or less as compared to pre-industrial levels). To avoid exceeding this limit, GHG emissions would need to drop by 80 per cent by mid-century. At current trends and even with the extension of the Kyoto Protocol, this is an unachievable target. "Greener" growth pathways need to be created now. Despite their large investment costs, they would also provide opportunities for more robust short-term recovery and global rebalancing.

Inflation remains subdued in most developed economies....

Inflation rates remain subdued in most developed economies. Continuing large output gaps and downward pressure on wages in many countries are keeping inflationary expectations low. Inflation in the United States moderated over 2012, down to about 2.0 per cent from 3.1 per cent in 2011. A further moderation in headline inflation is expected in the outlook for 2013. In the euro area, headline inflation continues to be above the central banks' target of 2 per cent. Core inflation, which does not include price changes in volatile items such as energy, food, alcohol and tobacco, has been much lower, at about

1.5 per cent, with no evidence of upward pressures. In the outlook, inflation is expected to drift down slowly. Inflation in the new EU members is also expected to lessen. Deflation continues to prevail in Japan, although the central bank has raised its inflation target to boost inflation expectations.

..and is receding in most but not all developing countries

Inflation receded in a majority of developing countries during 2012, but remains stubbornly high in some. In the outlook, anticipated increases in world food prices provoked by droughts in various producer regions, persistently high oil prices and some country-specific supply-side constraints may continue to put some pressures on inflation in developing countries in 2013 and into 2014. In Africa, while inflation moderated in many economies, the rate of inflation is still above 10 per cent in Angola, Nigeria, and elsewhere. Inflation is expected to remain subdued in most of East Asia, but is still a concern for most countries in South Asia, where inflation rates were over 11 per cent in 2012, on average, and are forecast to remain above or near 10 per cent in 2013 and 2014. Inflation remains low in most economies in West Asia, although it is still high (above 10 per cent) in Yemen and very high (30 per cent) in the Syrian Arab Republic. The inflation rate in Latin America and the Caribbean is expected to stay at about 6 per cent.

International trade and commodity prices

The expansion of world merchandise trade is decelerating sharply

Growth of world trade decelerated sharply for the second year in a row, dropping from 12.6 per cent in 2010 to 6.4 per cent in 2011 and 3.2 per cent in 2012. Feeble global economic growth, especially in Europe and other developed economies, is the major factor behind the deceleration. In the baseline outlook, world trade growth will pick up moderately in 2013 and return to near its long-term average growth rate of 5 per cent in 2014. However, developing countries were more resilient to the renewed slowdown and their importance in world trade continues to increase, along with their integration in global value chains.

Commodity prices remain high and volatile

For many commodities, the high price level reached in 2011 extended in 2012 with some significant bouts of volatility. After peaking during the first quarter of the year in the wake of the European Central Bank's (ECB) long-term refinancing operations having nurtured misperceptions about a rapid economic recovery, most commodity prices declined slightly during the second quarter. Prices of food and oil remained elevated in the third quarter, however, as a result of adverse weather conditions in many countries and renewed strategic risk in the Middle East. By contrast, a grim global economic outlook further depressed prices of minerals, metals and ores. In the outlook, commodity exporters that have benefited from improved terms of trade over the last few years remain exposed to downward price pressures. Financial speculation and the development of new commodity-backed financial products may further amplify commodity price volatility in a context of abundant liquidity. Food prices are expected to moderate somewhat with slowing global demand and assuming favourable weather conditions. However, given that markets are very tight and stock-to-use ratios for most staple foods are very low, even relatively minor supply shocks may easily cause new price spikes.

Expanding trade in services is increasing global greenhouse gas emissions

The strong recovery of trade in services experienced across all regions and groups of countries in 2010 began faltering during the last quarter of 2011. While the financial sector has contracted in some developed countries, the carbon emission-intensive transport and travel sectors keep expanding in developing countries. Freight transport services continue to grow along with the expansion of trade through global value chains. While increasingly important as a source of foreign-exchange earnings, especially for developing countries, expanding freight transport is also significantly contributing to global CO_2 emissions (figure O.3). Policymakers worldwide need to pay greater attention to this negative externality arising from the environmentally suboptimal organization of production through global value chains.

Figure 0.3
CO_2 emissions from transport and share of trade in world gross product move in tandem

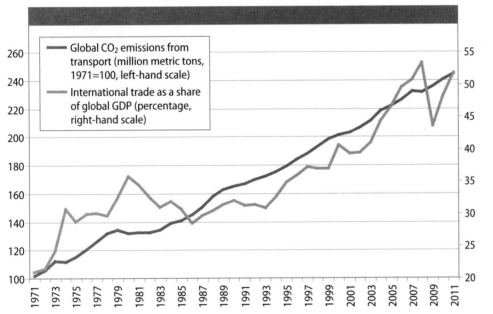

Global CO_2 emissions from transport (million metric tons, 1971=100, left-hand scale)

International trade as a share of global GDP (percentage, right-hand scale)

Source: World Bank.

International financing for development

Private capital flows remain volatile

Since the crisis, international private capital flows to emerging and developing countries have remained extremely volatile. While some stability appeared in international currency and capital markets during the early months of 2012, there was renewed volatility later, owing in part to growing fears among portfolio investors about the sustainability of public finances in Europe that prompted a "flight to safety". In addition, many European banks continue to face deleveraging pressures, which has led to cutbacks in lending to developing and transition economies. Signs of an economic slowdown in Brazil, China and India have reduced flows to these countries.

International reserves accumulation moderated

The pace of reserve accumulation by developing countries and economies in transition moderated somewhat in 2012, influenced by weaker capital inflows. Yet, the continued accumulation of international reserve holdings is reflective of continued concerns with global economic uncertainties and a perceived need for "self-insurance" against external shocks. The increased monetary reserves held in currencies of the major developed countries by far outweigh capital inflows and, as a result, developing countries and economies in transition continue to make substantial net financial transfers to developed countries. In 2012, these net outflows amounted to an estimated $845 billion, down from $1 trillion in 2011. LDCs, however, received positive net transfers of an estimated $17 billion in 2012 (figure O.4).

Figure 0.4
Continued net financial transfers from developing to developed countries

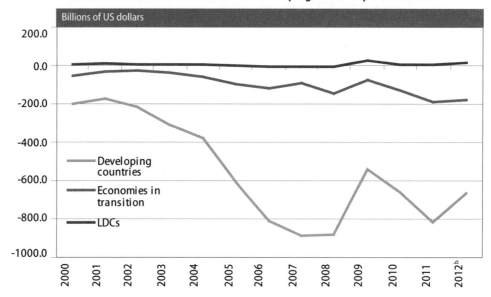

Source: UN/DESA.
Note: Figures for 2012 are partly estimated.

Official development assistance is falling

Net ODA flows from member countries of the Development Assistance Committee of the Organization for Economic Cooperation and Development (OECD) reached $133.5 billion in 2011, up from $128.5 billion in 2010. In real terms, however, this represents a fall of 3 per cent, widening the delivery gap in meeting internationally agreed aid targets to $167 billion. Preliminary results from the OECD survey of donors' forward spending plans indicate that Country Programmable Aid (CPA)—a core subset of aid that includes programmes and projects that have predicted trends in total aid—is expected to increase by about 6 per cent in 2012, mainly on account of expected increases in outflows of soft loans from multilateral agencies that had benefited from earlier fund replenishments. However, CPA is expected to stagnate from 2013 to 2015, reflecting the delayed impact of the global economic crisis and fiscal policy responses on donor country aid budgets.

Uncertainties and risks

A worsening of the euro area crisis, the "fiscal cliff" in the United States and a hard landing in China could combine to cause a new global recession

The baseline outlook is subject to major uncertainties and risks, mostly on the downside.

First, the economic crisis in the euro area could continue to worsen and become more disruptive. The ongoing perilous dynamics between sovereign debt distress and banking sector fragility are deteriorating the balance sheets of both Governments and commercial banks. The fiscal austerity responses are exacerbating the economic downturn, inspiring self-defeating efforts at fiscal consolidation and pushing up debt ratios, thereby triggering further budget cuts. The situation could worsen significantly with delayed implementation of the Outright Monetary Transactions programme and other supports for those members in need. Such delays could come as a result of political difficulties in reaching agreement between the countries in need of assistance and the troika of EU, ECB and IMF, and/or much larger detrimental effects of the fiscal austerity programmes and more difficulties in structural adjustments than anticipated. In such a scenario, as simulated through the United Nations World Economic Forecasting Model, the euro area could suffer an additional cumulative output loss of more than 3 per cent during 2013-2015 and the world as a whole of more than 1 per cent (see figure O.5).

Figure 0.5
Impact of downside risks on world economy will be substantial

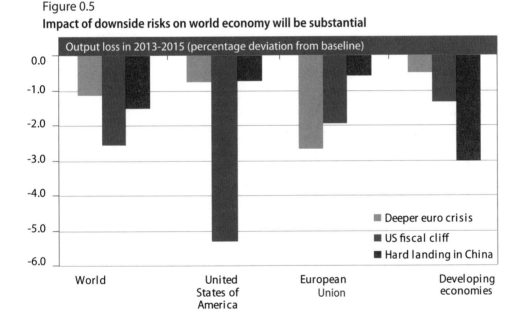

Source: UN/DESA, based on simulations with World Economic Forecasting Model.

Second, the United States could fail to avert the so-called fiscal cliff. A political gridlock preventing Congress from reaching a new budget agreement would put automatic fiscal cuts in place, including a drop in government spending by about $98 billion and tax increases of $450 billion in 2013; taken over 2013-2015, the automatic fiscal austerity would amount to about 4 per cent of GDP. In the fiscal cliff scenario, world economic growth would be halved to 1.2 per cent in 2013 and by 2015 global output would be 2.5 per cent lower than in the baseline projection. The output loss for developing countries would be about 1 per cent.

A third downside risk is the possibility of a hard landing of the economies of one or more of the large developing countries, including China. Growth slowed noticeably during 2012 in a number of large developing economies, such as Brazil, China and India, that had enjoyed a long period of rapid growth prior to the global financial crisis and managed to recover quickly at a robust pace in 2010 after the Great Recession. Given the uncertainties about their external demand and various domestic growth challenges, risks of further and larger-than-expected declines in the growth of these economies are not trivial. In the case of China, for instance, exports continued to slow during 2012, owing to weak demand in major developed economies. Meanwhile, growth in investment, which contributed to more than 50 per cent of GDP growth in the past decade, has been decelerating. The reasons for this are tighter housing market policies, greater caution regarding fiscal stimulus measures, and financing constraints faced by local governments in implementing new projects. Because of these factors, there are substantial risks for much lower GDP growth in China. If economic growth in China would slow to about 5 per cent per year (caused by a further deceleration in investment growth, continued tightening of the housing market and absence of new fiscal stimulus), developing countries as a group could suffer a cumulative output loss of about 3 per cent during 2013-2015 and the world as a whole of about 1.5 per cent.

Policy challenges

Present policy stances fall short of what is needed for economic recovery and addressing the jobs crisis

Weakening economic growth and policy uncertainties cast a shadow over the global economic outlook. As indicated, most developed countries have adopted a combination of fiscal austerity and expansionary monetary policies aimed at reducing public debt and lower debt refinancing costs in order to break away from the vicious dynamics between sovereign debt and banking sector fragility. Hopes are that this will calm financial markets and restore consumer and investor confidence. Together with structural reforms to entitlement programmes, labour markets and business regulation, such an improved environment should help restore economic growth and reduce unemployment. However, controlling debt stocks is proving to be much more challenging than policymakers expected.

An additional problem is that fiscal consolidation efforts of most developed countries rely more on spending retrenchment than improving revenue collection. The former tends to be more detrimental to economic growth in the short run, particularly when the economy is in a downward cycle. In many developed countries, public investment is being cut more severely than any other item, which may also prove costly to medium-term growth. In most cases, spending cuts also involve entitlement reforms, which immediately weaken automatic stabilizers in the short run by curtailing pension benefits, shortening the length of unemployment benefit schemes and/or shifting more of the burden of healthcare costs to households. Moreover, the fiscal austerity measures induce greater inequality in the short run, which could reduce social mobility and productivity growth in the long run.

Most developing countries and economies in transition have relatively stronger fiscal positions. Some have opted to put fiscal consolidation on hold in the face of global economic weakening. Fiscal deficits may rise in most low-income countries with slowing government revenue from commodity exports and the growing weight of food and energy subsidies. Concerns are also mounting in developing countries about the possible adverse effects of quantitative easing (QE) on the financial and macroeconomic stability of their economies as it may increase volatility in the international prices of commodities, capital flows and exchange rates.

Current policy stances seem to fall well short of what is needed to prevent the global economy from slipping into another recession.

More forceful and concerted actions are needed to generate growth and create jobs

The sobering outlook for the world economy and the enhanced downside risks call for much more forceful action. Those efforts will be challenging. At the same time, however, they will provide opportunities to better align policy actions addressing the immediate challenges with long-term sustainable development objectives.

Addressing policy uncertainties

A first challenge will be to reduce the high degree of policy uncertainty associated with the three key risks discussed in the downward scenario. These risks must be addressed immediately through shifts in policy approach and greater consideration of international spillover effects of national policies. In the euro area, the piecemeal approach to dealing with the debt crises of individual countries of the past two years should be replaced by a more comprehensive and integrated approach so as to address the systemic crisis of the monetary union. Policymakers in the United States should prevent a sudden and severe contraction in fiscal policy and overcome the political gridlock that was still present at the end of 2012. The major developing countries facing the risk of hard landings of their economies should engage in stronger countercyclical policy stances aligned with measures to address structural problems over the medium term. China, for instance, possesses ample policy space for a much stronger push to rebalance its economy towards domestic demand, including through increased government spending on public services such as health care, education and social security.

Making fiscal policy more countercyclical, more supportive of jobs creation and more equitable

In addition, fiscal policy should become more countercyclical, more supportive of jobs creation and more equitable. The present focus on fiscal consolidation in the short run, especially among developed countries, has proven to be counterproductive and to cause more protracted debt adjustment. The focus needs to shift in a number of different directions. A first priority of fiscal adjustment should be to provide more direct support to output and employment growth by boosting aggregate demand and, at the same time, spread out plans for achieving fiscal sustainability over the medium-to-long term. Moreover, fiscal multipliers tend to be more forceful during a downturn, but can be strengthened further by shifting budget priorities to growth-enhancing spending, undoing cuts in public investment and expanding subsidies on hiring. In addition, the distributional consequences of fiscal policies should be duly considered, not only for equity reasons, but also because of their implications for growth and employment generation. Finally, economic recovery can be strengthened in the short and longer run by promoting green growth through fiscal incentives and investments in infrastructure and new technologies.

Global financial market instability needs to be attacked at its root causes

Global financial market instability needs to be attacked where it originates. This challenge is twofold. First, greater synergy must be found between monetary and fiscal stimulus. Continuation of expansionary monetary policies among developed countries will be needed, but negative spillover effects into capital-flow and exchange-rate volatility must be contained. This will require reaching agreement at the international level on the magnitude, speed and timing of QE policies within a broader framework of targets to redress global imbalances. The second part of the challenge is to accelerate regulatory reforms of the financial sector at large, including shadow banking. This will be essential in order to avoid the systemic risks and excessive risk-taking that have led to the low-growth trap and financial fragility in developed countries and high capital flow volatility for developing countries.

Sufficient resources need to be made available to developing countries

Sufficient resources must be available to developing countries, especially those possessing limited fiscal space and facing large development needs. These resources will be needed to accelerate progress towards the achievement of the MDGs and for investments in sustainable and resilient growth, especially for the LDCs. Fiscal austerity among donor countries has also affected aid budgets, as seen in the decline of ODA in real terms in 2011. Further declines are expected in the outlook. Apart from delivering on existing aid commitments, donor countries should consider mechanisms to delink aid flows from their business cycles so as to prevent delivery shortfalls in times of crisis when the need for development aid is most urgent.

A scenario of concerted policies for more sustainable growth and jobs recovery is feasible

A jobs creation and green growth-oriented agenda as outlined above is compatible with medium-term reduction of public debt ratios and benign global rebalancing, according to a policy scenario analysis using the United Nations Global Policy Model. With continued existing policies, but assuming no major deepening of the euro crisis, growth of WGP would average, at best, about 3 per cent per year, far from sufficient to deal with the jobs crisis or bring down public debt ratios. The alternative scenario, based on the agenda outlined above, would support an acceleration of world economic growth to 4.5 per cent per year between 2013 and 2017, while public debt-to-GDP ratios would stabilize and start falling in 2016 or earlier. Employment levels in major developed countries would gradually increase and return to pre-crisis levels in absolute terms by 2014, and by 2017 after accounting for labour force growth. The employment recovery would thus come much sooner than in the baseline, although remaining protracted even with the suggested internationally concerted strategy for growth and jobs. An additional 33 million jobs per year on average would be created in developing and transition economies between 2013 and 2017.

Contents

Statisticals annex

Boxes

Figures

Tables

Explanatory Notes

The following symbols have been used in the tables throughout the report:

..   **Two dots** indicate that data are not available or are not separately reported.

–   **A dash** indicates that the amount is nil or negligible.

-           **A hyphen** indicates that the item is not applicable.

-           **A minus sign** indicates deficit or decrease, except as indicated.

.   **A full stop** is used to indicate decimals.

/   **A slash** between years indicates a crop year or financial year, for example, 2012/13.

-           **Use of a hyphen** between years, for example, 2012–2013, signifies the full period involved, including the beginning and end years.

Reference to "dollars" ($) indicates United States dollars, unless otherwise stated.

Reference to "billions" indicates one thousand million.

Reference to "tons" indicates metric tons, unless otherwise stated.

Annual rates of growth or change, unless otherwise stated, refer to annual compound rates.

Details and percentages in tables do not necessarily add to totals, because of rounding.

Project LINK is an international collaborative research group for econometric modelling, coordinated jointly by the Development Policy and Analysis Division of the United Nations Secretariat and the University of Toronto.

For **country classifications**, see statistical annex.

Data presented in this publication incorporate information available as at **30 November 2012**.

The following abbreviations have been used:

AMFm	Affordable Medicines Facility–malaria	**IMO**	International Maritime Organization
AMIS	Agricultural Market Information Systemn	**ISA**	International Services Agreement
ASEAN	Association of Southeast Asian Nations	**LDCs**	least developed countries
AUM	assets under management	**LME**	London Metal Exchange
BCBS	Basel Committee for Banking Supervision	**LTROs**	long-term refinancing operations
BIS	Bank for International Settlements	**mbd**	million barrels per day
BoJ	Bank of Japan	**MDGs**	Millennium Development Goals
CER	certified emissions reduction	**MFN**	most favoured nation
CIS	Commonwealth of Independent States	**MMFs**	money market funds
CO₂	carbon dioxide	**MNCs**	multinational corporations
COP	Conference of the Parties of the United Nations Framework Convention on Climate Change	**ODA**	official development assistance
		OECD	Organization for Economic Cooperation and Development
DAC	Development Assistance Committee (of the Organization for Economic Cooperation and Development)	**OMT**	outright monetary transactions
		OPEC	Organization of the Petroleum Exporting Countries
DCF	Development Cooperation Forum (of the United Nations)	**pb**	per barrel
ECB	European Central Bank	**PBC**	People's Bank of China
EDP	Excessive Deficit Procedure	**PPP**	purchasing power parity
EEDI	Energy Efficiency Design Index	**QE**	quantitative easing
EFSF	European Financial Stability Facility	**RBI**	Reserve Bank of India
EMU	Economic and Monetary Union	**REER**	real effective exchange rate
ESM	European Stability Mechanism	**RTAs**	regional trade agreements
ETFs	exchange-traded funds	**SBP**	State Bank of Pakistan
ETPs	exchange-traded products	**SDRs**	special drawing rights
EU	European Union	**SEC**	United States Securities and Exchange Commission
FAO	Food and Agricultural Organization of the United Nations	**SMEs**	small- and medium-sized enterprises
FDI	foreign direct investment	**TPP**	Trans-Pacific Partnership
Fed	Federal Reserve of the United States	**UNCSD**	United Nations Conference on Sustainable Development
FHFA	Federal Housing Finance Agency	**UNCTAD**	United Nations Conference on Trade and Development
FSB	Financial Stability Board		
G-SIFIs	global systemically important financial institutions	**UN/DESA**	Department of Economic and Social Affairs of the United Nations Secretariat
G20	Group of Twenty	**UNFCC**	United Nations Framework Convention on Climate Change
GCC	Gulf Cooperation Council		
GDP	gross domestic product	**WEF**	World Economic Forum
GHG	greenhouse gas	**WEFM**	World Economic Forecasting Model (of the United Nations)
GNI	gross national income		
GPM	Global Policy Model of the United Nations	**WEVUM**	World Economic Vulnerability Monitor (of the United Nations)
Gt	gigatons		
HICP	Harmonized Index of Consumer Prices	**WGP**	world gross product
HIPC	heavily indebted poor countries	**WTO**	World Trade Organization
IFFIm	International Finance Facility for Immunisation		
ILO	International Labour Organization		

Chapter 1
Global economic outlook

Prospects for the world economy in 2013-2014

Risk of a synchronized global downturn

Four years after the eruption of the global financial crisis, the world economy is still struggling to recover. During 2012, global economic growth has weakened further. A growing number of developed economies have fallen into a double-dip recession. Those in severe sovereign debt distress moved even deeper into recession, caught in the downward spiralling dynamics from high unemployment, weak aggregate demand compounded by fiscal austerity, high public debt burdens, and financial sector fragility. Growth in the major developing countries and economies in transition has also decelerated notably, reflecting both external vulnerabilities and domestic challenges. Most low-income countries have held up relatively well so far, but now face intensified adverse spillover effects from the slowdown in both developed and major middle-income countries. The prospects for the next two years continue to be challenging, fraught with major uncertainties and risks slanted towards the downside.

The world economy continues to struggle with post-crisis adjustments

Conditioned on a set of assumptions in the United Nations baseline forecast (box I.1), growth of world gross product (WGP) is expected to reach 2.2 per cent in 2012 and is forecast to remain well below potential at 2.4 per cent in 2013 and 3.2 per cent in 2014 (table I.1 and figure I.1). At this moderate pace, many economies will continue to operate below potential and will not recover the jobs lost during the Great Recession.

The slowdown is synchronized across countries of different levels of development (figure I.2). For many developing countries, the global slowdown will imply a much slower pace of poverty reduction and narrowing of fiscal space for investments in education, health, basic sanitation and other critical areas needed for accelerating the progress to achieve the Millennium Development Goals (MDGs). This holds true in particular for the least developed countries (LDCs); they remain highly vulnerable to commodity price shocks and are receiving less external financing as official development assistance (ODA) declines in the face of greater fiscal austerity in donor countries (see below). Conditions vary greatly across LDCs, however. At one end of the spectrum, countries that went through political turmoil and transition, like Sudan and Yemen, experienced major economic adversity during 2010 and 2011, while strong growth performances continued in Bangladesh and a fair number of African LDCs (box I.2).

The global slowdown will put additional strains on developing countries

Weaknesses in the major developed economies are at the root of continued global economic woes. Most of them, but particularly those in Europe, are dragged into a downward spiral as high unemployment, continued deleveraging by firms and households, continued banking fragility, heightened sovereign risks, fiscal tightening, and slower growth viciously feed into one another (figure I.3a).

Weakness in developed economies underpins the global slowdown

Several European economies are already in recession. In Germany, output has also slowed significantly, while France's economy is stagnating. A number of new

Table I.1
Growth of world output, 2006-2014

Annual percentage change								
							Change from June 2012 forecast[d]	
	2006-2009[a]	*2010*	*2011*[b]	*2012*[c]	*2013*[c]	*2014*[c]	*2012*	*2013*
World	**1.1**	**4.0**	**2.7**	**2.2**	**2.4**	**3.2**	**-0.3**	**-0.7**
Developed economies	-0.4	2.6	1.4	1.1	1.1	2.0	-0.1	-0.7
United States of America	-0.5	2.4	1.8	2.1	1.7	2.7	0.0	-0.6
Japan	-1.5	4.5	-0.7	1.5	0.6	0.8	-0.2	-1.5
European Union	-0.3	2.1	1.5	-0.3	0.6	1.7	-0.3	-0.6
EU-15	-0.5	2.1	1.4	-0.4	0.5	1.6	-0.3	-0.6
New EU members	2.1	2.3	3.1	1.2	2.0	2.9	-0.5	-0.8
Euro area	-0.4	2.1	1.5	-0.5	0.3	1.4	-0.2	-0.6
Other European countries	0.9	1.9	1.7	1.7	1.5	1.9	0.6	0.2
Other developed countries	1.2	2.8	2.4	2.3	2.0	3.0	0.0	-0.6
Economies in transition	2.2	4.4	4.5	3.5	3.6	4.2	-0.5	-0.6
South-Eastern Europe	1.6	0.4	1.1	-0.6	1.2	2.6	-1.2	-0.6
Commonwealth of Independent States and Georgia	2.2	4.8	4.8	3.8	3.8	4.4	-0.5	-0.6
Russian Federation	1.7	4.3	4.3	3.7	3.6	4.2	-0.7	-0.8
Developing economies	5.2	7.7	5.7	4.7	5.1	5.6	-0.6	-0.7
Africa	4.7	4.7	1.1	5.0	4.8	5.1	0.8	0.0
North Africa	4.2	4.1	-6.0	7.5	4.4	4.9	3.1	0.0
Sub-Saharan Africa	5.0	5.0	4.5	3.9	5.0	5.2	-0.2	0.0
Nigeria	6.6	7.8	7.4	6.4	6.8	7.2	0.1	0.0
South Africa	2.5	2.9	3.1	2.5	3.1	3.8	-0.3	-0.4
Others	6.3	5.5	4.4	3.9	5.5	5.3	-0.3	0.1
East and South Asia	7.1	9.0	6.8	5.5	6.0	6.3	-0.8	-0.8
East Asia	7.2	9.2	7.1	5.8	6.2	6.5	-0.7	-0.7
China	11.0	10.3	9.2	7.7	7.9	8.0	-0.6	-0.6
South Asia	6.4	8.3	5.8	4.4	5.0	5.7	-1.2	-1.1
India	7.3	9.6	6.9	5.5	6.1	6.5	-1.2	-1.1
Western Asia	2.3	6.7	6.7	3.3	3.3	4.1	-0.7	-1.1
Latin America and the Caribbean	2.5	6.0	4.3	3.1	3.9	4.4	-0.5	-0.3
South America	3.9	6.5	4.5	2.7	4.0	4.4	-0.9	-0.4
Brazil	3.6	7.5	2.7	1.3	4.0	4.4	-2.0	-0.5
Mexico and Central America	-0.1	5.4	4.0	4.0	3.9	4.6	0.6	0.0
Mexico	-0.6	5.5	3.9	3.9	3.8	4.6	0.5	-0.1
Caribbean	3.6	3.5	2.7	2.9	3.7	3.8	-0.4	-0.3
By level of development								
High-income countries	-0.2	2.9	1.6	1.2	1.3	2.2		
Upper middle income countries	5.3	7.4	5.8	5.1	5.4	5.8		
Lower middle income countries	5.8	7.4	5.6	4.4	5.5	6.0		
Low-income countries	5.9	6.6	6.0	5.7	5.9	5.9		
Least developed countries	7.2	5.8	3.7	3.7	5.7	5.5	-0.4	0.0
Memorandum items								
World trade[e]	-0.3	13.3	7.0	3.3	4.3	4.9	-0.8	-1.2
World output growth with PPP-based weights	2.3	5.0	3.7	3.0	3.3	4.0	-0.4	-0.7

Source: UN/DESA.

a Average percentage change.
b Actual or most recent estimates.
c Forecast, based in part on Project LINK and baseline projections of the UN/DESA World Economic Forecasting Model.
d See United Nations, *World Economic Situation and Prospects as of mid-2012* (E/2012/72).
e Includes goods and services.

Figure I.1
Growth of world gross product, 2006-2014ᵃ

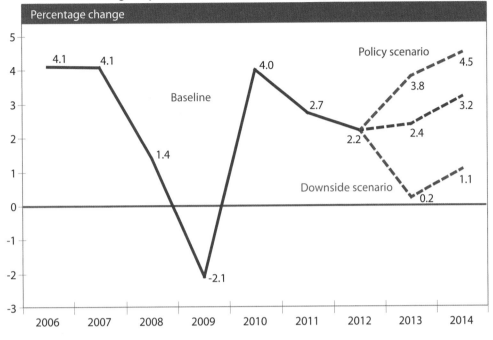

Percentage change

Source: UN/DESA.

a Growth rate for 2012 is partially estimated. Estimates for 2013 and 2014 are forecasts. See "Uncertainties and risks" section for a discussion of the downside scenario and box I.3 for a discussion of the policy scenario.

Figure I.2
Growth of GDP per capita by level of development, 2000-2014

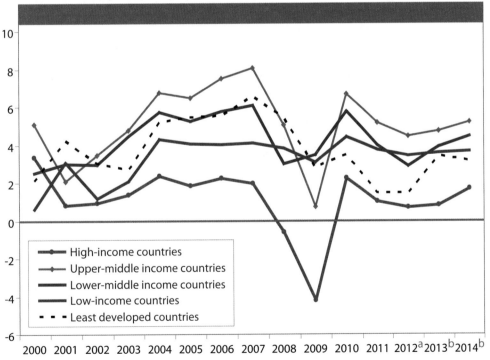

Source: UN/DESA.
a Estimates.
b United Nations forecasts.

Box I.1

Major assumptions for the baseline forecast

The forecast presented in the text is based on estimates calculated using the United Nations World Economic Forecasting Model (WEFM) and is informed by country-specific economic outlooks provided by participants in Project LINK, a network of institutions and researchers supported by the Department of Economic and Social Affairs of the United Nations. The provisional individual country forecasts submitted by country experts are adjusted based on harmonized global assumptions and the imposition of global consistency rules (especially for trade flows, measured in both volume and value) set by the WEFM. The main global assumptions are discussed below and form the core of the baseline forecast—the scenario that is assigned the highest probability of occurrence. Alternative scenarios are presented in the sections on "Uncertainties and risks" and "Policy challenges". Those scenarios are normally assigned lower probability than the baseline forecast.

Monetary policy

The Federal Reserve of the United States (Fed) is assumed to keep the federal funds interest rate at the current low level of between 0.00 and 0.25 per cent until mid-2015. It is assumed that the Fed will purchase agency mortgage-backed securities at a pace of $40 billion per month until the end of 2014, and will also continue its programme to extend the average maturity of its securities holdings through the end of 2012, as well as reinvest principal payments from its holdings of agency debt and agency mortgage-backed securities. The European Central Bank (ECB) is assumed to cut the minimum bid and marginal lending facility rates by another 25 basis points, leaving the deposit rate at 0 per cent. It is also assumed that the ECB will start to implement the announced new policy initiative, Outright Monetary Transactions (OMT), to purchase the government bonds of Spain and a few selected members of the euro area. The Bank of Japan (BoJ) will keep the policy interest rate at the current level (0.0-0.1 per cent) and implement the Asset Purchase Program, with a ceiling of ¥91 trillion, as announced. With regard to major emerging economies, the People's Bank of China (PBC) is expected to reduce reserve requirement rates twice in 2013 and reduce interest rates one more time in the same period.

Fiscal policy

In the United States, it is assumed that the 2 per cent payroll tax cut and emergency unemployment insurance benefits are extended for 2013, to be phased out gradually over several years. It is also assumed that the automatic spending cuts now scheduled to begin in January 2013 will be delayed, giving more time for the new Congress and president to produce a package of spending cuts and tax increases effective in 2014. The Bush tax cuts are assumed to be extended for 2013-2014. As a result, real federal government spending on goods and services will fall about 3.0 per cent in 2013 and 2014, after a fall of about 2.5 per cent in the previous two years.

In the euro area, fiscal policy is assumed to be focused on reducing fiscal imbalances. The majority of countries remain subject to the Excessive Deficit Procedure (EDP) under which they must submit plans to bring their fiscal deficits close to balance within a specified time frame. Typically, a minimum correction of 0.5 per cent per annum is expected, and the time frames range from 2012 to 2014. The time periods for achieving these targets will be extended in the most difficult cases. It is also assumed that in the event that tensions increase in sovereign debt markets, affected euro area countries will seek assistance from the rescue fund, thus activating the new OMT programme of the ECB. It is assumed that this will allow increases in bond yields to be contained and that the policy conditionality attached to the use of OMT finance will not entail additional fiscal austerity; rather, Governments requesting funds will be pressed to fully implement already announced fiscal consolidation measures.

In Japan, the newly ratified bill to increase the consumption tax rate from its current level of 5 per cent to 8 per cent by April 2014 and to 10 per cent by October 2015 will be implemented. Real government expenditure, including investment, is assumed to decline by a small proportion in 2013-2014, mainly owing to phasing out of reconstruction spending.

In China, the Government is assumed to maintain a proactive fiscal policy stance, with an increase in public investment spending on infrastructure in 2013.

Box I.1 (cont'd)

Exchange rates among major currencies

It is assumed that during the forecasting period of 2013-2014, the euro will fluctuate about $1.28 per euro. The Japanese yen is assumed to average about ¥80 per United States dollar, and the renminbi will average CNY6.23 per United States dollar.

Oil prices

Oil prices (Brent) are assumed to average about $105 per barrel (pb) in 2013-2014, compared to $110 pb in 2012.

policy initiatives were taken by the euro area authorities in 2012, including the Outright Monetary Transactions (OMT) programme and steps towards greater fiscal integration and coordinated financial supervision and regulation. These measures address some of the deficiencies in the original design of the Economic and Monetary Union (EMU). Significant as they may be, however, these measures are still being counteracted by other policy stances, fiscal austerity in particular, and are not sufficient to break economies out of the vicious circle and restore output and employment growth in the short run (figure I.3b). In the baseline outlook for the euro area, GDP is expected to grow by only 0.3 per cent in 2013 and 1.4 per cent in 2014, a feeble recovery from a decline of 0.5 per cent in 2012. Because of the dynamics of the vicious circle, the risk for a much worse scenario remains high. Economic growth in the new European Union (EU) members also decelerated during 2012, with some, including the Czech Republic, Hungary and Slovenia, falling back into recession. Worsening external conditions are compounded by fiscal austerity measures, aggravating short-term growth prospects. In the outlook, GDP growth in these economies is expected to remain subdued at 2.0 per cent in 2013 and 2.9 per cent in 2014, but risks are high for a much worse performance if the situation in the euro area deteriorates further.

The United States economy weakened notably during 2012, and growth prospects for 2013 and 2014 remain sluggish. On the up side, the beleaguered housing sector is showing some nascent signs of recovery. Further support is expected from the new round of quantitative easing (QE) recently launched by the United States Federal Reserve (Fed) whereby monetary authorities will continue to purchase mortgage-backed securities until the employment situation improves substantially. On the down side, the lingering uncertainties about the fiscal stance continue to restrain growth of business investment. External demand is also expected to remain weak. In the baseline outlook, gross domestic product (GDP) growth in the United States is forecast to decelerate to 1.7 per cent in 2013 from an already anaemic pace of 2.1 per cent in 2012. Risks remain high for a much bleaker scenario, emanating from the "fiscal cliff" which would entail a drop in aggregate demand of as much as 4 per cent of GDP during 2013 and 2014 (see "Uncertainties and risks" section). Adding to the already sombre scenario are anticipated spillover effects from possible intensification of the euro area crisis, a "hard landing" of the Chinese economy and greater weakening of other major developing economies.

Growth in the United States will slow, with significant downside risks

Economic growth in Japan in 2012 was up from a year ago, mainly driven by reconstruction works and recovery from the earthquake-related disasters of 2011. The Government also took measures to stimulate private consumption. Exports faced strong headwinds from the slowdown in global demand and appreciation of the yen. In the outlook,

The need for fiscal consolidation will reduce growth in Japan

Box I.2

Prospects for the least developed countries

The economies of the least developed countries (LDCs) are expected to rebound in 2013. GDP growth is projected to average 5.7 per cent in 2013, up from 3.7 per cent in 2012. However, most of the rebound is expected to come from improvements in economic conditions in Yemen and Sudan, following notable contractions of both economies in the face of political instability during 2010 and 2011.

In per capita terms, GDP growth for LDCs is expected to accelerate from 1.3 per cent in 2012 to 3.3 per cent in 2013. While an improvement, at this rate welfare progress will remain well below the pace of 5.0 per cent per annum experienced during much of the 2000s, prior to the world economic and financial crisis.

Economic performance varies greatly among LDCs, however. Numerous oil exporters such as Angola and Guinea will benefit from continued solid oil prices, propelling GDP growth to more than 7 per cent and 4 per cent, respectively, in 2013. LDCs with a predominant agricultural sector have seen volatile economic conditions. In Gambia, for example, where agriculture provides about one third of total output, poor crop conditions caused GDP to contract by 1.0 per cent in 2012. Much better harvests are expected to propel GDP growth to 6.2 per cent. Such sharp swings in the overall economic performance create multiple problems for policymakers. The inherent uncertainty not only complicates the planning and design of economic policies, especially those of a longer-term nature, but it also threatens the implementation of existing policy plans owing to sudden dramatic changes in economic parameters. In addition, unforeseen crises create needs—in the form of short-term assistance to farmers, for example—which divert scarce financial and institutional resources away from more structurally oriented policy areas. On the other hand, Ethiopia's robust growth of the past few years is expected to come down slightly but remain strong, partly owing to its programme of developing the agricultural sector.

A number of LDCs have also seen solid investment and consumption, supported by sustained inflows of worker remittances. This applies, for example, to Bangladesh, whose growth rate will continue to exceed 6.0 per cent in 2013 and 2014 despite a marked slowdown in external demand. Growth of remittance inflows to Bangladesh picked up to about 20 per cent year on year in the second half of 2012, following a strong rise in overseas employment earlier in the year.

The outlook for LDCs entails several downside risks. A more pronounced deterioration in the global economic environment would negatively affect primary commodity exporters through falling terms of trade, while others may be affected by falling worker remittances. Falling aid flows are expected to limit external financing options for LDCs in the outlook.

Japan's economy is expected to slow given the phasing out of private consumption incentives combined with a new measure increasing taxes on consumption, anticipated reductions in pension benefits, and government spending cuts. These measures responded to concerns about the extremely high level of public indebtedness. The impact of the greater fiscal austerity will be mitigated by reconstruction investments, which will continue but at a slower pace. GDP is forecast to grow at 0.6 per cent in 2013 and 0.8 per cent in 2014, down from 1.5 per cent in 2012.

Spillover effects from developed countries and domestic issues dampen growth in developing countries

The economic woes of the developed countries are spilling over to developing countries and economies in transition through weaker demand for their exports and heightened volatility in capital flows and commodity prices. Their problems are also home-grown, however; growth in investment spending has slowed significantly, presaging a continued deceleration of future output growth if not counteracted by additional policy

Figure I.3a
The vicious cycle of developed economies

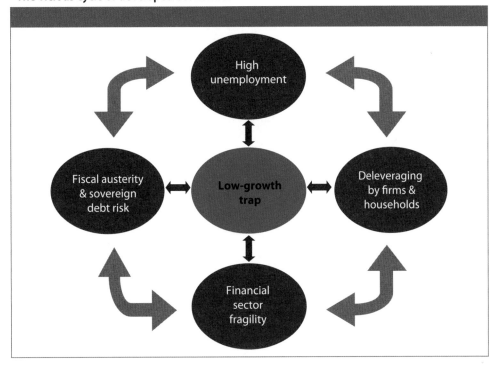

Source: UN/DESA.

Figure I.3b
Feeble policy efforts to break the vicious cycle

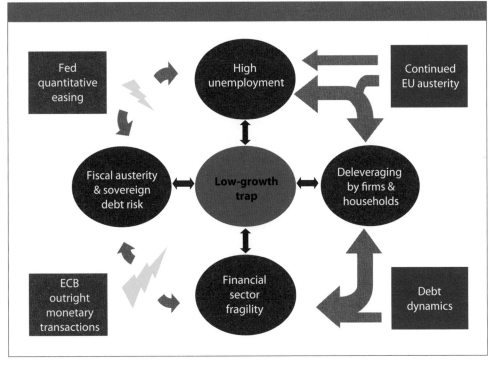

Source: UN/DESA.

measures. Several of the major developing economies that have seen fast growth in recent decades are starting to face structural bottlenecks, including financing constraints faced by local governments regarding investment projects in some sectors of the economy, and overinvestment leading to excess production capacity in others, as in the case of China (see "Uncertainties and risks" section).

On average, economies in Africa are forecast to see a slight moderation in output growth in 2013 to 4.8 per cent, down from 5.0 per cent in 2012. Major factors underpinning this continued growth trajectory include the strong performance of oil-exporting countries, continued fiscal spending in infrastructure projects, and expanding economic ties with Asian economies. However, Africa remains plagued by numerous challenges, including armed conflicts in various parts of the region. Growth of income per capita will continue, but at a pace considered insufficient to achieve substantial poverty reduction. Infrastructure shortfalls are among the major obstacles to more dynamic economic development in most economies of the region.

The economies in developing Asia have weakened considerably during 2012 as the region's growth engines, China and India, both shifted into lower gear. While a significant deceleration in exports has been a key factor for the slowdown, the effects of policy tightening in the previous two years also linger. Domestic investment has softened markedly. Both China and India face a number of structural challenges hampering growth (see below). India's space for more policy stimulus seems limited. China and other countries in the region possess greater space for additional stimulus, but thus far have refrained from using it. In the outlook, growth for East Asia is forecast to pick up mildly to 6.2 per cent in 2013, from 5.8 per cent estimated for 2012. GDP growth in South Asia is expected to average 5.0 per cent in 2013, up from 4.4 per cent of 2012, but still well below potential.

Contrasting trends are found in Western Asia. Most oil-exporting countries experienced robust growth supported by record-high oil revenues and government spending. By contrast, economic activity weakened in oil-importing countries, burdened by higher import bills, declining external demand and shrinking policy space. As a result, oil-exporting and oil-importing economies are facing a dual track growth outlook. Meanwhile, social unrest and political instability, notably in the Syrian Arab Republic, continue to elevate the risk assessment for the entire region. On average, GDP growth in the region is expected to decelerate to 3.3 per cent in 2012 and 2013, from 6.7 per cent in 2011.

GDP growth in Latin America and the Caribbean decelerated notably during 2012, led by weaker export demand. In the outlook, subject to the risks of a further downturn, the baseline projection is for a return to moderate economic growth rates, led by stronger economic performance in Brazil. For the region as whole, GDP growth is forecast to average 3.9 per cent in the baseline for 2013, compared to 3.1 per cent in 2012.

Among economies in transition, growth in the economies of the Commonwealth of Independent States (CIS) has continued in 2012, although it moderated in the second half of the year. Firm commodity prices, especially those of oil and natural gas, held up growth among energy-exporting economies, including Kazakhstan and the Russian Federation. In contrast, growth in the Republic of Moldova and Ukraine was adversely affected by the economic crisis in the euro area. The economies of small energy-importing countries in the CIS were supported by private remittances. In the outlook, GDP for the CIS is expected to grow by 3.8 per cent in 2013, the same as in 2012. The prospects for most transition economies in South-Eastern Europe in the short run remain challenging, owing to their close ties with the euro area through trade and finance. In these economies,

GDP growth is expected to average 1.2 per cent in 2013, a mild rebound from the recession of 2012 when economies in the subregion shrank by 0.6 per cent.

Lower greenhouse gas emissions, but far cry from "low-carbon" growth

Helped by weaker global economic growth, greenhouse gases (GHGs) emitted by the Annex I countries to the Kyoto Protocol are estimated to have fallen by about 2 per cent per year during 2011-2012 (see annex table A.22). This reverses the 3 per cent increase in GHG emissions by these countries in 2010. Emissions fell by 6 per cent in 2009 along with the fallout in GDP growth associated with the Great Recession. With the more recent decline, GHG emission reductions among Annex I countries are back on the long-run downward trend. Given the further moderation in global economic growth, emissions by these countries are expected to decline further during 2013-2014.[1] As a group, Annex I countries have already achieved the target of the Kyoto Protocol to reduce emissions by at least 5 per cent from 1990 levels during the 2008-2012 commitment period. Several important individual countries, however, such as the United States and Canada, are still to meet their own national targets. At the same time, GHG emissions in many developing countries are increasing at a rapid pace, such that globally, emissions continue to climb.

In all, the world is far from being on track to reduce emissions to the extent considered necessary for keeping carbon dioxide (CO_2) equivalent concentrations to less than 450 parts per million (consistent with the target of stabilizing global warming at a 2°C temperature increase, or less, from pre-industrial levels).[2] To avoid exceeding this limit, GHG emissions would need to drop by 80 per cent by mid-century. Given current trends and even with the extension of the Kyoto Protocol, this is an unachievable target. "Greener" growth pathways need to be created now, and despite large investment costs, they would also provide opportunities for more robust short-term recovery and global rebalancing (see "Policy challenges" and chapter II on the environmental costs of expanding trade through global value chains).

The world remains far from achieving its target for CO_2 equivalent concentrations

Job crisis continues

Unemployment remains elevated in many developed economies, with the situation in Europe being the most challenging. A double-dip recession in several European economies has taken a heavy toll on labour markets. The unemployment rate continued to climb to a record high in the euro area during 2012, up by more than one percentage point from one year ago. Conditions are worse in Spain and Greece, where more than a quarter of the working population is without a job and more than half of the youth is unemployed. Only a few economies

Unemployment remains high in developed economies

1　Projections are based on past trends in GDP growth and GHG emissions, accounting implicitly for the effects over time of policies aimed at decoupling (see notes to annex table A.22 for a description of the methodology). As far as the longer-term trends are concerned, the impact of more recent energy policy changes may not be adequately reflected.

2　A recent study by PricewaterhouseCoopers notes that "since 2000, the rate of decarbonisation has averaged 0.8% globally, a fraction of the required reduction. From 2010 to 2011, global carbon intensity continued this trend, falling by just 0.7%. Because of this slow start, global carbon intensity now needs to be cut by an average of 5.1% a year from now to 2050.... This rate of reduction has not been achieved in any of the past 50 years". (See PricewaterhouseCoopers LLP, "Too late for two degrees? Low carbon economy index 2012", November 2012, pp. 2-3, available from http://preview.thenewsmarket.com/Previews/PWC/DocumentAssets/261179_v2.pdf).

in the region, such as Austria, Germany, Luxembourg and the Netherlands, register low unemployment rates of about 5 per cent. Unemployment rates in Central and Eastern Europe also edged up slightly in 2012, partly resulting from fiscal austerity. Japan's unemployment rate retreated to below 5 per cent. In the United States, the unemployment rate stayed above 8 per cent for the most part of 2012, but dropped to just below that level from September onwards. However, the labour participation rate is at a record low, while the shares of long-term unemployment reached historic highs of 40.6 per cent (jobless for 6 months or longer) and 31.4 per cent (one year or longer). Long-term unemployment is also severe in the EU and Japan, where four of each ten of the unemployed have been without a job for more than one year. For the group of developed countries as a whole, the incidence of long-term unemployment (over one year) stood at more than 35 per cent by July 2012, affecting about 17 million workers. Such a prolonged duration of unemployment tends to have significant, long-lasting detrimental impacts on both the individuals who have lost their jobs and on the economy as a whole. The skills of unemployed workers deteriorate commensurate with the duration of their unemployment, most likely leading to lower earnings for those individuals who are eventually able to find new jobs. At the aggregate level, the higher the proportion of workers trapped in protracted unemployment, the greater the adverse impact on the productivity of the economy in the medium to long run.

Adequate job creation should be a key policy priority in developed economies. If economic growth stays as anaemic in developed countries as projected in the baseline forecast, employment rates will not return to pre-crisis levels until far beyond 2016 (figure I.4).

The employment situation varies significantly across developing countries, but

The employment situation varies across developing countries

Figure I.4
Post-recession employment recovery in the United States, euro area and developed economies, 2007 (Q1)-2011 (Q2) and projections for 2012 (Q3)-2016 (Q4)

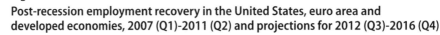

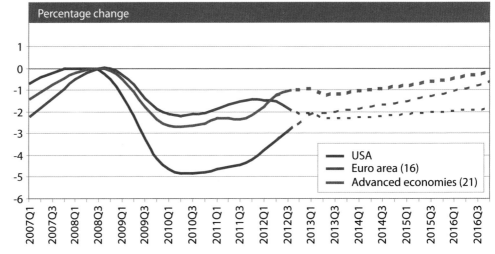

Source: UN/DESA, based on data from ILO and IMF.
Note: The chart shows percentage changes of total employment (as a moving average) with respect to pre-recession peaks. Projections (dashed lines) are based on estimates of the output elasticity of employment (Okun's law), following a similar methodology to that of ILO, *World of Work Report 2011* (Geneva).

the common challenges are to improve the quality of employment and reduce vulnerable employment as well as confront structural unemployment issues such as high youth unemployment and gender disparities in employment—all of which are key social and economic concerns in many developing countries.

Among developing countries, the unemployment rates in most economies in

East Asia and Latin America have already retreated to, or dropped below, levels seen prior to the global financial crisis. The growth moderation in late 2011 and 2012 has so far not led to a discernible rise in the unemployment rate in these two regions—a positive sign, with the caveat that a rise in the unemployment rate would usually lag in an economic downturn. If the growth slowdown continues, the unemployment rate could be expected to increase significantly. In Africa, despite relatively strong GDP growth, the employment situation remains a major problem across the region, both in terms of the level of employment and the quality of jobs that are generated. Labour conflicts also constitute a major downside risk to the economic performance of the region. Gender disparity in employment remains acute in Africa as well as in South Asia. Women are facing unemployment rates at least double those of men in some African countries, and the female labour force participation rate in India and Pakistan is much lower than that of males. Social unrest in North Africa and West Asia has been caused in part by high unemployment, especially among youth. The related disruptions in economic activity, in turn, have further pushed up unemployment rates in some countries. Among economies in transition, the unemployment rate in the Russian Federation declined to a record low of 5.2 per cent in August 2012, partly as a result of increased public spending, but also because of a shrinking active population. Notable job creation has also been recorded in Kazakhstan, but the unemployment rate has increased in Ukraine as a result of tighter fiscal policy and weaker external sector.

Inflation receding worldwide, but still a concern in some developing countries

Inflation rates remain subdued in most developed economies. Continuing large output gaps and downward pressure on wages in many countries are keeping inflationary expectations low. Inflation in the United States moderated over 2012, down to about 2 per cent from 3.1 per cent in 2011. A further moderation in headline inflation is expected in the outlook for 2013. In the euro area, headline inflation, as measured by the Harmonized Index of Consumer Prices (HICP), continues to be above the central bank's target of 2 per cent. Core inflation, which does not include price changes in volatile items such as energy, food, alcohol and tobacco, has been much lower at around 1.5 per cent, with no evidence of upward pressures. In the outlook, inflation is expected to drift down slowly. Inflation in the new EU members is also expected to lessen. Deflation continues to prevail in Japan, although the central bank has raised its inflation target to boost inflation expectations.

Inflation remains subdued in most developed economies…

Inflation receded in a majority of developing countries during 2012, but remains stubbornly high in some. In the outlook, higher oil prices and some country-specific supply-side constraints may continue to put upward pressure on inflation in developing countries in 2013 and into 2014. In Africa, while inflation moderated in many economies, the rate of inflation is still above 10 per cent in Angola, Nigeria and elsewhere. Inflation is expected to remain subdued in most of East Asia, but is still a concern for most countries in South Asia where inflation rates were, on average, over 11 per cent in 2012 and are forecast to remain above or near 10 per cent in 2013 and 2014. Inflation remains low in most economies in West Asia, though it is still high (above 10 per cent) in Yemen and very high (30 per cent) in the Syrian Arab Republic. The inflation rate in Latin America and the Caribbean is expected to stay at about 6 per cent.

…and is receding in most developing countries, although still high in some

Outlook for global commodity and financial markets

World trade slowed notably during 2012, along with weaker global output. The sovereign debt crisis and economic recession in the euro area and continued financial deleveraging in most developed economies affected capital flows to emerging markets and other developing countries, adding to uncertainty about economic prospects and enhancing market volatility. These factors, combined with spillover effects of expansionary monetary policies in developed economies, have also fueled volatility in primary commodity prices and exchange rates. Global imbalances, characterized by large savings surpluses in some economies and deficits in others, have narrowed markedly in the aftermath of the global financial crisis. However, the rebalancing has hardly been a benign process, having resulted mainly from demand deflation and weaker trade flows.

Sharp slowdown of world trade

Declining import demand in Europe dampened world trade growth in 2012

After plunging by more than 10 per cent in the Great Recession of 2009, world trade rebounded strongly in 2010. Since 2011, the recovery of the volume of world exports has lost momentum (figure I.5). Growth of world trade decelerated sharply during 2012, mainly owing to declining import demand in Europe, as the region entered into its second recession in three years, and anaemic aggregate demand in the United States and Japan. Developing countries and economies in transition have seen demand for their exports weaken as a result.

Figure I.5
World merchandise exports volume, January 2006-August 2012

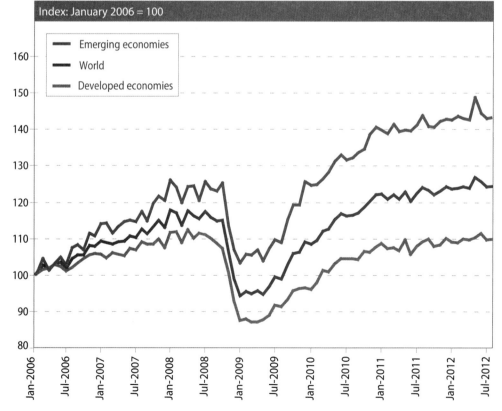

Source: CPB Netherlands Bureau for Economic Policy Analysis, rebased by UN/DESA.

The monthly trade data of different regions and countries showed a clear sequence of the weakening demand that originated in the euro area transmitting to the rest of the world. Import demand in Greece, Italy, Portugal and Spain started to decline in late 2011 and fell further during 2012, but the weakness in trade activity has spread further to the rest of Europe as well, including France and Germany. In tandem, imports of the United States and Japan also slowed significantly in the second half of 2012. East Asian economies that trade significantly with the major developed countries have experienced commensurate declines in exports. For example, the Republic of Korea, and Taiwan Province of China registered considerable drops in exports during 2012. China's exports also decelerated notably. Further down the global value chain, energy and other primary-exporting economies have seen demand for their exports weaken as well. Brazil and the Russian Federation, for instance, all registered export declines in varying degrees in the second half of 2012. Lower export earnings, compounded by domestic demand constraints have also pushed down GDP growth in many developing countries and economies in transition during 2012. This has led to flagging import demand from these economies, further slowing trade of developed countries.

At the same time, a rise in international protectionism, albeit modest, and the protracted impasse in the world multilateral trade negotiations, have also adversely affected international trade flows.[3] In the outlook for 2013 and 2014, the continued weak global growth outlook and heightened uncertainties lead to expectations that world trade will continue to expand at a rather tepid pace of 4.3 per cent in volume terms in 2013 and 4.9 per cent in 2014, compared to 3.3 per cent in 2012 and 6.8 per cent during 2005-2008.

Oil prices soften but risk premium remains

The price of oil fluctuated during 2012 (figure I.6); weaker global demand tended to push prices down, while heightened geopolitical risks in several oil-producing countries put upward pressure on prices. Global oil demand decelerated somewhat to 0.9 per cent in 2012. Global supply was affected by sanctions imposed by the EU and the United States on Syrian and Iranian oil exports. This was compensated to a large extent, however, by the preventive increase in oil production in Saudi Arabia, the resumption of production in Libya and higher-than-expected output in North America, Latin America and the Russian Federation. Yet, spare capacity dropped to 2.8 million barrels per day (mbd), down from an average of about 4 mbd during 2006-2011.

Oil prices fluctuated in 2012, with weaker demand offsetting geopolitical risks

In the outlook, world oil demand is expected to remain subdued during 2013 and 2014. Supply is expected to further expand in several oil-producing areas, including North America, the Russian Federation and Brazil, partially offset by declines in the North Sea and Central Asia. Saudi Arabia is expected to lower production, thereby increasing spare capacity. Continued geopolitical tensions in the Middle East will likely continue to put a risk premium on prices, however. As a result, Brent oil prices are forecast to decline somewhat and fluctuate around $105 per barrel (pb) in 2013-2014, down from an average of $110 pb in 2012.

Rising food prices

Food prices increased to a record high, but will moderate in 2013

Despite slowing global demand, food prices jumped to a record high in July 2012 (figure I.7). Global cereal production in 2012 is expected to fall by 2.7 per cent from previous

---

3   See *MDG Gap Task Force Report 2012: The Global Partnership for Development—Making Rhetoric a Reality* (United Nations publication, Sales No. E.12.I.5).

Figure I.6
Brent oil price, January 2000-October 2012

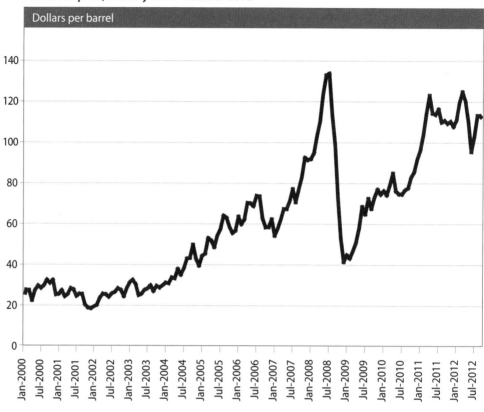

Source: UN/DESA.

Figure I.7
Daily grain prices, January 2007-October 2012

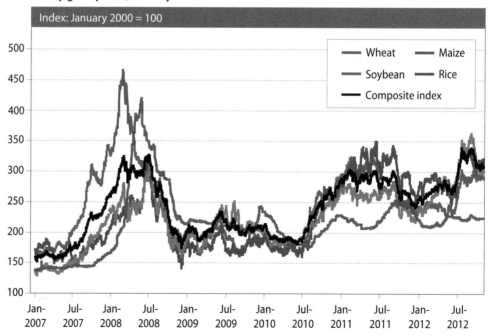

Source: International Grains Council.

year's record crop. The overall decrease reflects a 5.5 per cent reduction in wheat, and a 2.5 per cent decline in coarse grains, while the global rice crop is seen to grow by 0.7 per cent above last season's record. Severe droughts and poor weather this year in the United States, the Russian Federation, Ukraine and Kazakhstan have been the main cause of the reduced maize and wheat crops. According to the Food and Agricultural Organization (FAO), the decline would also reduce the world cereal stock-to-use ratio from 22.6 per cent in 2012 to 20.6 per cent in 2013, which compares with the low of 19.2 per cent registered in 2007-2008.[4] The situation is not yet considered a threat to global food security, however. In the outlook, food prices will likely moderate somewhat with slowing global demand. However, given that markets are very tight, even relatively minor supply shocks may easily cause new price spikes.

Softening non-food commodity prices

The prices of non-oil, non-food commodities started to decline in the second quarter of 2012 as a result of the slowdown in global demand (figure I.8). The appreciation of the United States dollar has also contributed to the weakness in the prices of non-food commodities, as these prices are dollar-denominated. Prices of base metals and ores continued their downward trend until mid-2012, before rebounding somewhat towards the end of the year, mainly influenced by financial factors (see chapter II). Global demand remained weak, while new mining projects implemented over the past decade have increased global supply.

Metal and ore prices will remain weak as a result of subdued demand

Figure I.8
Non-oil commodity prices, 2000-2014

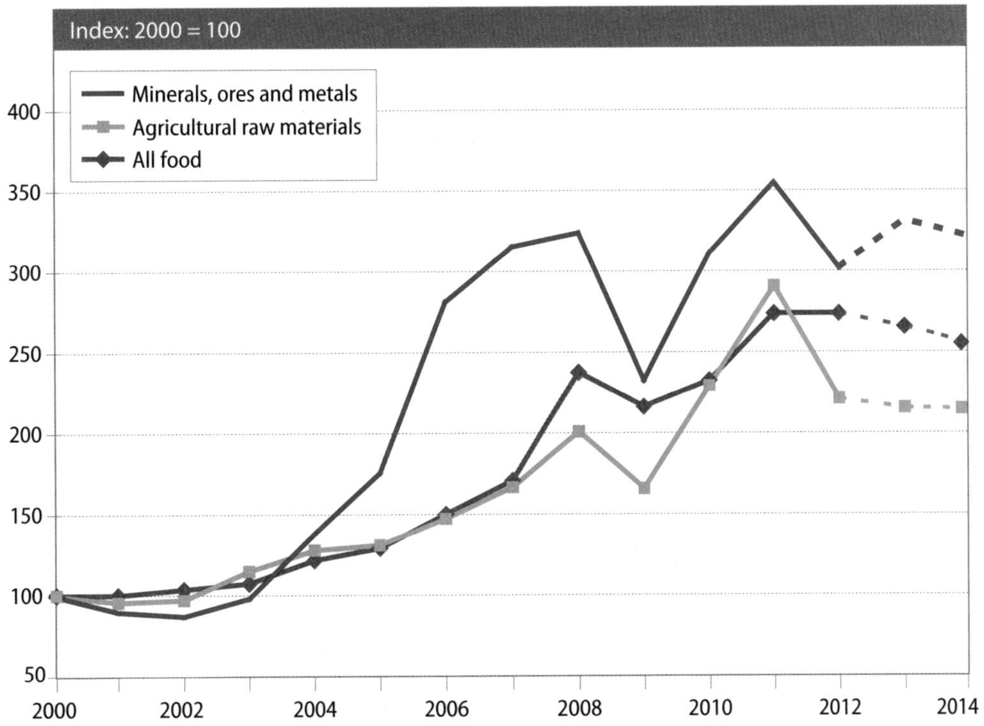

Index: 2000 = 100

Legend:
- Minerals, ores and metals
- Agricultural raw materials
- All food

Source: UN/DESA.

---

4   Food and Agricultural Organization of the United Nations, "World cereal production in 2012 down 2.7 percent from the 2011 record", FAO Cereal Supply and Demand Brief, 8 November 2012, available from http://www.fao.org/worldfoodsituation/wfs-home/csdb/en/.

The prices of metals and ores are likely to remain weak, as global demand is not expected to pick up quickly during 2013. Market conditions are likely to remain volatile, however. New rounds of monetary easing by major developed economies in a context of continued financial fragility, for instance, would likely induce more speculative financial flows into commodity markets, thereby keeping prices up and bringing more volatility into the market.

Continued volatility of capital flows to emerging markets

Emerging markets will continue to experience volatile capital flows

Global financial vulnerabilities remain unabatedly high. Bank lending has remained sluggish across developed economies. Financial conditions are likely to remain very fragile over the near term because of the time it will take to implement a solution to the euro area crisis and the shadow being cast over the recovery of the United States economy by the fiscal cliff. Most emerging markets are likely to continue experiencing volatile capital flows as they have over the past few years, strongly influenced by fragility in financial markets and QE policies in developed countries (figure I.9).

For the year 2012, net private capital inflows to emerging markets—that is, selected developing countries and economies in transition—are estimated to reach about $1 trillion, down by about 10 per cent from the previous year.[5] Next to ongoing deleveraging in developed countries, domestic factors specific to emerging market economies added to the downward pressure on net capital inflows in the first half of 2012. Slower growth in China and a few other Asian economies has lowered exchange-rate adjusted rate-of-return expectations of international investors. In North Africa and the Middle East, uncertainties

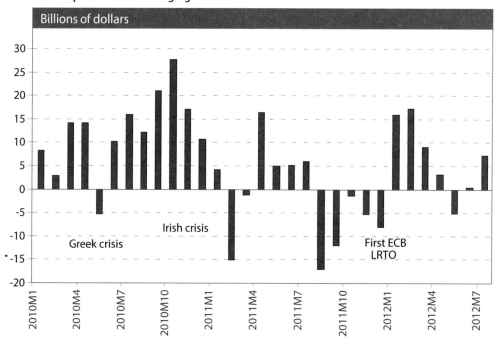

Figure I.9
Net capital flows to emerging markets

Source: IMF, WEO database,
October 2012.

5   Institute of International Finance, "Capital flows to emerging market economies", IIF Research Note, 13 October 2012. Data referring to private capital flows in this section cover about 30 emerging market economies and discuss net capital inflows separate from net outflows. In this sense the data differ from those presented in chapter III, which cover all developing and transition economies and apply the "net net flow" concept, that is net inflows less net outflows.

remain in the wake of political transformations and, in some cases, ongoing conflicts, creating an adverse environment for stronger capital inflows. Several Latin American countries, such as Brazil, have introduced more rigorous capital account regulation to limit short-term capital inflows and mitigate capital-flow and exchange-rate volatility.

The costs of external borrowing financing increased for developing countries and economies in transition when the crisis in the euro area escalated in mid-2012, but have since decreased and remain low in general (figure I.10).

Figure I.10
Daily yield spreads on emerging market bonds, January 2007-October 2012

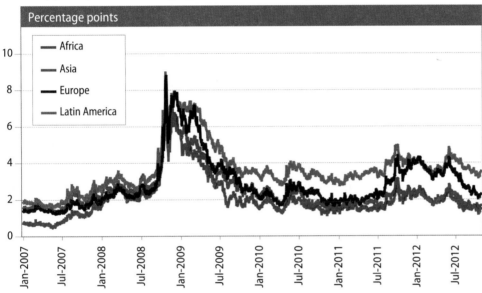

Source: JPMorgan Chase.

Net private capital inflows to emerging markets are not expected to increase by much on average in 2013, although volatility in markets would persist. New rounds of monetary easing announced by the central banks of developed countries are expected to provide some stabilizing impact on financial markets, which may help reduce risk aversion among investors. In view of the interest rate and growth differentials, investors are expected to retain interests in developing countries. At the same time, however, the continued need for deleveraging the bank system in developed countries keeps the risk of capital reversals high for emerging markets. Furthermore, uncertainties surround future growth prospects for some large developing economies (see "Uncertainties and risks" section), which could temper appetite for foreign investments in emerging markets.

Volatile capital inflows continue to be accompanied by large-scale capital outflows from emerging markets. Emerging market economies invested $1.3 trillion abroad in 2012, mostly associated with further increases in foreign exchange reserve holdings. Even though the degree of reserve accumulation was slightly less than in 2011, it signals continued concerns in emerging and developing country economies regarding world commodity and capital market volatility. While providing buffers against shocks and policy space to mitigate exchange-rate volatility, the massive reserve accumulation is also further weakening global demand.[6]

Capital inflows continue to be accompanied by large scale capital outflows from emerging markets

---

6   See, for example, the discussion in *World Economic and Social Survey 2010: Retooling Global Development* (United Nations publication, Sales No. E.10.II.C.1), chap V.

Net ODA flows from member countries of the Development Assistance Committee (DAC) of the Organization for Economic Cooperation and Development (OECD) reached $133.5 billion in 2011, up from $128.5 billion in 2010. In real terms, however, this represented a fall of 3 per cent, widening the delivery gap in meeting internationally agreed aid targets to $167 billion.[7] Preliminary results from the OECD survey of donors' forward spending plans indicate that Country Programmable Aid (CPA)—a core subset of aid that includes programmes and projects, which have predicted trends in total aid—is expected to increase by about 6 per cent in 2012, mainly on account of expected increases in outflows of soft loans from multilateral agencies that had benefited from earlier fund replenishments. However, CPA is expected to stagnate from 2013 to 2015, reflecting the delayed impact of the global economic crisis on donor country fiscal budgets.

Continued exchange-rate volatility

Exchange rates between major currencies remained relatively calm in response to QE measures

A large depreciation of the euro vis-à-vis other major currencies was the defining trend in global foreign exchange markets for the first half of 2012 (figure I.11), driven by the escalation of the debt crisis in the euro area. The euro rebounded somewhat in the second half of the year after the European authorities announced some new initiatives, including the OMT programme. The exchange rates between major currencies remained relatively calm in response to announcements of the OMT and further QE by the European Central Bank (ECB) and the Fed. In the outlook, given announced monetary policies in major developed economies and their generally weak growth prospects, it is difficult to ascertain a clear trend in the exchange rates among the major currencies.

Figure I.11
Exchange rates of major currencies vis-à-vis the United States dollar, January 2002-October 2012

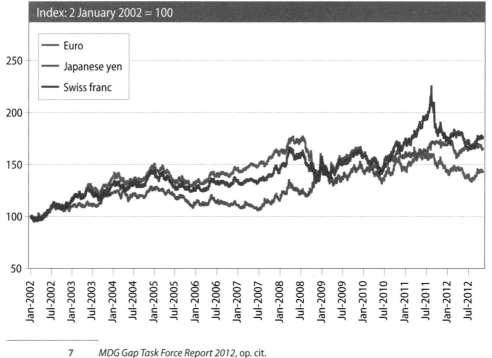

Source: UN/DESA, based on data from JPMorgan Chase.

---

7   *MDG Gap Task Force Report 2012*, op. cit.

After a precipitous fall in late 2011, the first half of 2012 saw currencies in most developing countries and the economies in transition depreciating further against the United States dollar (figure I.12). This trend was driven by two main factors: the reduction in capital inflows to these countries and the weaker growth prospects for these economies. Since mid-2012, the exchange rates of most of these currencies have stabilized, and some of them started to rebound after the launches of the new QE in major developed countries. In the outlook, continued implementation of the open-ended QE in major developed countries will likely increase the volatility in the exchange rates of the currencies of developing countries and the economies in transition.

Figure I.12

Exchange rates of selected developing country currencies vis-à-vis the United States dollar, January 2002-October 2012

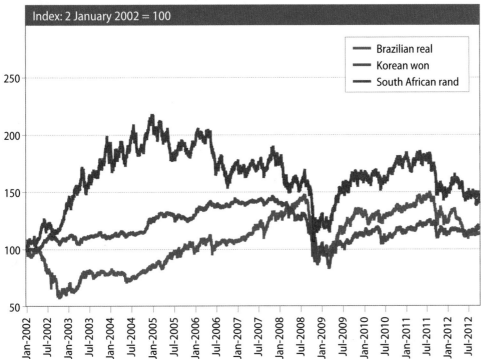

Source: UN/DESA, based on data from JPMorgan Chase.

No benign global rebalancing

Global imbalances, which refers to the current-account imbalances across major economies, have narrowed significantly in the aftermath of the global crisis. Even if widening slightly during 2012, they remain much smaller than in the years leading up to the crisis (figure I.13). Unfortunately, this trend cannot be seen as a sign of greater global financial stability and more balanced growth. External imbalances have fallen as a result of overall weakness in global demand and the synchronized downturn in international trade rather than through more structural shifts in savings rates and demand patterns.

The United States remained the largest deficit economy, with an estimated external deficit of about $467 billion (3.1 per cent of GDP) in 2012, down substantially

External imbalances have fallen as a result of overall weakness in global demand

Figure I.13
Global imbalances, 1997-2014

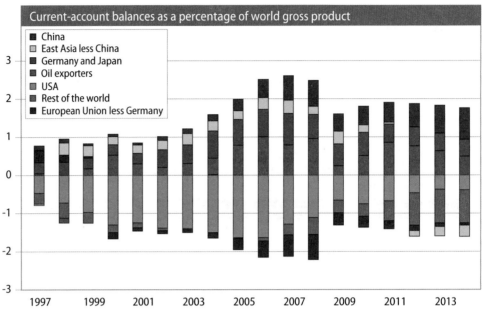

Current-account balances as a percentage of world gross product

Legend:
- China
- East Asia less China
- Germany and Japan
- Oil exporters
- USA
- Rest of the world
- European Union less Germany

Source: IMF World Economic Outlook database, October 2012 for historical data, and Project LINK for the 2012-2014 forecasts.

from the peak of $800 billion (6 per cent of GDP) registered in 2006. In mirror image, the external surpluses in China, Germany, Japan and a group of fuel-exporting countries have narrowed, albeit to varying degrees. China recorded an estimated surplus of slightly over 2 per cent of GDP in 2012, a sharp decline from a high of 10 per cent of GDP in 2007. Japan is expected to register a surplus of 4 per cent of GDP in 2012, also a significant reduction from its peak level of 5.0 per cent of GDP reached in 2007. While Germany's surplus declined only slightly, remaining above 5 per cent of GDP, the current account for the euro area as a whole turned from a deficit into a surplus of 1 per cent of GDP. Large surpluses relative to GDP are still present in oil-exporting countries, reaching 20 per cent of GDP or more in some of those in Western Asia.

The larger part of the adjustment reflects demand deflation in the global economy. In the United States, following several years of rebounding exports, both export and import demand weakened markedly in 2012. The corresponding narrowing of the saving-investment gap reflects a small decline in the savings rate and significant moderation in investment demand. The household saving rate, which increased from about 2.0 per cent of disposable household income before the financial crisis to about 5.0 per cent in the past few years, has started to fall again to about 3.8 per cent. The investment rate fell from 19.2 per cent in 2007 to 16.4 per cent of GDP in 2012. The government budget deficit dropped from 10.1 per cent of GDP in 2011 to 8.7 per cent in 2012, mainly as a result of further cuts in government spending, not increased government revenue. In the outlook, a further narrowing of the current-account deficit is expected in the United States in 2013 as a result of weakness caused by similar adjustments.

The decline in the external surplus of China was driven by a drop in export growth

In the surplus countries, the decline in the external surplus of China has mainly been driven by a significant drop in the growth of its exports caused by the weaker global economy, rather than a strengthening of imports pushed by domestic rebalancing. Both exports and imports in China decelerated substantially in 2012, even as China's exchange-rate policy has become more flexible. The Government has stepped up measures aiming to boost household consumption and rebalance the structure of the economy towards greater reliance on domestic demand, but thus far this has not resulted in any visible increase in the share consumption in GDP. The corresponding narrowing of the saving-investment ratio in China came mainly from a notable slowdown in the growth of investment, rather than a reduction in saving brought on by increased consumption.

In Japan, the narrowing of its external surplus has, to some extent, reflected the strengthening of its domestic demand—including increased imports of oil related to reconstruction in the aftermath of the devastating earthquake—but also a significant slowdown in exports.

The surpluses in oil-exporting countries are of quite a different nature as these countries will need to share the wealth generated by the endowment of oil with future generations through a continued accumulation of surpluses in the foreseeable future. Yet, some studies warn of a slowdown in oil exports for the Russian Federation in the medium run.[8]

In the euro area, the current-account deficits of member States in the periphery fell dramatically as a result of fiscal austerity and the severe contraction of private investment and consumption demand. Smaller current-account deficits were accompanied by large financial outflows triggered by panic in the banking sector of debt-distressed countries of the euro area. This reflects a stark reversal of the European economic integration process of past decades, when capital flowed from the core members to the peripheral members. In Germany, room remains for policies to stimulate more domestic demand so as to further narrow its external surplus.

Global imbalances persist, inducing wide imbalances in net asset and liability positions. The latest data show that the net external liability position of the United States widened to a record $4 trillion (more than 25 per cent of GDP) in 2011, a significant increase from $2.5 trillion in the previous year (figure I.14). The foreign assets owned by the United States totalled about $21 trillion by the end of 2011, while assets in the United States owned by the rest of the world totalled about $25 trillion.[9] Given the trends in global financial markets in 2012 and the current-account deficit trends discussed above, the net external liability position of the United States is estimated to have increased further during 2012.

Given current trends, the global imbalances are not expected to widen by a margin significant enough in the coming two years as to become an imminent threat to the stability of the global economy. However, the large net liability position of the United States poses a continued risk to the medium-term stability of exchange rates among major currencies, as investors and monetary authorities holding large dollar-reserve holdings may fear a strong depreciation of the dollar over time and which would accelerate such a process in possible disorderly fashion. Should the global economy fall into another recession, the imbalances could narrow further through demand deflation. It would thus seem

Persistent global imbalances have induced wide imbalances in net asset and liability positions

---

8   See Ernst & Young, "The future of Russian oil exploration: Beyond 2025", available from http://www.ey.com/Publication/vwLUAssets/Perspectives-of-Oil-and-Gas-explorations-2011-EN/$FILE/Perspectives-of-Oil-and-Gas-explorations-2011-EN.pdf.

9   The United States acquisitions of foreign assets increased by about $484 billion during the year, but valuation adjustments lowered the value of foreign assets owned by the United States by $702 billion, mostly from decreases in prices of foreign stocks. On the other hand, foreign acquisitions of the assets in the United States increased by about $1 trillion, and valuation adjustments raised the value of foreign-owned assets in the United States by $353 billion, mostly from price increases of the United States Treasury bonds. In short, the large increase in the net external liability position of the United States during 2011 mainly reflected a substantial change in the valuation of the assets and liability, with net flows accounting for a smaller part.

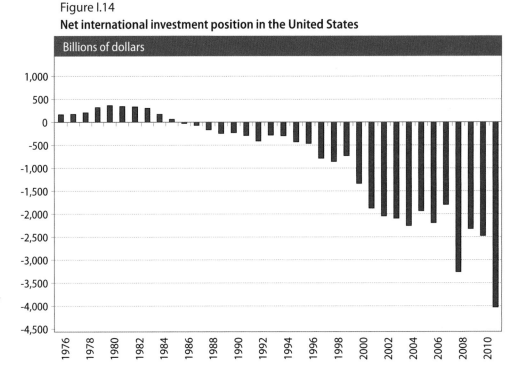

Figure I.14
Net international investment position in the United States

Source: UN/DESA, based on United States Bureau of Economic Analysis data.
Note: Data for 2009 and 2010 has been revised; data for 2011 is preliminary.

that international policy coordination should not have the rebalancing of current-account positions as its primary focus in the short term, but rather should give priority to concerted efforts to reinvigorate the global recovery, job creation and greater policy coherence to break out of the vicious circles.

Uncertainties and risks

The baseline outlook presented above is subject to major uncertainties and risks, mostly on the downside. The economic crisis in the euro area could continue to worsen and become more disruptive. The United States could fail to avert a fiscal cliff. The slowdown in a number of large developing countries, including China, could well deteriorate further, potentially ending in a "hard landing". Geopolitical tensions in West Asia and elsewhere in the world might spiral out of control. Given dangerously low stock-use ratios of basic grains, world food prices may easily spike with any significant weather shock and take a toll on the more vulnerable and poorest countries in the world. The discussion in this section focuses on the likelihood of the occurrence of the first three of these risks and what impact there would be on the global economy should they materialize.

Risk of a deeper crisis in the euro area

The euro area crisis continues to be the biggest threat to global growth

The crisis in the euro area continues to loom as the largest threat to global growth. The economies in the euro area have been suffering from entanglement in a number of vicious circles. The dangerous dynamics between sovereign debt distress and banking sector fragility are deteriorating the balance sheets of both Governments and commercial banks. The fiscal austerity responses are exacerbating the economic downturn, inspiring self-defeating efforts at fiscal consolidation and pushing up debt ratios, thereby triggering further budget cuts.

As a result, the region has already fallen into another recession three years after the global Great Recession of 2009, with unemployment rates rising to record highs since the debut of the euro. The situation in Greece remains particularly dire, despite the fact that fears of an imminent exit from the monetary union have eased and Greek government bond yields have subsequently retreated from their peaks following the debt restructuring in early 2012. GDP continues to plunge, however, even after having already fallen by nearly 20 per cent since 2007. Unless the troika of the EU, the ECB and the IMF relax the terms of conditionality on the target and the time span of Greek fiscal adjustment, and also provide more support, the economy will be unable to extricate itself from the present crisis any time soon.

The focus of attention shifted towards Spain in mid-2012. Spain is the fourth largest economy of the euro area, with a GDP twice the size of Greece, Ireland and Portugal combined. The country's borrowing costs surged when the Government asked for international financing to recapitalize the banks in early June 2012. Yields on 10-year sovereign bonds peaked at 7.6 per cent in late July, surpassing the level Greece, Ireland and Portugal faced when they were forced to ask for international assistance to address debt distress. Financial market contagion spread to Italy, which also has seen significant increases in sovereign borrowing costs.

These developments posed heightened systemic risks for the monetary union. In response, the ECB announced a new OMT programme in September through which it can make potentially unlimited purchases of sovereign bonds with a maturity of three years or shorter issued by selected debt-distressed countries. The OMT programme aims to reduce borrowing costs for these countries. However, the ECB can only purchase bonds under the OMT programme if countries have applied for international assistance via both the European Financial Stability Facility (EFSF) and the European Stability Mechanism (ESM), which comes with policy conditionality attached.

After the announcement, sovereign yields of Spain and a few other countries retreated substantially (figure I.15). In late September, Spanish authorities presented a budget that aims to cut the projected 2013 deficit by €40 billion ($51.4 billion). Government spending is to be cut by 8.9 per cent, while public infrastructure spending is to drop from 1.3 per cent to 0.89 per cent of GDP, among other austerity measures. A recent bank stress test showed a capital shortfall of €59.3 billion for Spanish banks. It will be feasible to repair this with the €100 billion in European aid the Spanish Government has already requested for recapitalization of its banks.

The OMT programme initiated by the ECB, if implemented as planned, potentially could significantly reduce debt refinancing costs for Spain and debt-distressed euro area countries. Uncertainties remain, however, on a number of issues unfolding in the future. For example, the agreement made earlier by euro area leaders to directly recapitalize Spanish banks without increasing the country's sovereign debt was considered to be a key initiative to effectively short-circuit the vicious feedback between sovereign debt and bank fragility. Subsequently, however, some euro area member countries have voiced a somewhat different interpretation in that the direct bank recapitalization would work only for banks getting into trouble in the future, not for those being rescued under the current programme for Spain. If this interpretation would hold in practice, Spain's government deficit would be much higher than originally projected and could trigger severe additional fiscal adjustment.

The OMT programme of the ECB could significantly reduce debt refinancing costs, but uncertainties remain

Figure I.15
Yields on two-year government bonds of selected euro area countries, January 2010-October 2012

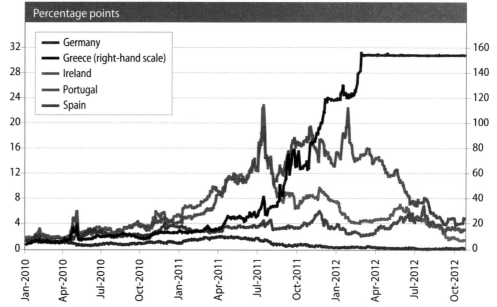

Source: JPMorgan Chase.

Question remains as to whether Spain actually needs such deep budget cuts. In contrast with Greece, some analysts argue that Spain's woes started in the private sector as the housing bubble burst, drastically reducing government tax revenue and prompting a rescue of banks. Before that, the Government had relatively low debt levels and a modest deficit. From this perspective, fiscal austerity would not address the root cause of the problem in Spain, but only exacerbate the economic downturn and cause more unemployment.

In any case, even if the policy initiatives announced to date are implemented as planned, they seem to be insufficient to break the downward spiral many euro area members face in the short run and inadequate to boost a solid growth in the medium run. Given all the uncertainties and risks, a number of researchers have already studied the scenarios and economic ramifications of the possible exit of some euro area members.[10] The pessimistic scenario, discussed further below, does not assume any break-up of the euro area or the exit of any of its members, however. The real implications of such an event are extremely difficult to gauge because of the large amount of financial market uncertainty that would arise and the complex, but as yet unknown, set of institutional rearrangements that would result.

Instead, the downside scenario presented below looks at possibility of a much deeper recession in the euro area than delineated in the baseline. The further downturn

The announced policy initiatives seem to be insufficient to break the downward spiral

---

10   Global Insight estimates that an exit of Greece would come with substantial international spillover effects. It estimates that the simulated output loss for the United States could be as much as 2.5 per cent, pushing the economy into recession in 2013. (See IHS Global Insight, "US Executive Summary", November 2012). Oxford Economics ("Central banks take out additional insurance", Global Scenario Service, September 2012) estimates that an exit of Greece in the third quarter of 2013 would lower euro area GDP by 3.5 per cent and WGP would drop 1.3 per cent below the baseline for 2014. In a fuller euro area break-up with Greece, Portugal, Ireland, Spain, Italy, and Cyprus exiting in the first quarter of 2014, Oxford Economics estimates output losses could be as high as 10 per cent and those for the world as a whole would also be commensurately higher.

could be caused by a delayed implementation of the OMT programme and other support measures for those members in need. Delays could occur through political difficulties in reaching agreement between the countries in need of assistance and the troika of EU, ECB and IMF, and/or much larger detrimental effects of the fiscal austerity programmes and more difficulties in structural adjustments than anticipated in the baseline forecast.[11]

Uncertainties about the "fiscal cliff" in the United States

Unless Congress can reach an agreement to avert it, the United States will face a sharp change in its government spending and tax policy at the end of 2012. Because of the potentially severe implications, it has been coined the "fiscal cliff". The tax cuts endorsed during the Administration of George W. Bush worth $280 billion per year (often referred to as the "Bush tax cuts"), the 2 percentage point payroll tax reduction worth $125 billion, and the emergency unemployment compensation worth $40 billion introduced during the first term of the Obama Administration, were all designed to expire at the end of 2012. More specifically, the expiration of the Bush tax cuts would imply an increase in income tax rates across all income levels by about 5 percentage points in 2013. Among the other changes associated with the expiration of Bush tax cuts are the phasing out of the reduction in the Federal Child Tax Credit and an increase in the maximum tax rate for long-term capital gains by about 5 percentage points. The expiration of the 2-percentage-point reduction in employee payroll taxes would imply a decline in aggregate disposable income by about $125 billion. Moreover, the expiration of emergency unemployment compensation, which was first passed into law in 2008 and has been extended in the past four years, would imply a reduction in consumption spending by about $40 billion.[12] On the expenditure side, automatic budget cuts will be activated, cutting expenditure by $98 billion.[13] Together these actions amount to a downward adjustment in aggregate demand of no less than 4 per cent of GDP.

The risk was still clear and present in the immediate aftermath of the November 6 presidential and congressional elections in the United States. In the worst case, political gridlock would prevent Congress from reaching any agreement, leading to a full-scale drop in government spending by about $98 billion and substantial hikes in taxes amounting to $450 billion in 2013. It is reasonable to assume that after realizing the costs to the economy, policymakers will feel compelled to reach an agreement on reinstating those tax reduction measures and on ceasing the automatic spending cuts in the second half of 2013.

The United States may see major changes in government spending and tax policy at the end of 2012

---

11 More specifically, the scenario of a deeper euro crisis presented in table I.2 below assumes further fiscal tightening in the debt-distressed countries and no use of the OMT programme. As a result, bond yields and borrowing costs increase, while consumer and business confidence drop further, affecting private consumption and investment demand.

12 For more details, see JPMorgan Chase Bank NA, "The US fiscal cliff: an update and a downgrade", Economic Research Note, 18 October 2012, available from https://mm.jpmorgan.com/EmailPubS ervlet?h=c7s2j110&doc=GPS-965096-0.pdf; and Joseph Brusuelas, "Fiscal cliff", Bloomberg Brief, 25 September 2012, available from http://www.bloombergbriefs.com/files/2012-9-25-Fiscal-Cliff-Special-Issue.pdf.

13 These automatic cuts are specified in the Budget Control Act which was adopted as a result of the failure of the Joint Select Committee on Deficit Reduction (the so-called "Supercommittee") to reach an agreement in 2011 as to how to bring the budget deficit down to sustainable levels over the next ten years.

A hard landing of some large developing economies

Growth slowed noticeably during 2012 in a number of large developing economies, such as Brazil, China and India, which all enjoyed a long period of rapid growth prior to the global financial crisis and managed to recover quickly at a robust pace in 2010. For example, growth in Brazil dropped from a peak of 7.5 per cent in 2010 to an estimated 1.3 per cent in 2012; in China, from 10.4 per cent to 7.7 per cent; and in India, from 8.9 per cent to 5.5 per cent.

Given the uncertainties about their external demand and various domestic growth challenges, risks of further and larger-than-expected declines in the growth of these economies are not trivial. In this section, China is used as an example to illustrate such risks and their implications for these economies and for the rest of the world.

China's exports continued to slow during 2012, owing to weak demand in major developed economies. For 2012 as whole, real exports for China may register growth of about 5-6 per cent, compared to an average growth of about 20 per cent in the past 10 years. Meanwhile, growth in investment, which contributed to more than 50 per cent of GDP growth in the past decades, has been decelerating. Growth in nominal fixed investment has declined from 25 per cent a year ago to 20 per cent currently. As fixed investment accounts for almost 50 per cent of GDP, this deceleration alone will reduce GDP growth by 2.5 percentage points. Compared with 2009, when China's exports dropped by more than 10 per cent, it appears that the present deceleration in GDP growth comes mainly on account of domestic demand.

The slowdown in investment growth in China has been driven primarily by two factors. First, the Government has adopted policies to control the risk of asset price bubbles in the housing sector, including requirements for larger down payments and limits on the number of housing units people can buy. Real estate investment, which accounts for about 25 per cent of total fixed investment, increased by 15 per cent in the first half of 2012, but the pace of growth was down from 33 per cent recorded a year ago. Acquisition of land for home construction has been declining at an annualized pace of about 20 per cent since the beginning of 2012. Because this is a key source of revenue for local governments in China, their fiscal space has been heavily reduced. Slower real estate investment growth also has considerable damaging effects on supplying industries.

Second, the central Government has become more cautious about fiscal stimulus. Most of the 2009-2010 large-scale fiscal stimulus package, costing about 4 trillion yuan, was used for infrastructure investment and formed an important driver of economic growth in those years. However, after it was phased out in 2011, increasing concerns have been expressed in China over unintended side effects created by the stimulus and vast excess production capacity emerging in some industrial sectors. The Government seems set to put more effort into restructuring the economy, rather than trying to create more aggregate demand stimulus. This is based on the assumption that a rebalancing of the economy through an increase in the share of household consumption in GDP could compensate for a decline in the investment rate and a slowdown in exports. It assumes that with such rebalancing the economy could still grow at a robust pace of 7.5 per cent (which is the official growth target for 2012). However, thus far it has proven difficult to boost consumption in the short run and, moreover, industrial restructuring and future GDP growth would require making substantial new investments today.

Furthermore, local governments have been facing financing constraints in the implementation of new projects. Fixed investment projects managed by local governments account for more than 90 per cent of total fixed investment in value terms. The financing constraints have emerged because of less revenue from land sales and lack of bank lending as the banks await positive signals from the central Government.

Because of these factors, there are substantial risks for much lower GDP growth in China. The downside scenario presented below assumes a slowdown in growth to about 5 per cent per year, particularly if fixed investment growth decelerates further, subtracting another 5-10 percentage points per year in 2013-2014. Other assumptions for this alternative scenario for the Chinese economy include the central Government maintaining the tightening measures in the housing sector and no fiscal stimulus.

In the downside scenario, it is assumed that growth in China would slow to about 5 per cent

Risk of a double-dip global recession

Table I.2 summarizes the global economic consequences of the three scenarios discussed above, based on simulations using the United Nations World Economic Forecasting Model.

The euro crisis scenario focuses on the relatively high risk of deeper fiscal cuts in the debt-distressed countries. For reasons mentioned above, the much worse case, but, for now, less likely scenario of a break-up of the monetary union is not considered here. More specifically, in this first scenario, Greece, Italy, Portugal and Spain are expected to take further austerity measures in 2013, with deeper cuts than assumed in the baseline. As a result, the estimated output losses in these economies would be between 1 and 2 percentage points in 2013. The deeper recession is assumed to spread to other economies through trade channels and, more importantly, through greater financial uncertainty as confidence in the euro and prospects for recovery erodes further. As a result, the economy of the euro area would shrink by 0.9 per cent compared with the baseline forecast for 2013, thus further deepening the euro area recession that set in throughout 2012. During 2013-2015, the cumulative output loss for the euro area as a whole would amount to 3.3 per cent. The further weakening in the euro area would spill over to the rest of the world and the cumulative loss of global output would amount to 1.1 percentage points. The other developed economies, such as the United States and Japan, would all suffer notable losses. The deepening of the euro crisis would cost developing countries about 0.5 per cent of GDP on average.

A deepening of the euro crisis would cause a loss of global output of more than 9 per cent

In the fiscal cliff scenario, world economic growth would slow to 1.2 per cent in 2013, compared to 2.4 per cent in the baseline. The cumulative output loss between 2013 and 2015 would be 2.5 percentage points. The United States economy would enter into recession and Japan and the EU would also be severely affected, with output losses of about 2 percentage points during 2013-2015. Mexico and Central America would be hardest hit among developing countries, losing about 3.0 percentage points owing to close economic ties with the United States. East Asian economies would see cumulative output losses of about 1.6 percentage points.

The fiscal cliff would have an even larger impact

A hard landing of the Chinese economy, with GDP growth slowing to 5 per cent in 2013, would also have a visible impact on the world economy. China accounts for about 8 per cent of WGP and 10 per cent of world trade. Compared with the baseline forecast, a 3 percentage point deceleration in the pace of growth of the Chinese economy would cause a cumulative global output loss of 1.5 percentage points during 2013-2015.

Given its close economic ties with China, Japan would be most affected, suffering a GDP loss of 1.6 percentage points. GDP of the United States and the EU would drop by 0.7 and 0.6 percentage points, respectively, over 2013-2015 compared with the baseline. Much of their output losses would be caused by lower exports of capital goods to China.

A hard landing of the Chinese economy would also have a visible impact on the world economy

Table I.2
Downside scenarios for the world economy[a]

Percentage deviation from baseline GDP level	Output loss (-)											
	Deeper euro area crisis			United States fiscal cliff			Hardlanding in China			Three scenarios combined		
	2013	2014	2015	2013	2014	2015	2013	2014	2015	2013	2014	2015
World	**-0.3**	**-0.7**	**-1.1**	**-1.2**	**-2.1**	**-2.5**	**-0.4**	**-1.0**	**-1.5**	**-2.2**	**-4.3**	**-5.9**
Developed economies	-0.4	-0.9	-1.5	-1.7	-2.7	-3.2	-0.1	-0.4	-0.8	-2.5	-4.7	-6.4
United States of America	-0.1	-0.4	-0.8	-3.8	-5.2	-5.3	-0.1	-0.3	-0.7	-4.1	-6.3	-7.3
Japan	-0.2	-0.4	-0.6	-0.6	-1.2	-2.1	-0.4	-0.9	-1.6	-1.7	-3.5	-5.8
European Union	-0.7	-1.8	-2.7	-0.5	-1.2	-1.9	-0.1	-0.3	-0.6	-1.6	-4.1	-6.5
EU-15	-0.7	-1.8	-2.8	-0.5	-1.2	-2.0	-0.1	-0.3	-0.6	-1.6	-4.2	-6.7
New EU members	-0.6	-1.1	-1.3	-0.2	-0.6	-1.1	-0.1	-0.3	-0.6	-1.4	-2.8	-3.7
Euro area	-0.9	-2.1	-3.3	-0.5	-1.2	-1.8	-0.1	-0.3	-0.6	-1.7	-4.6	-7.3
Other European countries	-0.4	-0.9	-1.2	-0.2	-0.8	-1.4	-0.1	-0.3	-0.7	-1.1	-2.8	-4.2
Other developed economies	-0.1	-0.2	-0.3	-0.6	-1.3	-1.7	-0.1	-0.3	-0.7	-0.8	-2.0	-3.0
Economies in transition	-0.3	-0.5	-0.6	-0.2	-0.5	-0.7	-0.1	-0.3	-0.6	-0.9	-1.8	-2.4
South-Eastern Europe	-0.5	-0.8	-0.9	-0.1	-0.4	-0.7	0.0	-0.2	-0.3	-1.1	-1.9	-2.4
Commonwealth of Independent States and Georgia	-0.3	-0.5	-0.6	-0.2	-0.5	-0.8	-0.1	-0.4	-0.7	-0.9	-1.8	-2.4
Russian Federation	-0.3	-0.5	-0.6	-0.2	-0.5	-0.8	-0.1	-0.4	-0.7	-0.8	-1.8	-2.4
Developing economies	-0.2	-0.3	-0.5	-0.3	-0.9	-1.3	-1.1	-2.3	-3.0	-1.7	-3.7	-5.1
Africa	-0.5	-0.5	-0.6	-0.6	-1.0	-1.0	-0.4	-0.8	-1.1	-1.8	-2.5	-2.9
North Africa	-0.9	-0.8	-0.9	-0.9	-1.2	-1.1	-0.2	-0.4	-0.7	-2.7	-2.9	-3.1
Sub-Saharan Africa	-0.3	-0.3	-0.4	-0.5	-0.9	-0.9	-0.5	-0.9	-1.3	-1.5	-2.3	-2.8
Nigeria	-0.4	-0.5	-0.7	-1.1	-1.8	-1.7	-0.1	-0.4	-0.7	-1.8	-3.0	-3.5
South Africa	-0.3	-0.2	-0.3	-0.3	-0.5	-0.5	-1.1	-1.8	-2.3	-1.9	-2.6	-3.2
Others	-0.3	-0.3	-0.4	-0.4	-0.7	-0.8	-0.2	-0.6	-0.9	-1.1	-1.8	-2.3
East and South Asia	-0.1	-0.3	-0.5	-0.3	-0.9	-1.4	-1.6	-3.3	-4.2	-2.2	-4.8	-6.4
East Asia	-0.2	-0.4	-0.6	-0.3	-1.0	-1.6	-2.0	-3.9	-4.9	-2.6	-5.6	-7.4
China	-0.2	-0.4	-0.7	-0.4	-1.1	-1.8	-3.0	-5.7	-6.8	-3.7	-7.6	-9.6
South Asia	-0.1	-0.2	-0.3	-0.1	-0.4	-0.5	-0.3	-0.8	-1.5	-0.6	-1.5	-2.5
India	-0.1	-0.2	-0.2	-0.1	-0.4	-0.5	-0.1	-0.3	-0.5	-0.4	-0.9	-1.4
Western Asia	-0.1	-0.2	-0.3	-0.2	-0.5	-0.7	-0.1	-0.3	-0.6	-0.6	-1.2	-1.9
Latin America and the Caribbean	-0.2	-0.3	-0.4	-0.5	-1.2	-1.7	-0.4	-0.9	-1.5	-1.0	-2.5	-3.7
South America	-0.1	-0.2	-0.3	-0.2	-0.6	-0.9	-0.4	-1.0	-1.6	-0.8	-2.0	-3.1
Brazil	-0.1	-0.2	-0.3	-0.1	-0.4	-0.7	-0.4	-1.1	-1.7	-0.8	-1.9	-2.9
Mexico and Central America	-0.3	-0.4	-0.6	-1.0	-2.6	-3.2	-0.5	-0.9	-1.4	-1.4	-3.7	-5.2
Mexico	-0.3	-0.4	-0.6	-1.0	-2.7	-3.4	-0.5	-1.0	-1.5	-1.4	-3.9	-5.5
Caribbean	-0.1	-0.2	-0.4	-0.5	-1.2	-1.6	0.0	-0.1	-0.3	-0.7	-1.7	-2.5
Least developed countries	-0.2	-0.3	-0.4	-0.3	-0.6	-0.8	-0.2	-0.5	-0.7	-0.8	-1.6	-2.1

Source: UN/DESA.

a See section on "Uncertainties and risks" for assumptions for these scenarios.

Developing Asia would also feel the consequences through trade channels, especially as it experiences decreased demand for intermediate products in the context of global value chains (see chapter II for further discussion). Economies in Latin America, Africa and Western Asia would be most impacted by lower demand for primary commodities, losing about 1 per cent of their aggregate income.

It is difficult to ascertain the probability of these three risks materializing simultaneously. However, considering the magnitude of the global consequences of each of these events separately, if these events were to occur at the same time, thereby reinforcing each other, the global economy would fall into another Great Recession.

Policy challenges

Current macroeconomic policy stances

Weakening economic growth and policy uncertainties cast a shadow over the global economic outlook. As indicated, most developed countries have adopted a combination of fiscal austerity and expansionary monetary policies, aiming to reduce public debt and lower debt refinancing costs in order to break away from the vicious dynamics between sovereign debt and banking sector fragility. These policy measures were expected to calm financial markets and restore consumer and investor confidence. Supported by structural reforms of entitlement programmes, labour markets and business regulation, the improved environment is expected to help restore economic growth and reduce unemployment. However, reducing debt stocks is proving to be much more challenging than policymakers expected. Public debt rollover requirements remain very high and continue to expose fiscal balances to the whims of financial markets. Helped by the QE policies of central banks, borrowing costs have been contained and are elevated only for a subset of debt-distressed euro area countries. While the QE programmes have helped lower long-term interest rates, their impact on economic growth will be rather limited at this stage of the recovery.

> Most developed countries have adopted a combination of fiscal austerity and expansionary monetary policies

An additional problem is that fiscal consolidation efforts of most developed countries rely more on spending retrenchment than improving revenue collection. The former tends to be more detrimental to economic growth in the short run, particularly when the economy is in a downward cycle.[14] In many developed countries, public investment is being cut more severely than any other item, which may also prove costly to medium-term growth. In most cases, spending cuts also involve entitlement reforms, which immediately weaken automatic stabilizers in the short run by curtailing pension benefits, shortening the length of unemployment benefit schemes and/or shifting more of the burden of healthcare costs to households. Moreover, the fiscal austerity measures have been found to induce greater inequality in the short run.[15] The impact tends to be stronger when unemployment effects are higher, when there is no compensation for the cost of entitlement reform to lower- and middle-income groups, and when revenue increases are pursued through increases in sales or value-added tax rates. Rising inequality by itself tends to weaken the recovery, as lower-income groups tend to have higher spending pro-

---

14   See *World Economic Situation and Prospects 2012* (United Nations publication, Sales No. E.12. II.C.2), box I.3.

15   International Monetary Fund, *Fiscal Monitor: Taking stock—A progress report on fiscal adjustment* (Washington, D.C., October 2012).

pensities. The distributional impact of spending and revenue measures thus should be a concern to macroeconomic policymakers. In short, downside risks for developed countries remain extremely high, because the present policy stances are, on balance, not supportive of growth and job creation, and thus fail to definitively break out of the vicious circle.

Most developing countries and economies in transition have relatively stronger fiscal positions. Some have opted to put fiscal consolidation on hold in the face of global economic weakening. Fiscal deficits may rise in most low-income countries that have slowing government revenue from commodity exports and the growing weight of food and energy subsidies. Concerns are also mounting in developing countries about the possible adverse effects of QE on the financial and macroeconomic stability of their economies through increased volatility in international prices of commodities, capital flows and exchange rates. Such concerns underlie the further accumulation of reserves and justify maintaining capital controls. Facing a slowdown in growth and inflation, central banks in many developing countries and economies in transition have eased monetary policy during 2012. In the outlook, further monetary easing will be likely in many of these countries, except for those with persistently high inflation, such as South Asia and Africa.

The need for more forceful and concerted actions

Given the looming uncertainties and downside risks discussed in the previous section, current policy stances seem to fall well short of what is needed to prevent the global economy from slipping into another recession. More forceful and concerted actions should be considered.

First, the policy uncertainties associated with the three key risks discussed in the downward scenario need to be addressed immediately through shifts in approach and greater consideration of international spillover effects of national policies. In the euro area, the piecemeal approach to dealing with the debt crises of individual countries of the past two years should be replaced by a more comprehensive and integrated approach, so as to address the systemic crisis of the monetary union and mitigate the key risks for the stability of the global economy. While individual countries may still need to confront issues in their domestic economic structures and institutions, crucial collective efforts are needed to close the institutional gaps and mend the pervasive deficiencies of the EMU, including through laying solid foundations for fiscal and banking unions. Although important steps in this direction are being taken or considered, the present state of affairs requires much swifter and more forceful action. Only when concrete actions are taken that will restore confidence in the union can other more technical policy measures be put in place to deal with such issues as how to resolve debt overhang and how to break the linkage between sovereign risk and bank fragility. Policymakers in the United States should prevent a sudden and severe contraction in fiscal policy—the so-called fiscal cliff—and overcome the political gridlock that was still present at the end of 2012. As holds for the EU, the global ramifications of failing to do so should be considered. It is only feasible to work out the current debt problems over the long run, and a fiscal consolidation plan will be credible only when rooted in an explicit strategy of economic growth and jobs creation. The major developing countries facing the risk of hard landings of their economies should engage in stronger countercyclical policy stances aligned with measures to address structural problems over the medium term. China, for instance, possesses ample policy space for a much stronger push to rebalance its economy towards domestic demand, including through increased government spending on public services such as health care, education and

Policy uncertainties should be addressed immediately and a different approach must be taken

social security—all of which will help lower precautionary household savings and increase consumption, thus reducing dependence on external demand.

Second, more specifically, fiscal policy should become more countercyclical, more supportive of jobs creation and more equitable. The present focus on fiscal consolidation in the short run, especially among developed countries, has proven to be counterproductive and to cause more protracted debt adjustment. The focus needs to shift in a number of different directions:

- As a starting point, a first priority of fiscal adjustment should be to provide more direct support to output and employment growth by boosting aggregate demand and, at the same time, spread out plans for achieving fiscal sustainability over the medium-to-long term. Introducing cyclically adjusted or structural budget targets will allow for keeping a countercyclical stance while aiming for fiscal sustainability over the medium term.

- Fiscal multipliers tend to be more forceful during a downturn, but can be strengthened further by shifting budget priorities to growth-enhancing spending, undoing cuts in public investment and expanding subsidies on hiring (which may be targeted towards new labour entrants and the long unemployed) as well as enhancing public work programmes and employment schemes. On the tax side, reducing taxes on labour and changing tax codes to reduce labour income tax wedges for youth, women, and older workers are options that provide short-term boosts to employment as well as labour supply.

- The distributional consequences of fiscal policies should be duly considered, not only for equity reasons, but also because of their implications for growth and employment generation. As indicated, rising inequality tends to have a dampening effect on aggregate demand and hence on economic growth. Shifting spending priorities to enhance employment effects will help avoid such an outcome, as much as would maintaining an adequate degree of progressivity in taxation and access to social benefits. Many middle- and low-income countries may wish to reconsider across-the-board subsidies on food and fuel; these tend to come with a heavy fiscal cost, while the benefits may accrue most to higher-income groups. Better targeting would provide more effective income protection to the poor at potentially much lower fiscal cost.

- Economic recovery can be strengthened in the short and longer run by promoting green growth through fiscal incentives and investments in infrastructure and new technologies. Lessons can be learned from several developing countries, such as the Republic of Korea, which have successfully provided economic stimulus through green infrastructure investment and energy-saving incentives. This has been found to generate strong employment effects, suggesting that investing in green growth can be a win-win solution. Moreover, these measures are imperative to substantially accelerating reductions in greenhouse gas emissions—an essential step in combating climate change. Developing countries also stand to gain, provided they obtain technological and financial support to adopt the still higher-cost clean energy technologies without jeopardizing economic development prospects.

Third, global financial market instability needs to be attacked at its roots. This challenge is twofold. First, greater synergy must be found between monetary and fiscal stimulus. Continuation of expansionary monetary policies among developed countries

Fiscal policy should become more countercyclical, more supportive of jobs creation and more equitable

Global financial market instability needs to be attacked at its root causes

will be needed, but negative spillover effects into capital-flow and exchange-rate volatility must be contained. This will require reaching agreement at the international level on the magnitude, speed and timing of QE policies within a broader framework of targets to redress the global imbalances. The second part of the challenge is to accelerate regulatory reforms of the financial sector. This will be essential in order to avoid the systemic risks and excessive risk-taking that have led to the low-growth trap and financial fragility in developed countries and high capital flow volatility for developing countries. Steps have been proposed in some national jurisdictions, but implementation is lagging behind. Moreover, insufficient coordination between national bodies appears to result in a regulatory patchwork. Global financial stability is unlikely to be achieved in the absence of a comprehensive, binding and internationally coordinated framework. This is needed to limit regulatory arbitrage, which includes shifting high-risk activities from more to less strictly regulated environments. Among other measures, such a framework should include strict limits on positions that financial investors can take in commodity futures and derivatives markets—measures that may also help stem volatility in capital flows and commodity prices.

Sufficient resources need
to be made available to
developing countries

Fourth, sufficient resources must be available to developing countries, especially those possessing limited fiscal space and facing large development needs. These resources will be needed to accelerate progress towards the achievement of the MDGs and for investments in sustainable and resilient growth, especially for the LDCs. Fiscal austerity among donor countries has also affected aid budgets, as seen in the decline of ODA in real terms in 2011. Further declines may be expected in the outlook. Apart from delivering on existing aid commitments, donor countries should consider mechanisms to delink aid flows from their business cycles so as to prevent delivery shortfalls in times of crisis when the need for development aid is most urgent. In this regard, internationally agreed taxes (such as airline levies, currency transaction taxes or carbon taxes), along with the possibility of leveraging idle special drawing rights (SDRs) for development finance could be considered, as suggested in a recent United Nations report.[16]

A jobs creation and green growth-oriented agenda as outlined above is compatible with medium-term reduction of public debt ratios and benign global rebalancing, as shown in a scenario of internationally concerted policies simulated using the United Nations Global Policy Model (GPM).[17] With continued existing policies, but assuming no major deepening of the euro crisis, growth of WGP would average, at best, about 3 per cent per year on average, far from sufficient to deal with the jobs crisis or bring down public debt ratios. The alternative scenario, based on the agenda outlined above, includes a shift in fiscal policies away from austerity and towards more job creation through, inter alia, more spending on infrastructure; energy efficiency, social programmes and tax and subsidy measures to stimulate private investment projects in these areas; continued expansionary monetary policies aligned with stronger capital account regulation to stem capital flow volatility; and enhanced development assistance to the poorest nations. The GPM simulations show that under such a policy scenario, WGP would grow at an average rate of 4.5 per cent between 2013 and 2017, public debt-to-GDP ratios would stabilize and

---

16   *World Economic and Social Survey 2012: In Search of New Development Finance* (United Nations publication, Sales No. E.12.II.C.1).

17   The scenario is an update of the ones presented in *World Economic Situation and Prospects 2012*, op. cit., pp. 33-36; and United Nations Economic and Social Council, "World economic situation and prospects as of mid-2012 (E/2012/72).

start falling from 2016 or earlier. Employment levels in major developed countries would gradually increase and return to pre-crises levels in absolute terms by 2014 and by 2017 after accounting for labour force growth. The employment recovery thus would come much sooner than in the baseline, although remaining protracted even with the suggested internationally concerted strategy for growth and jobs. An additional 33 million jobs per year on average would be created in developing and transition economies between 2013 and 2017 (see box I.3).

Box I.3

An internationally coordinated strategy for jobs and growth

An alternative policy scenario based on the recommendations in this chapter has been created using the United Nations Global Policy Model (GPM). The key finding is that such a scenario would avoid a widespread double-dip recession; instead, it would allow for a benign rebalancing of the global economy. Job losses caused by the global financial crisis would see recovery and a shift towards more sustainable fiscal balances and debt levels would begin, setting the global economy on a more sustained (and sustainable) path to growth.

The key differences with the baseline policy assumptions are that:

- Policies, especially those in developed economies, shift away from premature fiscal austerity and towards a more countercyclical stance, thereby supporting aggregate demand in the short run. This is done cautiously, however. Public spending is allowed to grow, but more slowly than GDP. As tax revenues grow in response to overall income growth, budget deficits narrow and debt-to-GDP ratios decline over time.

- In all countries, Governments enhance public spending on social and physical infrastructure and public investment as well as expanding fiscal incentives for private investors promoting "green" growth (including through greater energy efficiency and clean energy generation). This also applies to developing countries where most additional public spending is directed to infrastructure investment, including capacity in sustainable agriculture and renewable energy. Green growth investments are generally perceived to have greater job creation effects than existing "brown" technologies. This is also assumed to be the case in the GPM.

- Industrial policy incentives implemented by developing countries are assumed to be supportive of economic diversification and reduced dependence on commodity exports.

- Central banks and other financial regulators in developed countries further step up action to prevent soaring interest rates on sovereign bonds and accelerate regulatory action that reduces bank fragility and helps commercial lending to grow again.

- The policy scenario further assumes that these national policies are part of an internationally concerted strategy. Policy coordination would ensure that there is sufficient aggregate fiscal stimulus in the short run, while differentiating stimulus across countries in accordance with available fiscal and other macroeconomic policy space (based on initial levels of indebtedness, sovereign borrowing costs and size of external surplus). Furthermore, it is assumed that monetary policy action is better coordinated internationally to prevent the strategy underlying the alternative scenario from being disrupted by excessive exchange-rate and capital flow volatility. Through concerted efforts, developing countries (low-income countries, in particular), are provided with adequate access to official development assistance and other external financing to complement domestic resources for financing new investments in infrastructure and sustainable energy and agriculture.

Box I.3 (cont'd)

Under these assumptions, growth of world gross product would accelerate to about 4.5 per cent per year, with both developed and developing economies accelerating output growth by between 1 and 2 percentage points compared with the baseline (see figures A and B). Shortly after the new policies are in place, the jobs deficit caused by the global financial crisis of 2008-2009 would start to close, especially in the developed countries. Employment levels in major developed countries would gradually increase and return to pre-crisis levels in absolute terms by 2014, and by 2017 after accounting for labour force growth. The employment recovery would thus come much sooner than in the baseline, although it would remain protracted, even with the suggested internationally concerted strategy for growth and jobs. An additional 33 million jobs per year on average would be created in developing and transition economies between 2013 and 2017.

The simulation also shows that more rapid recovery of growth and employment helps to stabilize public debts. After an initial increase, government deficits would quickly decrease, stabilizing public debt ratios in the medium term and reducing them thereafter (see Appendix table). As countries with an external surplus apply more fiscal stimulus, private investment and consumption would increase, leading to higher imports and a reduction of global current account imbalances. With investments targeting higher energy efficiency and production of renewable energy, world energy prices would stabilize on lower levels over the medium run. Meanwhile, investment in sustainable agricultural production would allow meeting a growing demand for food and stabilize world food prices.

Source: UN/DESA Global Policy Model (http://www.un.org/esa/policy/publications/ungpm.html).

Figure A: **Employment levels of selected countries or country groups**

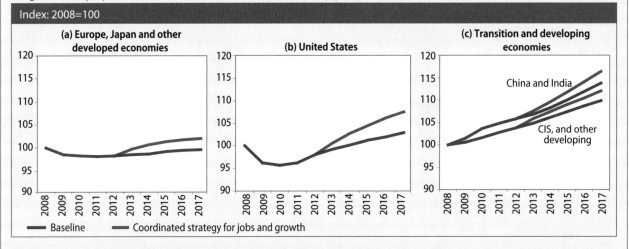

Figure B: **GDP growth rates of selected countries or country groups**

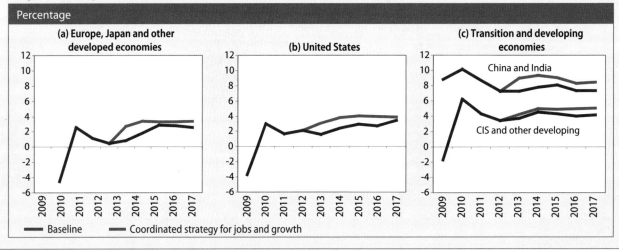

Appendix

An internationally coordinated strategy for jobs and growth, 2012-2017

	2012	2013	2014	2015	2016	2017
GDP Growth (percentage)						
United States	2.1	3.1	3.8	4.0	4.0	3.9
Europe	-0.2	2.9	3.8	3.7	3.6	3.7
Japan and other developed countries	2.0	2.4	2.5	2.5	2.6	2.7
China and India	7.3	9.0	9.3	9.0	8.3	8.5
CIS and Western Asia (major oil exporters)	3.7	3.3	3.6	3.5	3.7	3.8
Other developing countries	3.3	4.7	5.6	5.5	5.5	5.6
Employment created above the baseline (millions)						
United States	0.0	2.1	3.8	5.0	6.3	5.7
Europe	0.0	3.0	4.9	5.1	5.2	4.8
Japan and other developed countries	0.0	1.1	1.7	2.0	2.4	2.6
China and India	0.0	11.3	15.0	18.3	21.7	10.8
CIS and Western Asia (major oil exporters)	0.0	2.3	3.9	5.4	6.8	6.5
Other developing countries	0.0	7.9	13.2	17.7	21.7	2.5
Growth of government spending (constant prices, percentage per annum)						
United States	-2.4	-0.7	2.1	4.2	4.2	3.5
Europe	-1.6	1.6	1.6	0.7	0.9	1.6
Japan and other developed countries	0.9	1.7	2.2	-0.6	2.6	2.9
China and India	8.5	9.0	8.9	8.9	8.9	8.9
CIS and Western Asia (major oil exporters)	4.0	4.9	4.8	4.7	4.7	4.6
Other developing countries	4.8	6.8	6.8	6.8	6.7	6.7
Growth of private investment (constant prices, percentage per annum)						
United States	5.2	11.2	11.6	10.5	10.0	6.3
Europe	-0.7	4.0	7.2	6.4	5.8	6.8
Japan and other developed countries	2.6	4.6	3.3	3.1	3.4	2.8
China and India	5.3	8.6	8.1	7.6	5.6	5.4
CIS and Western Asia (major oil exporters)	8.5	3.5	3.2	1.8	3.9	3.8
Other developing countries	4.7	5.0	6.4	6.9	7.6	7.8
Net government financial surplus (percentage of GDP)						
United States	-11.0	-8.5	-6.9	-6.0	-5.4	-4.9
Europe	-7.2	-6.0	-4.9	-3.8	-2.9	-2.3
Japan and other developed countries	-7.9	-7.1	-6.6	-5.5	-5.3	-5.1
China and India	-3.3	-2.5	-1.8	-1.3	-1.2	-1.2
CIS and Western Asia (major oil exporters)	0.1	-0.1	-0.2	-0.1	-0.1	-0.1
Other developing countries	-3.1	-2.4	-1.7	-1.3	-1.0	-0.8
Net private sector financial surplus (percentage of GDP)						
United States	8.5	5.7	3.8	2.5	1.6	0.8
Europe	8.3	7.5	6.6	5.5	4.6	3.9
Japan and other developed countries	7.1	6.5	6.3	5.7	5.7	6.0
China and India	4.0	2.8	2.2	1.9	2.3	2.5
CIS and Western Asia (major oil exporters)	5.4	4.8	3.9	3.5	2.9	2.6
Other developing countries	2.4	2.0	1.5	1.3	1.1	1.0

Appendix (cont'd)	2012	2013	2014	2015	2016	2017
Current account deficit (percentage of GDP)						
United States	-2.6	-2.9	-3.1	-3.5	-3.9	-4.1
Europe	1.1	1.5	1.7	1.7	1.7	1.7
Japan and other developed countries	-0.8	-0.6	-0.2	0.1	0.5	0.8
China and India	0.6	0.3	0.4	0.6	1.1	1.4
CIS and Western Asia (major oil exporters)	5.4	4.8	3.7	3.4	2.8	2.4
Other developing countries	-0.7	-0.4	-0.2	0.0	0.1	0.2
Government debt (percentage of GDP)						
United States	76.4	75.9	73.6	70.6	67.0	63.1
Europe	74.5	73.6	72.1	70.5	67.4	64.9
Japan and other developed countries	138.3	136.0	133.0	129.7	127.0	125.1
China and India	23.8	22.5	20.1	18.0	17.3	16.9
CIS and Western Asia (major oil exporters)	40.5	42.8	45.5	47.4	49.1	50.2
Other developing countries	36.6	36.6	36.3	36.0	35.9	35.9
Memo:						
Growth of Gross World Product at market rate (percentage)	2.3	3.8	4.5	4.5	4.5	4.6
Growth of Gross World Product at ppp rate (percentage)	3.1	4.6	5.2	5.2	5.1	5.2
Global creation of employment above baseline (millions)	0.0	27.8	42.6	53.6	64.1	32.9
Average employment creation in developing countries above baseline (millions)	0.0	21.5	32.2	41.4	50.3	19.8
Growth of exports of good and services (percentage)	3.2	5.9	5.6	6.0	5.0	5.0
Real world price of energy (index)	1.4	1.5	1.4	1.5	1.5	1.5
Real world price of food & primary commodities (index)	1.2	1.2	1.3	1.3	1.4	1.4
Real world price of manufactures (index)	1.0	1.0	1.0	1.0	1.0	1.0

Source: UN/DESA Global Policy Model, available from http://www.un.org/en/development/desa/policy/publications/un_gpm.shtml.

Chapter 2
International trade

Sharp slowdown of world merchandise trade

The vigorous recovery in world trade in the immediate aftermath of the Great Recession has quickly lost its momentum. Growth of world trade, as measured in the volume of world imports and exports, moderated sharply for the second year in a row, dropping from 12.6 per cent in 2010 to 6.4 per cent in 2011 and 3.2 per cent in 2012 (figure II.1). The deceleration of world trade has been closely associated with the weakening of global demand, resulting mainly from stalling economic activity in Europe and anaemic aggregate demand in the United States of America and Japan. Developing countries and the economies in transition are increasingly feeling the effects of the slowdown through integrated global networks of production and trade. As a result, global output and trade have slowed in tandem.

Figure II.1
Synchronized slowdown of world merchandise trade and output, 2002-2014

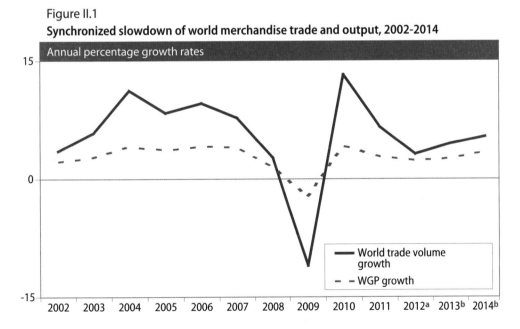

Source: UN/DESA.
a Partly estimated.
b Projections.

In the euro area, import demand in countries such as Italy, Greece, Portugal and Spain started to contract in late 2011, as austerity measures combined with the woes of debt distress and bank fragility to cause a drop in aggregate demand. Import demand of these countries contracted by more than 6 per cent in real terms in 2012, and declined by more than 20 per cent in nominal terms[1] during several months of the year. By the first quarter

Weak demand has spread through global networks of production and trade

---

1   Nominal terms are in United States dollars.

of 2012, weak demand had spread to the rest of Europe. Imports by France and Germany plummeted by more than 10 per cent in nominal terms (annualized rate) during the second quarter of the year, but expanded modestly in real terms over the year. As intraregional trade accounts for about 70 per cent of total European Union (EU) trade, this was also reflected in commensurate export declines in most European countries. Import demand also slowed significantly in the United States and Japan, especially during the second half of 2012.

As a result, East Asian countries, such as the Republic of Korea, Singapore and Taiwan Province of China that have strong trade ties with the major developed countries, saw their exports decline during most of 2012. China's export volume growth also decelerated and came to a halt in mid-2012, along with other emerging countries such as Brazil and India. Further down the global value chain, primary commodity-exporting countries followed suit, with many registering export declines in the second half of 2012. In turn, weaker exports and GDP growth have depressed import demand in developing countries, further softening trade with developed economies.

Four years after the start of the Great Recession, external demand, as measured by the volume of world imports, is still far below pre-crisis trend levels, which now appear unsustainable, especially for developed countries. In the baseline outlook (see chapter I), global economic activity is expected to remain weak in 2013 before picking up modestly in 2014. As a result, international trade will likely continue drifting further below trend levels in both developed and, to a lesser extent, in developing countries (figure II.2). In 2009, the import volume of developed countries dropped 26 per cent below the pre-crisis trend level. The gap narrowed slightly in 2010-2011, but widened again in 2012. In the baseline scenario, the gap is expected to remain as large as 25 per cent in 2014. The import volume of developing countries also fell well below the trend (about 17 per cent) in 2009, but recovered more strongly during 2010-2011, reducing the gap to 7 per cent. As the global economic recovery is expected to remain elusive, however, the gap is also expected to widen further to 9 per cent for developing countries in 2014.

Import demand is drifting further below pre-crisis trends

Figure II.2
Imports of developed and developing countries, 2000-2014

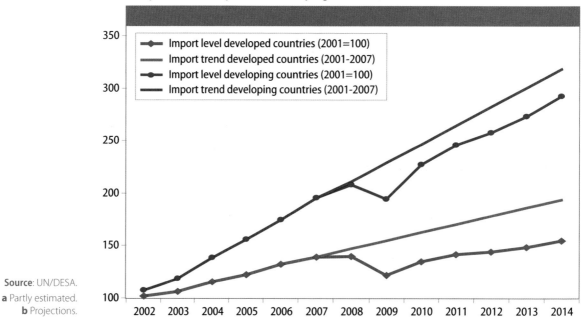

- Import level developed countries (2001=100)
- Import trend developed countries (2001-2007)
- Import level developing countries (2001=100)
- Import trend developing countries (2001-2007)

Source: UN/DESA.
a Partly estimated.
b Projections.

Nonetheless, as their economies and export sectors continue to show greater resilience, the share of developing countries in world trade has increased by 6 percentage points over the last five years, reaching 42 per cent in 2012. Furthermore, developing country import growth currently contributes to about half of world import demand growth, compared to 43 per cent before the crisis. Trade in developing countries—with their high potential growth and increasing integration into global supply chains—is expected to grow faster than in developed economies. However, the potential economic gains for these countries may be accompanied by increasing contributions to the already steadily rising global carbon emissions (box II.1). Global economic woes could further complicate

---

Box II.1

Global production chains, freight transport and climate change

International trade is a driver of economic growth in many countries and a pillar of globalization. Simultaneously, the transport of traded goods, intensified by the rise of global production chains and multinational corporations (MNCs) that generate growing flows of trade in tasks and intrafirm trade, produces significant carbon dioxide (CO_2) emissions. This negative externality associated with the environmentally suboptimal organization of global production chains and international trade flows is, by and large, ignored by policymakers.

Currently, about 90 per cent of merchandise trade (excluding intra-EU trade) is shipped by sea. As maritime shipping only accounts for 2.7 per cent of global CO_2 emissions,[a] the significance of trade-related emissions is sometimes downplayed.[b] The picture changes drastically, however, when considering intra-EU trade and transport of goods from ports to their destination using emission-intensive modes of transportation. Internationally traded goods are estimated to generate on average 50 per cent more CO_2 emissions than locally traded goods. The estimate is much higher for traded manufactured goods, especially for electronics and machinery, which represent a significant share of intrafirm trade.[c] As traded goods embody about 21 per cent of global CO_2 emissions,[d] transport associated with merchandise trade alone may thus contribute to more than 7 per cent of global CO_2 emissions.[e]

Over the past four decades, the volume of merchandise trade has grown at an annual rate of 5 per cent, about 2 per cent faster than global economic growth. Rapid trade growth partly stems from the globalization of consumption and, more importantly, of production. The latter is supported by the rise in global production chains' integration of capital and advanced technologies from developed countries and cheap labour from developing countries. While efficient and profitable from the point of view of MNCs, this restructuring of production processes has given rise to a vast expansion of intrafirm trade, which currently accounts for almost 50 per cent of imports in the United States and probably about one third of total international trade.[f]

Expanding world trade is bound to come with greater environmental costs if left unabated. In the absence of counteracting policies (see below) and if both the trade volume and trade-related CO_2 emissions would continue to grow at an annual rate of 5 per cent, both would double within 15 years. The share of trade in world gross product (WGP) would continue to increase, fostering the expansion of transport and CO_2 emissions (figure). Trade volume would increase from more than 10 billions tons (Bt) in 2011 to over 20 Bt in 2026 and trade-related CO_2 emissions would rise from 2.2 gigatons (Gt) to 4.4 Gt during the same period. Faced with these trends that move away from climate change mitigation targets, policymakers are actively promoting measures that are to reduce emissions generated by freight transport. Thus far, however, the approach is focused only on the transport sector without taking into account the broader implications of the environmentally damaging organization of global production chains and steadily increasing trade flows.

a International Maritime Organization, "Second IMO GHG Study 2009", available from http://www.imo.org/blast/blastDataHelper.asp?data_id=27795&filename=GHGStudyFINAL.pdf.

b See World Trade Organization, "The impact of trade opening on climate change", available from http://www.wto.org/english/tratop_e/envir_e/climate_impact_e.htm.

c Anca D. Cristea and others, "Trade and the greenhouse gas emissions from international freight transport", NBER Working Paper, No. 17117 (Cambridge, Massachusetts: National Bureau of Economic Research, June 2011).

d Glen P. Peters and Edgar G. Hertwich, "CO_2 embodied in international trade with implications for global climate policy", *Environmental Science & Technology*, vol. 42, No. 5 (1 March 2008), pp. 1401-1407.

e See Stern Review on the Economics of Climate Change, available from http://webarchive.nationalarchives.gov.uk/+/http://www.hm-treasury.gov.uk/independent_reviews/stern_review_economics_climate_change/sternreview_index.cfm.

f Rainer Lanz and Sébastien Miroudo, "Intra-firm trade: patterns, determinants and policy implications", OECD Trade Policy Paper, No. 114 (24 June 2011).

Box II.1 (cont'd)

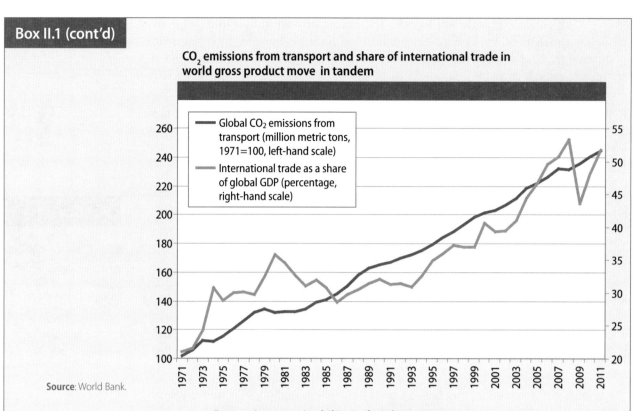

CO_2 emissions from transport and share of international trade in world gross product move in tandem

Legend:
- Global CO_2 emissions from transport (million metric tons, 1971=100, left-hand scale)
- International trade as a share of global GDP (percentage, right-hand scale)

Source: World Bank.

Promoting sustainability in freight transport

About 80 per cent of merchandise trade (including intra-EU trade) is shipped by sea. This is a relatively energy-efficient mode of transport that has expanded at an average annual rate of 3 per cent over the last 30 years. If seaborne trade would continue to grow at this pace without any global action being taken to reduce CO_2 emissions in that sector, seaborne trade and related CO_2 emissions would double by 2035.

The International Maritime Organization (IMO) asserts that measures affecting ship and fuel technology could improve energy efficiency and reduce the emission intensity (CO_2/ton-mile) by 25 to 75 per cent below current levels. As mandated under the United Nations Framework Convention on Climate Change (UNFCCC), IMO adopted in 2011 a set of global rules to control CO_2 emissions from international shipping. The package included technical and operational measures in the form of the Energy Efficiency Design Index (EEDI) and the Ship Energy Efficiency Management Plan (SEEMP). These measures will enter into force in 2013 and apply to all ships of 400 gross tonnage and above. However, the EEDI will only apply to new ships. Given the long life cycle of ships and the relatively young average age of the current fleet, emission reduction due to EEDI will not materialize in the near future.

The shipping industry is also taking action. This year, for instance, SinoPacific Shipbuilding Group launched a new generation of fuel-saving and environmentally friendly bulk carriers, which reduce fuel consumption by 13 per cent compared to the equivalent size bulk carriers currently operating.

Various opportunities have further emerged for improving environmental sustainability in ports, such as: enhanced port infrastructure and efficient terminal layout designs that reduce time and processes required to move cargo; switching to greener modes of transport for hinterland access, such as by rail or inland waterways; the adoption of energy efficiency programmes; and the use of renewable energy. By implementing such measures, the Rotterdam Shortsea Terminal reduced its CO_2 emission by nearly 70 per cent.[g]

Efforts to achieve sustainability in maritime transport demand an integral approach, as international trade is carried through multimodal transportation systems. CO_2 emissions largely emanate from land modes, in particular haulage by road, which is projected to expand significantly in

g Harry Geerlings and Ron van Duin, "A new method for assessing CO_2-emissions from container terminals: a promising approach applied in Rotterdam", Journal of Cleaner Production, vol. 19, Issues 6-7 (April-May 2011), pp. 657-666.

Box II.1 (cont'd)

developing countries in the next decades. The rate of surface freight activity worldwide—including rail, medium-duty truck and heavy truck (in trillions of ton-kilometres)—is expected to increase by an average annual rate of 2.3 per cent and double within the next thirty years.[h] With these trends, trade-driven economic growth and environmental sustainability will remain incompatible objectives, unless emissions from land freight transport are more effectively addressed.

There are ways to improve sustainability in land freight transport and logistics through a comprehensive and integrated approach, but this may require trading off energy efficiency gains with transport costs and, potentially, the speed and reliability of services. This entails, inter alia, optimizing the performance of multimodal logistics chains, improving the competitiveness of environmentally friendly modes of transport, leveraging technologies capable of improving energy efficiency, logistical efficiency, and reducing emissions, as well as creating integrated transport networks and dedicated freight corridors that are efficient and environmentally friendly.

Initiatives are being developed at the industry level to improve energy efficiency in vehicles and expand the use of ICT-driven applications to optimize operations. By reducing fuel consumption, kilometres driven, and frequency of vehicles travelling empty or partially loaded, the latter could help achieve a 16 per cent global reduction in land freight transport emissions by 2020.[i]

Current efforts to reduce CO_2 emissions from freight transport are, however, insufficient to achieve the energy and environmental sustainability required by internationally agreed climate targets. Greater efforts are needed to reach more integrated approaches that encompass all modes of transportation. Multilateral approaches that jointly address economic and environmental challenges are required to ensure the coherence between international trade, transport and environmental policies.

h World Business Council for Sustainable Development, "Mobility 2030: Meeting the Challenges to Sustainability", The Sustainable Mobility Project (Geneva, July 2004), available from http://www.wbcsd.org/web/publications/mobility/mobility-full.pdf.

i The Climate Group, "Smart 2020: Enabling the low carbon economy in the information age", a report by The Climate Group on behalf of the Global eSustainability Initiative, 2008, available from http://www.smart2020.org/_assets/files/02_Smart2020Report.pdf.

reaching an agreement in the climate negotiations, illustrated by the inadequate progress in setting sufficiently ambitious binding carbon targets for all countries at the Eighteenth Conference of Parties (COP-18) to the United Nations Framework Convention on Climate Change (UNFCCC).

Regional trade patterns

Import demand declined across all groups of countries and regions in 2012, except Africa (figures II.3 and II.4). Although trade flows remained robust in most regions during the first half of the year, the contagion of downward-spiralling demand progressively spread from Europe and other developed economies to the rest of the world during the second half of 2012.

As its economy fell back into recession, import volume in the euro area contracted by 0.1 per cent in 2012, after having increased by 4.8 per cent in the previous year. Subdued growth in import volume in core euro area countries did not completely offset sharp declines in periphery countries that had been weakened by hard-hitting austerity measures. Export volume growth decelerated from 6.9 per cent in 2011 to 2.8 per cent in 2012, and remained positive, even in the debt-distressed countries. Unlike in the euro area, import demand slightly increased in the United Kingdom of Great Britain and Northern Ireland, despite severe fiscal austerity measures. Exports from the United Kingdom declined, however, contributing to the economic downturn. Growth in the volume of exports from the EU at large (all 27 members) decelerated to 2.3 per cent in 2012, but remained positive, helped by comparatively stronger demand from other regions and a weaker euro.

In North America, import volume growth decelerated from 5.2 per cent in 2011 to 3.1 per cent in 2012. Exports remained a driver of economic activity, despite a

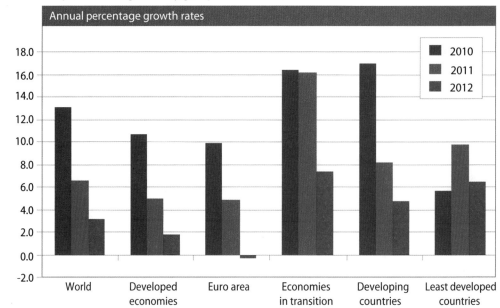

Figure II.3
Import volume growth by groups of countries, 2010-2012

Source: UN/DESA.

drop in volume growth from 6.3 per cent in 2011 to 3.7 per cent in 2012. Japan's exports rebounded weakly by 0.8 per cent in 2012. As its economy recovered from the destruction inflicted by the 2011 earthquake, tsunami and nuclear disasters, import volume growth stood at a steady 5 per cent, despite turning negative for several months in the second half of 2012.

Import demand slows more strongly in East and South Asia than other developing country regions

In East and South Asia, the growth of import demand slowed more than in other developing country regions in 2012. Nonetheless, these two populous subregions remain key drivers of trade growth, especially among developing regions, including through their mediating role in global value chains. In most East Asian countries, export growth decelerated slightly more than import growth in 2012, leading to smaller trade surpluses. Weaker demand from developed countries and China was transmitted through global production networks and lowered prices of primary commodities, such as rubber and copper, leading to a deceleration of Asian export growth from 6.9 per cent in 2011 to 3.4 per cent in 2012. Chinese export and import volumes have expanded at an annual rate of about 6 per cent in 2012, much lower than the average annual rate of above 20 per cent during the 2000s. Import demand growth stalled sharply in South Asia, dropping from 18.3 per cent in 2011 to 3.8 per cent in 2012, partly as a consequence of currency depreciations in the region. Export volumes also declined significantly, especially in the Islamic Republic of Iran as a consequence of international sanctions.

As oil prices reached a record yearly average in 2012, oil-exporting countries in Western Asia registered unprecedented trade surpluses. Energy exporters in the Commonwealth of Independent States (CIS) also kept up trade surpluses, despite the fact that import demand increased faster than exports in 2012 (7.9 per cent and 3.8 per cent, respectively). Exporters of non-energy commodities were more severely affected by declining prices, especially for metals, minerals and agricultural raw materials, reflecting deteriorating global growth prospects. Although weakening external demand affected exports

Figure II.4
Import volume growth in selected regions, 2010-2012

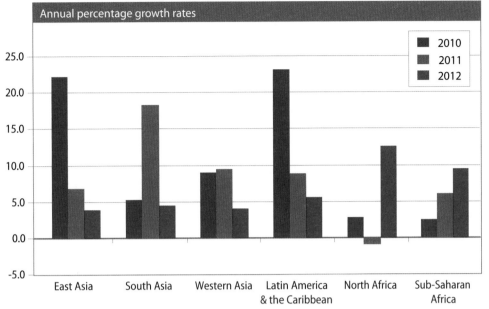

Annual percentage growth rates

Legend: 2010, 2011, 2012

Regions (x-axis): East Asia, South Asia, Western Asia, Latin America & the Caribbean, North Africa, Sub-Saharan Africa

Source: UN/DESA.

in several countries in South America, import demand growth in the Caribbean and Latin America at large remained robust at over 5 per cent in 2012. In Africa, import and export volume growth declined slightly in most countries in 2012. However, a small number of significant outliers, such as Libya and Nigeria, experienced a spectacular rebound after having faced steep export declines in 2011. Owing to these exceptional rebounds, Africa was the only region which saw its growth rate of trade volume increase in 2012.

Primary commodity markets

Underpinned by initially strengthening industrial activity,[2] strong demand from developing countries, and more optimistic market sentiment following the European Central Bank's (ECB) long-term refinancing operations (LTROs),[3] the United Nations Conference on Trade and Development price index[4] rose significantly in the first quarter of 2012 for three groups of commodities: all food;[5] agricultural raw materials; and minerals, ores and metals. From the second quarter on, however, prices fell as a result of the economic slowdown in China and the intensification of sovereign debt crises in the euro area.

Prices of food and base metals and ores diverged in the third quarter. The food market tightened because of supply disruptions created by adverse weather in the United States, Australia and the Black Sea region. The surge in maize, wheat and soybean prices put a strain on the food market. By contrast, the prices of many important base metals

Monetary easing heightens commodity price volatility

Adverse weather pushed up food prices

---

2   World Bank, *Global Economic Prospects: Managing Growth in a Volatile World*, vol. 5 (Washington, D.C., June 2012).

3   See United Nations, Economic and Social Council, World economic situation and prospects as of mid-2012 (E/2012/72).

4   Unless otherwise stated, all indices used in this section are United Nations Conference on Trade and Development (UNCTAD) price indices, measured in United States dollars.

5   The category of all food includes food, tropical beverages, and vegetable oilseeds and oils.

and ores continued their downward trend in July and August of 2012 as global economic prospects remained gloomy. Copper prices declined significantly compared with 2011. At the same time, productive investment in aluminium, nickel and zinc markets over the last decade have increased supply, exerting long-term downward pressure on prices.

In September, several major central banks engaged in further unconventional monetary policies to revive their economies. While the full impact of these policies on employment generation and economic growth remains unclear, commodity markets responded quickly, with the prices of gold and key base metals rising significantly.[6]

Food and agricultural commodities

Food prices surged throughout 2012

During the first nine months of 2012, the food price index remained high, despite short-term price fluctuations. Led by high prices of maize, wheat and soybeans, the price index rose sharply to 283 points in July 2012, an increase of 11 per cent from January 2012. However, the price pattern differed within various commodity sub-groups.

Maize and wheat stocks fell to four-to-six-year lows

During the first quarter of 2012, the food price index rose by around 7 per cent. Prices stabilized in the following three months before jumping to a record high in July, mainly resulting from tight maize and wheat supply and low stock levels. In the United States, severe drought in the corn belt reduced yield prospects and drove the price of maize to an all-time high in July. Poor weather also adversely affected the outlook for

Figure II.5
Agricultural commodities price indices, January 2000-September 2012

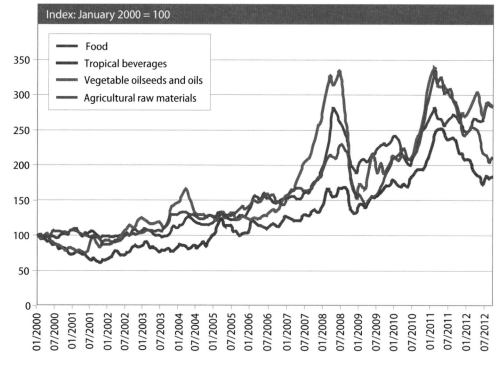

Source: UNCTAD.

---

6   In September 2012, the average gold price surged to $1,744 an ounce, 1.6 per cent lower than its historical peak in September 2011. The prices of copper, aluminium, nickel, lead, zinc and tin also rose considerably compared to August 2012.

wheat production in Kazakhstan, the Russian Federation and Ukraine. Global stocks for maize and wheat are expected to fall to six- and four-year lows, respectively, by the end of 2012/2013.[7]

The price of rice continued to be relatively stable, however, as stock levels remain high and supply and demand are broadly in balance. The rice-pledging programme in Thailand—which subsidizes farmers by setting a fixed price for their rice harvests—significantly reduced the country's rice exports in 2011. To date, the impact of this government policy on the global rice market is limited thanks to adequate rice stocks and stable supply from other major exporting countries such as India and Viet Nam. However, the dynamics of the world rice market might change quickly if other exporting countries also intervene in the market through policy measures, such as subsidies or export bans/restrictions.

The spike in major cereal prices has raised concerns that another food crisis may be in the offing. The countries of the Group of Twenty (G20) are closely monitoring global food markets through the Agricultural Market Information System (AMIS) launched in June 2011. While increased transparency may contribute to a better alignment of spot prices with fundamentals in physical markets, it does not address the instability caused by financial speculation in derivatives markets, and may thus limit the effectiveness of this initiative.[8]

The Group of Twenty fosters transparency in physical food markets, but stops short of interfering with derivatives markets

High maize prices have also revived the debate on using grains as feedstock to produce biofuels. Under increasing calls for adjustments in the EU and United States biofuel policies, the European Commission has proposed to cap crop-based biofuels to 5 per cent of transport fuel until 2020.[9]

The vegetable oilseeds and oils price index soared by 10 per cent during the four months to April 2012. The index jumped again in the third quarter, mainly driven by soybean prices, which reached a record high of $684 per ton, an increase of 21 per cent from June 2012. A combination of factors contributed to the price surge: concerns about reduced United States supply caused by adverse weather conditions, robust demand from Asia, and tight stocks.

During the first half of 2012, the tropical beverages price index continued its downward trend, which started in May 2011, with only a slight recovery in the third quarter of 2012. Coffee prices fell by 33 per cent from their peak of $2.13 in April 2011 down to $1.42 per pound in June 2012.[10] In July, coffee prices rebounded to $1.52 a pound, owing to concerns over the impact of heavy rainfall on Brazil's coffee supply.

The price of cocoa beans fluctuated between $1.03 and $1.07 per pound during the 7 months to July 2012. The relatively stable prices resulted from the offsetting effects of an expected production decline in West Africa, caused by erratic weather, as well as a sharp fall in cocoa grindings in Europe and North America—both affected by the economic crisis—versus resilient demand growth in emerging markets.[11] In August

---

7   International Grains Council, Grain Market Report, GMR No. 427, 25 October 2012.

8   See UNCTAD, *Price Formation in Financialized Commodity Markets: The Role of Information* (United Nations publication, UNCTAD/GDS/2011/1).

9   See Barbara Lewis and Michele Kambas, "EU Commission to cap food-based biofuels in major shift", Reuters, 17 September 2012, available from http://www.reuters.com/article/2012/09/17/us-eu-biofuel-idUSBRE88G0IL20120917.

10   The coffee prices refer to coffee composite indicator prices which consist of the prices for Arabic and Robusta coffee.

11   In August 2012, the International Cocoa Organization forecast that world cocoa bean production would decline by 8.1 per cent during the 2011/2012 cocoa season compared to the previous season, and reach 3.962 million tons.

and September, prices increased based on uncertainties surrounding the supply from Côte d'Ivoire, which started to reform its cocoa marketing system in early 2012.

The agricultural raw materials price index recovered briefly during the first two months of 2012 before declining steadily in the subsequent six months. In September, the price index rebounded slightly after reaching a 33-month low in August. Cotton prices exhibited a similar trend. Various factors contributed to the bearish market, including the expected surge in global stocks, a supply surplus, renewed concerns over the euro area economy and the strengthening of the United States dollar.[12]

Minerals, ores and metals

Prices of metals proved to be sensitive to monetary easing, while being depressed by the weakening global economy

The minerals, ores and metals price index rebounded in 2012 in the wake of the LTRO, before declining in the second quarter, mainly owing to worsening global economic prospects, reaching a two-year low in July. Following monetary easing in major developed economies, the price index rose again in September. (See box II.2 for an assessment of the influence of financial factors on markets for minerals and metals in particular.)

Copper prices fluctuated as a result of volatile world economic prospects. In the first quarter, the average London Metal Exchange (LME) cash price surged to $8,307 per ton, up 11 per cent from its level in the fourth quarter of 2011. The surge was driven by abundant liquidity in financial markets, as well as by strong demand from China (partly for stockpiling). The average LME cash price decreased by 5 per cent during the second quarter. Though copper prices rebounded in the third quarter, they were still 14 per cent below levels reached in the same period in 2011.

Figure II.6
Price indices of selected metals, January 2008-September 2012[a]

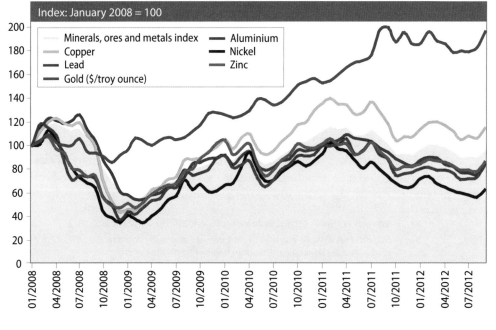

Index: January 2008 = 100

Legend:
— Minerals, ores and metals index
— Copper
— Lead
— Gold ($/troy ounce)
— Aluminium
— Nickel
— Zinc

Source: UNCTAD.
a Gold is not included in the UNCTAD minerals, ores and metals price index.

---

12   According to the International Cotton Advisory Committee (ICAC) press release of 1 June 2012, global cotton stocks would represent 61 per cent of global consumption by the end of July 2013, the highest stocks-to-use ratio reached since 1998/99.

Prices of nickel, aluminium, lead and zinc climbed in early 2012, driven by strong demand and the then prevailing optimism about global economic prospects. Since March, however, sluggish demand, coupled with oversupply, has pushed prices downward. The price of nickel, a crucial raw material in the production of stainless steel, hit a 38-month low in August 2012. Chronic oversupply, high stocks and weakened demand have driven the average aluminium cash price on the LME down to $1,838 per ton, the lowest level since October 2009. In June and August 2012, the prices of lead and zinc hit their lowest levels since August 2010.[13] In September, however, the prices of these metals surged sharply at the announcement of further monetary easing by the central banks of several developed economies.

Box II.2

Financial investment and physical commodity holdings

Financial investors continue venturing into commodity markets. Commodity assets under management (AUM) increased almost fortyfold between 2001 and April 2011, when they reached a record of $458 billion. Assets declined sharply thereafter but rebounded to reach $439 billion in September 2012, 11 per cent above their level at the beginning of the year.[a] Since mid-2008, financial investors have been looking for new ways to access commodities as an asset class. They became less interested in traditional broad-based passive index investment instruments, which only allow betting on rising prices. Instead, to optimize investment strategies in unstable markets, financial investors have increasingly opted for more active instruments, allowing bets on both rising and declining prices.[b] As a result, index investment as a share of total commodity AUM declined from 65-85 per cent in 2005-2007 to 32 per cent in September 2012.[c]

Exchange-traded products (ETPs), particularly futures-based exchange-traded funds (ETFs), have become the largest investment vehicles in commodity markets (figure). ETFs issue shares which are traded like equities on a securities exchange. Physically-backed ETFs have also become increasingly attractive for financial investors, because they offer the advantage of establishing a direct link between financial investment and physical inventories and thereby give investors direct exposure to commodity spot prices. This avoids uncertainty related to possible differences between spot prices and prices of futures contracts, to which traditional index funds and futures-based ETFs are exposed.

Until recently, physically-backed ETFs were confined to precious metals. In 2010, however, some European banks started to offer such vehicles related to industrial metals, especially copper. While accumulated investment has remained limited, this situation could change rapidly. At the time of writing in November 2012, the United States Securities and Exchange Commission (SEC) was deliberating whether to approve two requests to list and trade physically-backed copper ETFs.[d] Opponents of the approval, which include large industrial firms, have expressed concern that the resulting large purchase of physical copper holdings would cause rising prices and reduced availability of physical copper. Such concerns are related to recent events in aluminium markets where the arrival of investment banks was followed by a record-level surge of the premium that consumers pay for metal—surpassing the benchmark price set at the London Metal Exchange (LME), the world's leading exchange for non-ferrous metals.[e] This surge led to fears that allowing financial investors to accumulate and store physical copper holdings could lead to inflated prices that would destabilize the market and, ultimately, disrupt metal supply and industrial production. Sizeable effects could indeed occur, given that the two planned ETFs combined would absorb more than 180,000 metric

a Barclays, The Commodity Investor, October 2012.

b UNCTAD, *Trade and Development Report 2011: Post-crisis policy challenges in the world economy* (United Nations publication, Sales No. E.11.II.D.3), chap. V.

c Barclays, The Commodity Investor, *op. cit.*

d See Securities and Exchange Commission Release No. 34–67965; SR–NYCEArca-2012-28, 2 October 2012, available from http://www.sec.gov/rules/sro/nysearca/2012/34-67965.pdf.

e Jack Farchy, "Banks force aluminium market shake-up", *Financial Times*, 12 September 2012, available from http://www.ft.com/intl/cms/s/0/c3b3e02e-fcf3-11e1-a4f2-00144feabdc0.html#axzz2DXWwGjEH.

---

13   According to the International Lead and Zinc Study Group, supply exceeded demand by 49,000 tons (about 0.8 per cent of demand) and 135,000 tons (about 1.9 per cent of demand), respectively, in the global refined lead and zinc metal market during the first seven months of 2012.

Box II.2 (cont'd)

Source: Barclays.

f Josephine Mason, "Copper users attack ETF plans ahead of SEC ruling", Reuters, 20 July 2012, available from http://in.reuters.com/article/2012/07/19/copper-etf-jpmorgan-idINL2E8IJF7P20120719. See also Vandenburg & Feliu LLP, "Comments of Vandenberg & Feliu LPP on proposed rule change to list and trade shares of the JPM XF Physical Copper Trust pursuant to NYSE Arca equities rule 8.201", 9 May 2012, available from http://www.sec.gov/comments/sr-nysearca-2012-28/nysearca201228-1.pdf.

g Chris Kelly and Silvia Antonioli, "Copper hits new 4-1/2 month top, demand worries resurface", Reuters, 19 September 2012, available from http://af.reuters.com/article/metalsNews/idAFL5E8KJA2W20120919.

h Izabella Kaminska, "Outing the aluminum squeeze, Deripaska style", *Financial Times*, 13 September 2012, available from http://ftalphaville.ft.com/blog/2012/09/13/1159071/outing-the-aluminum-squeeze-deripaska-style/.

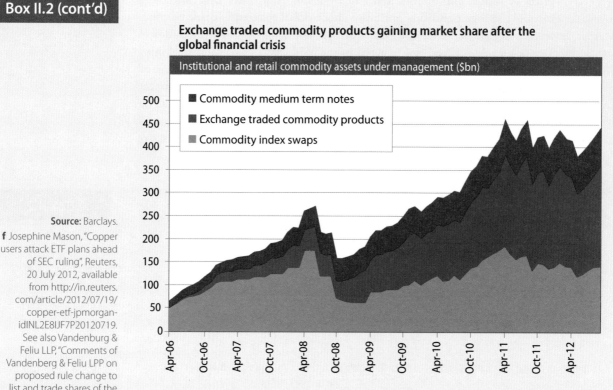

Exchange traded commodity products gaining market share after the global financial crisis

Institutional and retail commodity assets under management ($bn)

■ Commodity medium term notes
■ Exchange traded commodity products
■ Commodity index swaps

tons of copper,[f] which corresponds to about 80 per cent of recorded copper inventories held at the LME global network of warehouses in mid-September 2012.[g]

But even if the Securities and Exchange Commission eventually rejects approval of these two ETFs, the physical commodity operations of financial investors are likely to continue affecting prices through other mechanisms. Ownership of warehouses or storage tanks, for instance, allow banks to realize certain profits based on so-called contango financing. "Contango" indicates situations in which prices of futures contracts with more distant delivery dates exceed those of near-term contracts. When markets are well supplied, producers would normally reduce their activities to support prices. However, banks may encourage producers to maintain their level of activity by accepting their inventory as collateral for secured financing. The encumbered collateral, which would be kept off market and hedged through derivatives, would not only generate inventory fee revenues, but also end up yielding a positive return on derivatives for banks because of the forward contango structure.[h] The fact that banks can modulate the level of stored physical commodities independently of market fundamentals tends to add to price volatility. More generally, the fact that these inventories typically remain unreported creates information asymmetry in the market and makes it impossible for commercial market participants to determine the price that would solely reflect supply and demand fundamentals. Ultimately, banks' efforts to expand their business activities to include the management of physical commodity inventories create information asymmetries and increase the risk of the emergence of conflicts of interest and perverse incentives detrimental to other market participants. Considering all of the above elements together raises doubts on the social value of these new financial instruments and practices.

After reaching $1,743 per ounce in February 2012, gold prices retreated in the following months, owing to weaker demand from the jewellery industry and from investors. The price of gold quickly recovered and hit a 12-month high in September as expansionary monetary policies in major developed economies renewed inflation concerns.

The first four months of 2012 saw little movement in iron ore prices, with spot prices in Brazil fluctuating about $144 per dry metric ton.[14] Since May 2012, however, prices dropped sharply and hit a 34-month low in September. The plunge was caused in large part by the shrinking demand for steel from China's construction and manufacturing industries, high levels of Chinese stocks, and sufficient iron ore supply. The financial turbulence in the euro area and slowdown of other emerging economies, such as Brazil, also contributed to the price decline.

The oil market

Global oil demand continued to increase at an annual rate of about 1 per cent in 2012, mirroring the global economic slowdown. Anaemic growth in developed economies has led to a 0.6 per cent decline in oil demand from the Organization for Economic Cooperation and Development (OECD) countries. Weakening economic growth in emerging economies, particularly China and India, capped oil demand growth from non-OECD countries at 2.8 per cent. Global oil production, in contrast, increased by 3 per cent to an average of 90.8 million barrels per day (mbd) during the first nine months of the year, thereby generating excess supply of more than 1 mbd on average during that period. This rare situation mainly resulted from the substantial production increase of 6 per cent in the Organization of the Petroleum Exporting Countries (OPEC). The sanctions-induced decline in Iranian oil output by 0.8 mbd was more than compensated for by the 1.3 mbd of Libyan crude that returned to international markets in early January, and by the activation of almost 2 mbd of Saudi spare capacity since the beginning of the Arab Spring. As a consequence, oil stocks in the OECD countries and major emerging countries increased slightly over the first half of 2012.

During the first three quarters of 2012, the average price of oil remained almost unchanged with respect to last year. Brent, for instance, averaged $112 per barrel (pb), compared with $111 for 2011 as a whole, and the average spread between Western Texas Intermediate and Brent crudes stayed around $16. Prices remained volatile, however, with Brent fluctuating within a band of $40, and one out of every five trading days ending with a price change in excess of $2, excluding intraday volatility (figure II.7). Quantitative easing measures, the imposition of sanctions on Iranian oil exports, and certain declarations by political leaders in the Middle East punctuated most of the significant turnarounds in the oil market.

Following the first LTRO of the ECB on 21 December 2011, stock markets surged in January. The year thus started with abundant liquidity in financial markets and misperceptions about a rapid economic recovery. A portion of the liquidity injected into the financial system ended up being invested in commodity derivatives markets. Daily volumes for monthly Brent crude futures contracts increased by 49 per cent in the six months following the first LTRO (figure II.8). In a context of near-zero interest rates, the rising risk premium on oil prices associated with growing tensions in the Middle East attracted further speculative trading in derivatives markets, increasing hedging costs for physical

Average oil prices reached record highs despite weak demand growth and excess supply

Abundant financial market liquidity and geopolitical tensions are keeping prices high and volatile

---

14   The pricing mechanisms of iron ore have experienced a fundamental change in recent years. In 2010, a quarterly index-based pricing mechanism was substituted for a decades-long annual benchmark pricing system. With shorter pricing cycles, the price volatility has increased and promoted the rapid expansion of iron ore derivative markets in the past two years. Currently, there are a large number of published iron ore prices and indices, such as The Steel Index (TSI), Metal Bulletin and Platts. In this section, iron ore prices for Brazil (IMF estimates) were used as a reference.

Figure II.7

Increasing volatility of the Brent oil price, 1987-2012

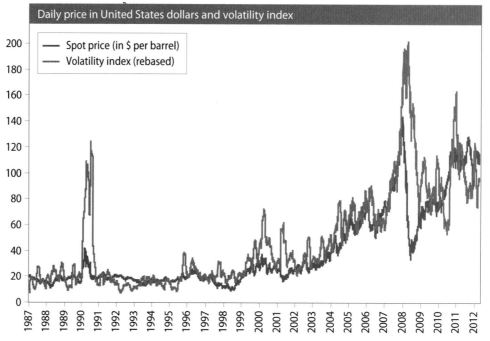

Source: UN/DESA, based on data from the United States Energy Intelligence Agency.

Note: Volatility is measured as a 40-day moving average of the standard deviation of the nominal oil price.

traders. As futures prices are used by many traders as a reference to price transactions in the spot market,[15] the Brent spot price rose, hovering above $120 from mid-February to mid-April. The possibility of a Hormuz Strait blockade, trapping 20 per cent of global oil supply (or 17 mbd) and a significant share of world liquefied natural gas supply in the Gulf region, also strengthened incentives for preventive hoarding by physical traders. Despite oversupply reaching 0.9 mbd during the first quarter, Brent price peaked at $128 in mid-March.

At the end of March, Saudi officials intervened in the hope of shaping expectations and declared they would "correct the myth that there is, or could be, a shortage".[16] As Saudi spare capacity is insufficient to compensate for a supply shortage of such magnitude,

---

15   See the evidence presented in UNCTAD, *Trade and Development Report 2011: Post-crisis policy challenges in the world economy* (United Nations publication, Sales No. E.11.II.D.3), chap. V and *Price Formation in Financialized Commodity Markets, op. cit*. A number of studies also stress the growing financialization of commodity markets, that is, the growing correlation existing between commodity and other financial markets as a consequence of the diminishing influence of physical traders and the rising influence of money managers devising trading strategies based on high-frequency trading. See David Bicchetti and Nicolas Maystre, "The synchronized and long-lasting structural change on commodity markets: evidence from high frequency data", UNCTAD Discussion Paper, No. 208 (UNCTAD/OSG/DP/2012/2); Michael Greenberger, "The relationship of unregulated excessive speculation to oil market price volatility", paper prepared for the International Energy Forum, (The University of Maryland, Center for Health & Homeland Security, 15 January 2012); Robert A. Kaufmann, "The role of market fundamentals and speculation in recent price changes for crude oil," *Energy Policy*, vol. 39, No. 1 (January), pp. 105-115; Robert Pollin and James Heintz, "How Wall Street speculation is driving up gasoline prices today", PERI Research Brief (University of Massachusetts Amherst, Political Economy Research Institute, June 2011); and Kenneth J. Singleton, "Investor flows and the 2008 boom/bust in oil prices", 23 March 2011, available from http://ssrn.com/abstract=1793449. For a summary of the controversy, see *World Economic Situation and Prospects 2010* (United Nations publications, Sales No. E.10.II.C.1), box II.1.

16   Ali Naimi, "Saudi Arabia will act to lower soaring oil prices", *Financial Times*, 28 March 2012), available from www.ft.com/cms/s/0/9e1ccb48-781c-11e1-b237-00144feab49a.html#axzz2DXWwGjEH.

Figure II.8
**Brent price and open interest in daily volumes for ICE Brent crude futures,
January 2010-November 2012**

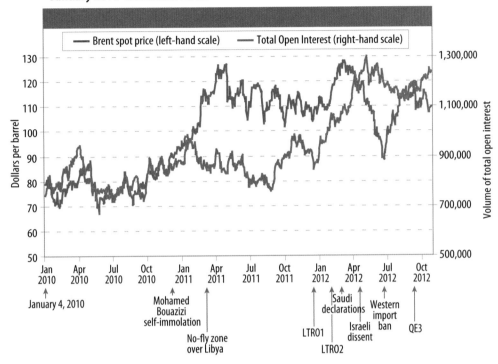

Source: United States
Energy Intelligence Agency
and Intercontinental
Exchange (ICE).

and additional output would itself be trapped in the Gulf region given that half of Saudi exports transit through the Hormuz Strait, these declarations seem to have had a limited effect.

At the end of April, dissent in the Israeli security establishment surfaced and weakened fears for an imminent military strike at the time, causing a decline in the Brent price. The fall accelerated as Saudi output increased in anticipation of the ban on Iranian oil imports imposed by the EU and the United States that came into force on 28 June. The Brent price continued to decline until the third week of June, bottoming below trend at $88. In late June, the price of Brent jumped by 7 per cent at the announcement that a bank recapitalization agreement had been reached in the euro area[17] and then continued rising to above $110 in August, hovering around its yearly average annual price during the subsequent months.

To a lesser extent, other events also affected oil price developments. The ban on Syrian crude oil exports imposed by the United States and the EU at the end of 2011, South Sudan's shut down of oil production in January 2012, supply outages in other countries, and rising demand in Japan all exerted upward pressures on oil prices. On balance, however, market conditions were characterized by excess supply during the first three quarters of the year, not warranting the record-high average oil price observed during that period. It is therefore likely that abundant liquidity in financialized commodity markets had a disproportionate and distorting effect on oil prices.

In the outlook, global oil demand is assumed to further expand by 1 per cent in 2013, to 90.5 mbd, as declining demand from OECD countries partly offsets growing

Temporarily fading geopolitical risks and use of Saudi spare capacity cause short-lived price plunge

Oil demand is expected to remain subdued in 2013

---

17 See UNCTAD, "Don't blame the physical markets: financialization is the root cause of oil and commodity price volatility", Policy Brief, No. 25 (September 2012).

demand in emerging markets. On the supply side, non-OPEC countries are expected to post an increase in output of 1.3 per cent in 2013, to 53.9 mbd, driven by expanding output in Canada and the United States. Supply in non-OECD countries, which provide about 55 per cent of non-OPEC output, is expected to rise by 0.4 percent as oil production increases in Brazil and in countries of the former Soviet Union.

As a consequence, the Brent price is assumed to average $105 pb in 2013 in a market in which prices continue to be strongly influenced by the risk premium associated with geopolitical tensions, tight spare capacity among OPEC producers, and financial market conditions. The outlook is subject to significant uncertainty. A blockade of the Hormuz Strait could create major supply shortages and trigger unprecedented price surges. Decreasing tensions in the Middle East or weaker-than-expected economic activity in developing countries, in contrast, would create significant downward pressure on oil prices.

Volatile terms of trade

Terms of trade improved for mineral and oil exporters

Trade affects national income through two channels: the prices of exports and imports and the volume of demand.[18] Changes in the terms of trade, which is defined as the ratio of export prices over import prices, provide a synthetic measure of international price shocks associated with trade. Among developing countries, exporters of oil and other minerals and mining products have enjoyed strong improvements in their terms of trade since 2000. For exporters of agricultural products the terms of trade remained fairly stable, while they deteriorated for countries exporting manufactures (figure II.9). Non-agricultural commodity exporters saw the strongest declines in the terms of trade during the height of the global financial crisis, but recovered rapidly thereafter. The swings for exporters of agricultural commodities and manufactures were much less pronounced.

Energy exporters face the sharpest terms-of-trade fluctuations

The magnitude of trade shocks resulting from changes in both prices and volumes has varied greatly across regions and country groups with different export structures (figures II.10a and II.10b).[19] Across all regions, the negative trade shock in 2009 was followed by a strong rebound in 2010-2011. The shock of 2009 resulted primarily from the stark decline in global demand (more than 3 percent of WGP), as well as from falling import and export prices in every region (for the world as a whole, the terms of trade shocks are netted out). Economies in transition, Africa and Western Asia had to cope with the largest trade shocks.

Non-oil commodity exporters also faced sharp price swings

Energy exporters faced the sharpest price fluctuations over the last few years. Mineral and agricultural exporters also faced strong swings in export prices, but in many cases these were mitigated in terms of their impact on the trade balance by parallel swings in energy prices on the import side. Least developed countries (LDCs) as a group do not seem to have been affected as severely by terms-of-trade shocks, but this relatively milder impact mainly reflects the large heterogeneity in export dependence within this group, which is composed of energy and minerals exporters among a number of African LDCs, agricultural exporters among other African LDCs, and agriculture and manufacturing exporters in Asia. Individually, these countries tend to be highly vulnerable to trade shocks.

---

18   The effects of each of these factors can be quantified with some degree of accuracy by combining information from COMTRADE (import and export structure), UNCTAD and other sources (international prices), Netherlands Bureau for Economic Policy Analysis (CPB) and other sources (volume changes of imports and exports). See the World Economic Vulnerability Monitor technical note available from http://www.un.org/en/development/desa/policy/publications/wevm/monitor_note.pdf.

19   For more details about the estimation of trade shocks, see the World Economic Vulnerability Monitor technical note, ibid.

Figure II.9
Barter terms of trade of selected groups of countries by export structure, 2000-2014

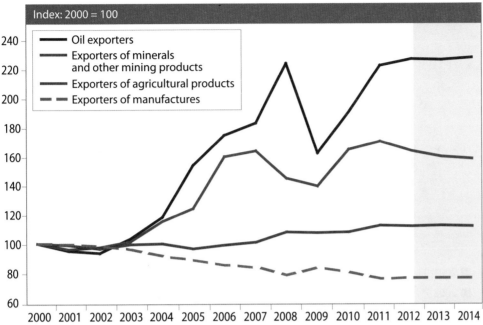

Index: 2000 = 100

Legend:
— Oil exporters
— Exporters of minerals and other mining products
— Exporters of agricultural products
- - Exporters of manufactures

Source: UNCTAD and UN/DESA World Economic Vulnerability Monitor.

Figure II.10a
Trade shocks by main geographic regions and country groupings, 2001-2014

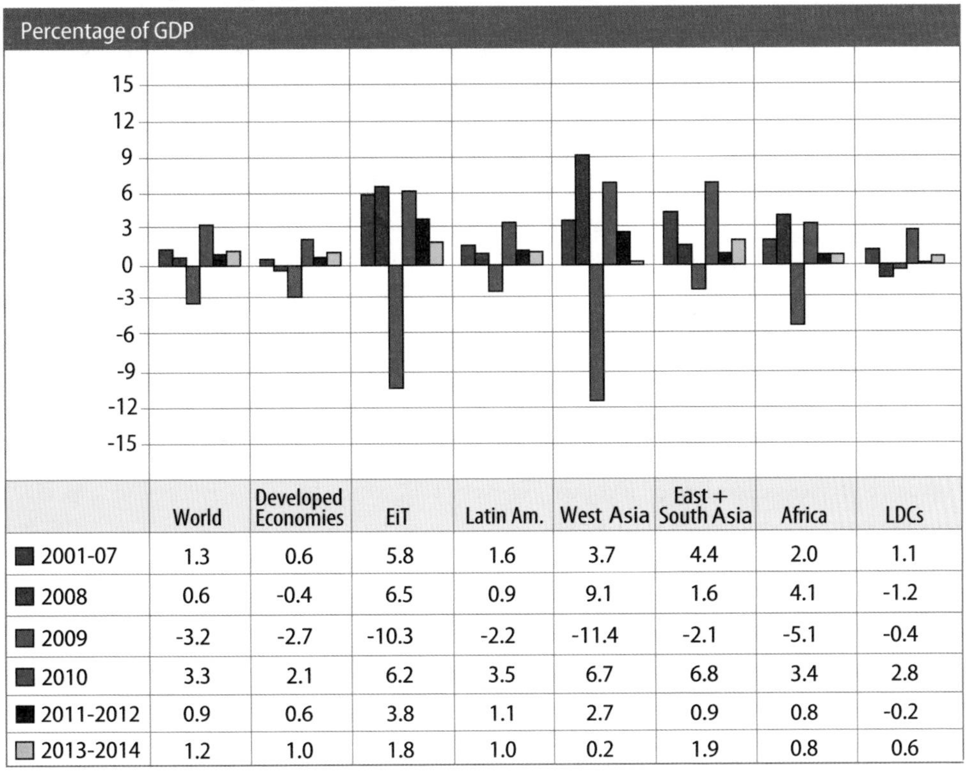

Percentage of GDP

	World	Developed Economies	EiT	Latin Am.	West Asia	East + South Asia	Africa	LDCs
2001-07	1.3	0.6	5.8	1.6	3.7	4.4	2.0	1.1
2008	0.6	-0.4	6.5	0.9	9.1	1.6	4.1	-1.2
2009	-3.2	-2.7	-10.3	-2.2	-11.4	-2.1	-5.1	-0.4
2010	3.3	2.1	6.2	3.5	6.7	6.8	3.4	2.8
2011-2012	0.9	0.6	3.8	1.1	2.7	0.9	0.8	-0.2
2013-2014	1.2	1.0	1.8	1.0	0.2	1.9	0.8	0.6

Source: UN DESA World Economic Vulnerability Monitor (WEVUM), available from http://www.un.org/en/development/desa/policy/publications/wevm.shtml. Data for 2013 and 2014 are baseline United Nations projections.

Figure II.10b
Trade shocks by country groupings according to export specialization, 2001–2014

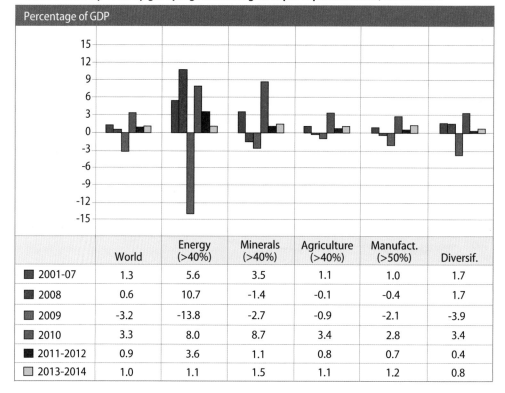

Percentage of GDP						
	World	Energy (>40%)	Minerals (>40%)	Agriculture (>40%)	Manufact. (>50%)	Diversif.
■ 2001-07	1.3	5.6	3.5	1.1	1.0	1.7
■ 2008	0.6	10.7	-1.4	-0.1	-0.4	1.7
■ 2009	-3.2	-13.8	-2.7	-0.9	-2.1	-3.9
■ 2010	3.3	8.0	8.7	3.4	2.8	3.4
■ 2011-2012	0.9	3.6	1.1	0.8	0.7	0.4
☐ 2013-2014	1.0	1.1	1.5	1.1	1.2	0.8

Source: UN DESA World Economic Vulnerability Monitor (WEVUM), available from http://www.un.org/en/development/desa/policy/publications/wevm.shtml. Data for 2013 and 2014 are baseline United Nations projections.

Export diversification reduces vulnerability to trade shocks

Developing economies with greater export diversification have experienced milder trade shocks and been able to keep import levels relatively stable. This, in turn, has provided a more stable domestic policy environment, inter alia, because a large share of imports is used as inputs for manufacturing industries.

In the outlook, trade shock projections in 2013-2014 appear to be relatively mild. This reflects the fact that the estimated growth rates of trade volume per region are moderately positive, together with the fact that most commodity prices are assumed to experience a further correction from the spikes observed in 2010-2011. Under these conditions, countries with greater degrees of diversification may continue to benefit from relatively stable, albeit moderate, external demand.

Growing trade in services

The recovery of trade in services started to falter in the last quarter of 2011

Trade in services experienced a robust recovery following the Great Recession, especially in developing countries. World services trade grew by almost 10 per cent in 2010, but remained subdued in developed countries. In 2011, the value of trade in services further increased by 10.6 per cent, surpassing its pre-crisis peak level by 8.0 per cent to reach $4.2 trillion. Its rate of growth converged across developed and developing countries as well as LDCs. Economies in transition registered growth rates close to 18 per cent in 2011, driven by the continuing boom of travel services in countries such as Azerbaijan, Georgia and Kazakhstan (figures II.11 and II.12).

Figure II.11
Services exports by major country groupings, 2007-2011

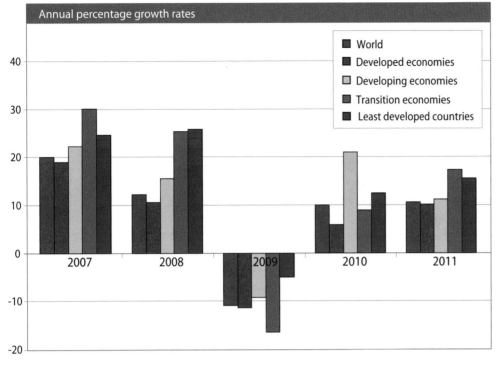

Source: UNCTAD.

Figure II.12
Services imports by major country groupings, 2007-2011

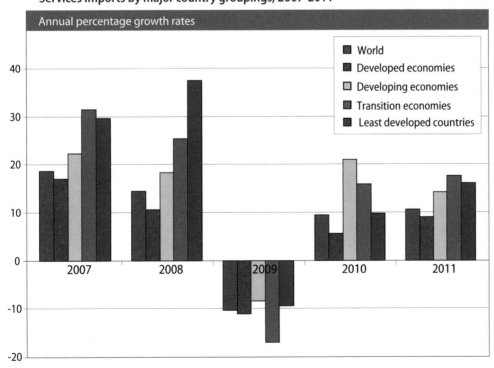

Source: UNCTAD.

In the fourth quarter of 2011, world services exports rose by only 3 per cent year-on-year, a drop of 8.5 per cent compared to the previous quarter. Expansion remained sluggish in the first quarter of 2012 and came to a halt in the second quarter, decelerating along with global output and merchandise trade.[20]

Developing countries see increasing market shares in world services trade

In 2011, the value of world services trade represented 12 per cent of WGP. Merchandise trade, in contrast, represented more than 50 per cent. The share of developing countries in total world services trade remains well below their share in total world merchandise trade, estimated at about 42 per cent. Over the last five years, however, the market share of developing countries in total world services trade increased by 5 percentage points. In 2011, the market shares of developing countries in world services exports and imports were 29.8 per cent and 36.3 per cent, respectively (table II.1). Developing countries thus remain net importers of services. Economies in transition and LDCs experienced fast growth in their tradable services industries over the last 15 years, but their share in world services trade has remained almost constant because of low initial levels. Their trade in services balance remains in deficit as well.

Services sectors recovered unevenly in the wake of the global financial crisis. High technology sectors, such as communication services and computer and information services, recovered swiftly because these sectors are still in the early stages of development in many developing countries and still have significant room for growth. Travel services have also been at the core of trade in services growth worldwide. Transport has been a leading sector in Africa and Latin America.

Table II.1
Shares and rankings of top regions and countries in trade in services

Exports	Share (percentage)		World rank	
	2007	2011	2007	2011
Regions				
Developed economies	71.7	67.3	1	1
Developing economies	25.7	29.8	2	2
Transition economies	2.6	2.9	3	3
Least developed countries	0.5	0.6	4	4
Top 10 exporters				
United States	14.1	14.1	1	1
United Kingdom	8.3	6.5	2	2
Germany	6.4	6.1	3	3
China	3.5	4.3	7	4
France	4.3	4.0	4	5
Japan	3.7	3.4	5	6
Spain	3.7	3.3	6	7
India	2.5	3.2	11	8

---

20 World trade estimates are aggregated from individual reporters' quarterly balance-of-payments statistics taken from the IMF and Eurostat, supplemented with estimates for missing data, as well as national sources. Quarterly figures may not add up to annual figures published elsewhere in World Trade Organization (WTO) or UNCTAD statistical publications or online databases, owing to statistical discrepancies.

Table II.1 (cont'd)	Share (percentage)		World rank	
	2007	2011	2007	2011
Netherlands	3.2	3.2	9	9
Singapore	2.4	3.0	12	10
Other top developing country exporters				
Hong Kong SAR[a]	2.4	2.9	13	11
Korea, Republic of	2.1	2.2	15	15
Russian Federation	1.1	1.3	25	22
Taiwan Province of China	1.0	1.1	26	24
Thailand	0.9	1.0	27	26
Macao SAR[a]	0.4	0.9	40	27
Brazil	0.7	0.9	31	28
Turkey	0.8	0.9	29	29
Malaysia	0.8	0.8	28	32
Imports				
Regions				
Developed economies	66.4	60.1	1	1
Developing economies	30.4	36.3	2	2
Transition economies	3.2	3.6	3	3
Least developed countries	1.3	1.7	4	4
Top 10 importers				
United States	11.3	10.5	1	1
Germany	7.9	7.1	2	2
China	4.0	5.8	5	3
United Kingdom	6.1	4.3	3	4
Japan	4.6	4.1	4	5
France	3.9	3.5	6	6
India	2.2	3.1	14	7
Netherlands	3.0	2.9	8	8
Italy	3.7	2.8	7	9
Ireland	2.9	2.8	10	10
Other top developing country importers				
Singapore	2.3	2.8	13	11
Korea, Republic of	2.6	2.4	11	13
Russian Federation	1.8	2.2	17	15
Saudi Arabia	1.9	1.9	16	18
Brazil	1.1	1.9	26	19
China, Hong Kong SAR	1.3	1.4	20	21
Thailand	1.2	1.3	24	23
United Arab Emirates	1.0	1.2	28	24

Source: UNCTAD.

a Special Administrative Region of China.

Box II.3

International tourism

International tourism growth remains robust amid global slowdown

Despite persistent economic turbulence, international tourist arrivals expanded by 4 per cent during the first eight months of 2012 compared to the same period last year, reaching a record of 705 million overnight visitors. As a result, the milestone of one billion tourists should be reached by the end of the year. While still robust, growth of international tourist arrivals slightly decelerated over the last two years, from 6.6 per cent in 2010 to 5.0 per cent in 2011.

As tourists tend to cut more on spending than on travel in difficult times, international tourism receipts grew more modestly by 4 per cent in 2011, but nevertheless reached a record of $1 trillion. With revenues from international passenger transport estimated at $203 billion in 2011, total tourism receipts that registered as services exports in the balance of payments amounted to $1.2 trillion in 2011.

The export value of travel and passenger transport account for 30 per cent of the world's exports of commercial services and 5.5 per cent of overall exports of goods and services (figure A). As a worldwide export category, tourism ranks fifth after fuel, chemicals, food and automotive products.

Figure A: **Tourism as a share of trade and trade in services by subregion**

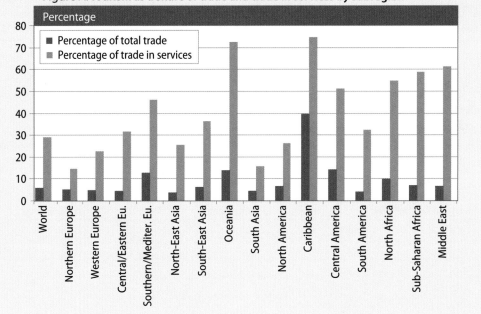

During the first eight months of 2012, tourist arrivals increased by 7 per cent in Asia and the Pacific, boosted by rebounding Japanese inbound and outbound tourism as well as by the continued strong performance of other major source markets in South and South-East Asia. Growth of tourist arrivals in Europe declined from 6 per cent in 2011 to 3 per cent in 2012, with stronger performance in Central and Eastern Europe. Stalling tourism activity in Southern and Mediterranean Europe was partly created by the recovery of destinations in North Africa, which grew by 10 per cent following rebounding activity in Tunisia. In sub-Saharan Africa, tourist arrivals increased by 4 per cent, bringing the continental average growth rate to 6 per cent. The return of tourists to Egypt limited the decline of tourist arrivals in the Middle East to 1 per cent. The number of overnight visitors grew by 4 per cent in the Americas. While it expanded robustly by 6 per cent on average in Latin America, destinations in North America grew at 3 per cent, a relatively high rate for a mature subregion.

In terms of tourism expenditures abroad, demand from both emerging and advanced economy source markets during the first six to nine months of 2012 remained steady. Among the 10 major source markets, spending on overseas tourism rose by 30 per cent in China, 15 per cent in

Source: UNWTO (estimates based on data from 2010).

Note: International tourism, including travel and passenger transport.

Box II.3 (cont'd)

the Russian Federation, but also by 9 per cent in the United States, 7 per cent in Japan, 6 per cent in Canada, 5 per cent in Germany and 4 per cent in Australia.

According to the latest survey of the World Tourism Organization (UNWTO) Panel of Experts, prospects for international tourism expansion are weakening, but remain positive. International tourism is expected to grow by 3 per cent to 4 per cent in 2012, before declining slightly in 2013.

Sustainable tourism

Travel and tourism are both victim and vector of climate change. Because climate so directly defines the length and quality of tourism seasons, affects tourism operations, and influences environmental conditions that both attract and deter visitors, the sector is considered to be highly climate sensitive. The effects of climate change therefore can have a significant impact on tourism business and destinations, particularly in the vulnerable small island developing States and least developed countries.

At the same time, travel and tourism help feed climate change by accounting for approximately 5 per cent of global carbon dioxide (CO_2) emissions, which are the main contributor to the greenhouse gas effect and global warming (see also box II.1).[a] Transport accounts for 75 per cent of CO_2 emissions by the tourism sector. Air travel emissions make up about 40 per cent of the total and are expanding at an average annual rate of 3.2 per cent. While slower than the growth in the number of air travel passengers and tourist arrivals, the trend keeps adding to CO_2 emissions (figure B).

Figure B: CO_2 emissions from air transport, passenger carried and tourist arrivals move in tandem

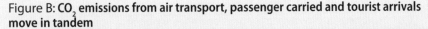

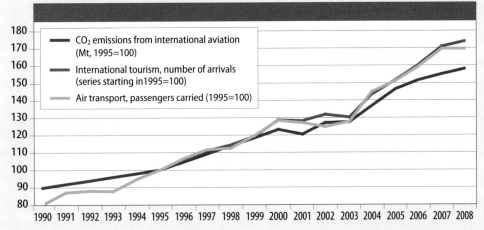

- CO₂ emissions from international aviation (Mt, 1995=100)
- International tourism, number of arrivals (series starting in1995=100)
- Air transport, passengers carried (1995=100)

Sources: World Bank and International Transport Forum.

a World Tourism Organization and United Nations Environment Programme, *Climate Change and Tourism: Responding to Global Challenges* (Madrid, World Tourism Organization, 2008), available from http://www.unwto.org/sdt/news/en/pdf/climate2008.pdf.

b See the G20 Los Cabos Leaders Declaration of 19 June 2012, available from http://www.g20.utoronto.ca/2012/2012-0619-loscabos.html.

c See General Assembly resolution 66/288 of 27 July 2012, paras. 130 and 131, available from http://www.un.org/ga/search/view_doc.asp?symbol=%20A/RES/66/288.

d For a description of the optimistic assumptions and the green growth scenario, see United Nations Environment Programme, *Green Economy Report*, Part II: Investing in energy and resource efficiency: Tourism", annex 3, available from http://www.unep.org/greeneconomy/Portals/88/documents/ger/11.0_Tourism.pdf.

The G20 recently recognized the role of travel and tourism as "a vehicle for job creation, economic growth and development" and made the commitment to "work towards developing travel facilitation initiatives in support of job creation, quality work, poverty reduction and global growth".[b]

In efforts to curb emissions in the coming decades, the tourism industry continues to develop mitigation and adaptation strategies. In this regard, "The future we want",[c] the outcome document of the 2012 United Nations Conference on Sustainable Development (UNCSD, also known as "Rio+20"), emphasized the significant contribution that well-designed and well-managed tourism can make to advancing the three dimensions of sustainable development: economic, social and environmental.

The shift towards sustainable tourism can create jobs and reduce poverty, while also improving environmental outcomes. With tourism expected to expand in the coming decades, the challenge of cutting back emissions is even larger. Investing in the greening of tourism can reduce the costs related to energy, water and waste and enhance the value of biodiversity, ecosystems and cultural heritage, while at the same time curbing the expansion of tourism-related CO_2 emissions. Under a green growth scenario based on optimistic assumptions,[d] CO_2 emissions generated by tourism in 2050 would only be half compared to a business-as-usual scenario and they would have returned to their current level after an initial increase.

Recovery of service activities directly affected by the global financial crisis was more sluggish. Financial services were the most severely affected by the global financial turmoil. Construction services were hit by the bursting of the housing bubble in developed economies and transportation services growth stalled because of the weak rebound of global trade. International tourism receipts increased by 4 per cent in real terms in 2011 as it continued to recover from the losses incurred during the global crisis.

Developing and transition economies further improved their ranking among the world's top 10 exporters and importers of services during 2007-2011 (table II.1). China moved from the seventh to the fourth position in world exports, and from the fifth to the third position of world imports. China is a major contributor to Asian predominance (81 per cent) in total developing country services trade. In the top 10 developing countries and economies in transition, 6 of the top exporters also rank among the top 10 importers.

Trade policy developments

The Doha Round

The Doha Round of multilateral trade negotiations of the World Trade Organization (WTO), launched in November 2001, continues to be at a complete stalemate with no clear prospects for the foreseeable future. As requested at the Eighth WTO Ministerial Conference in December 2011, participants have been exploring the possibility of focusing on a limited number of negotiating areas as part of a likely "smaller package" to complete negotiations, probably by the time of the next WTO Ministerial Conference in Bali, Indonesia, at the end of 2013. The G20 Summit at Los Cabos in June 2012 also supported such a partial approach.

A smaller package could potentially reflect results of negotiations on trade facilitation—focused on strengthening multilateral rules and procedures to streamline the movement, release and clearance of goods at the border and in transit—where some tangible progress has been achieved. However, progress in negotiations is still challenged by many developing countries for whom trade facilitation efforts entail high implementation costs without any of their key trade and development concerns being addressed. An outcome on trade facilitation would therefore also require agreement on support measures, including financial and technical assistance, in order for developing countries to meet implementation costs. Such agreement is yet to be negotiated.

A smaller package would also cover results of negotiations on a plurilateral International Services Agreement (ISA), which has been contemplated by a group of about 20 countries. Some of them intend to negotiate the ISA as a closed agreement in which benefits will not be extended to all WTO members on a most favoured nation (MFN) basis. Although still in a consultation phase, such an approach, if implemented, would mean a critical departure from the "single undertaking" concept of the WTO, involving risks for the multilateral trading system based on the unconditional MFN treatment.

Therefore, completing the Round with a smaller package will be difficult. To be balanced and attractive for developing countries, LDCs in particular, any such package would need to be supplemented by meaningful provisions that are of interest to them, such as giving full duty-free and quota-free market access on a lasting basis for all LDCs, and elimination of developed-country subsidies on agricultural exports and cotton production.

Another important obstacle to the negotiation process is the perception—perhaps not wholly justified but yet increasingly widespread—that the Doha Round would be about an outdated set of twentieth century issues. As such, it would contribute too little, too late to the aspirations of globalizing businesses today and be inadequate to provide the enabling policy environment needed to support the inclusive and sustainable growth and development pathways called for by the G20 and numerous United Nations summits and high level conferences, including the Conference on Sustainable Development (Rio+20) and UNCTAD XIII.

The failure to complete the Doha Round is not only detrimental to the credibility of the multilateral trading system, but is also deterring progress in building consensus on other complex multilateral issues, such as the sustainable development agenda. More generally, the incapacity to reach comprehensive and balanced results in the Round for more than a decade reflects wider global governance deficits and eventually may call multilateralism itself into question as the preferred approach to solving global issues.

Apart from trade negotiations, there were several trade policy developments, mostly related to the accessions of countries still outside the WTO, including Montenegro, Samoa and Vanuatu. The accession of the Russian Federation on 22 August 2012 marked the completion of an 18-year-long negotiating process. With Russia's membership, the WTO now covers approximately 97 per cent of world trade and is closer to universal membership. The Russian Federation took on an array of commitments and obligations, ranging from binding import tariffs on agricultural and manufactured goods below currently applied rates to improved market access for foreign services providers in a number of sectors, such as telecommunications, transportation, financial and distribution services.

The Russian Federation joins the WTO

In general, Russia's accession package offers new trade opportunities for WTO members, particularly developing countries. It also contains an extensive set of systemic obligations serving as a multilateral basis for Russia's further integration into the world economy. On the other hand, the effects of WTO membership on Russia's domestic economy are not straightforward, particularly with regards to agriculture and several industrial sectors, and were subject to an intensive but inconclusive internal discussion prior to the ratification of the accession terms (see box IV.1 in chapter IV).

New guidelines on accessions of LDCs to the WTO were agreed to in July 2012. These guidelines are expected to streamline and facilitate accession of LDCs by offering them some additional policy space and flexibility. For example, acceding LDCs will be required to bind all their agricultural tariff lines at an overall average rate of 50 per cent, and 95 per cent of their non-agricultural tariff lines at an overall average rate of 35 per cent, while 5 per cent of their industrial tariff lines could be left unbound.

New guidelines facilitate accession of LDCs to the WTO

Preferential trade agreements

Against the deadlock in the Doha Round, the uncoordinated process of negotiating preferential bilateral and regional trade agreements (RTAs) has gained further momentum. According to recent WTO estimates, there are now almost 400 preferential trade agreements in force, with each WTO member belonging, on average, to 13 separate agreements. The expanding number of such agreements further adds to an already complex system of trade preferences with often substantially different regulatory frameworks across agreements. Despite expected overall benefits to their parties, the effects of RTAs in regard to trade relationships with third countries are often less positive. One issue of particular importance for small- and medium-sized enterprises is that the fragmentation of trade

Fragmentation of trade rules undermines the consistency of the multilateral trading system rules brought by RTAs has the effect of increasing compliance costs for their participants. Multinational corporations (MNCs), by contrast, are in a better position to handle and exploit the regulatory maze. In more general terms, preferential trade agreements have also had the effect of weakening the multilateral trading system by including "WTO-plus" and "WTO-extra" rules with their own dispute settlement mechanisms.

Fragmentation of trade rules and regulations is more evident in regard to North-South agreements. While RTAs comprised of high-income markets are largely related to "deep" integration, often based on sophisticated regulatory frameworks of major developed markets, South-South RTAs more often reflect the dynamics and priorities of regional integration among developing countries. They are still focused on traditional market access issues like the reduction of tariffs, which remain relatively higher as compared to those in North-South trade (box II.4). Deeper integration is still an open issue in many South-South RTAs as it will require additional rule-making in the trade regulatory framework, especially with regard to non-tariff measures.

Twenty-first century agreements increasingly address the aspirations of globalizing businesses

The Trans-Pacific Partnership (TPP) is probably the most actively negotiated North-South RTA today. The TPP is being negotiated among 11 developed and developing countries[21] and is presented as a comprehensive and high-standard RTA aimed at almost full liberalization of trade in goods and services and establishing commitments that reach beyond multilateral rules under the WTO. It is also viewed by some as an alternative to the stalled Doha Round as a twenty-first century agreement that addresses new and cross-cutting issues reflecting the needs of an increasingly globalized economy and evolving global production and supply chains.

Apart from market access in goods and services, TPP negotiations are focused on setting rules that extend beyond those in the WTO and cover such areas as intellectual property rights, services, government procurement, investment, rules of origin, competition policy, labour and environmental standards. In addition, for the first time, rule-making is sought in completely new areas like state-owned enterprises, regulatory coherence and supply chain competitiveness.

Provisions on labour standards remain controversial

One of the most controversial issues that the TPP negotiations are trying to address relates to the scope and depth of provisions on labour standards and worker rights. According to some reports, TPP would require its participants to adopt and enforce the four internationally accepted labour rights that are contained in the 1998 International Labour Organization (ILO) Declaration on Fundamental Principles and Rights at Work: the freedom of association and the effective recognition of the right to collective bargaining; the elimination of all forms of compulsory or forced labour; the effective abolition of child labour; and the elimination of discrimination in respect of employment and occupation. These provisions would be enforceable under the TPP dispute settlement mechanism, while violations could be subject to potential trade sanctions.

Attempts to enforce labour standards through trade agreements have a long history. This linkage has traditionally been strongly opposed by many developing countries on the grounds that it may serve to artificially increase production costs of domestic businesses and operations of MNCs, thus undermining their comparative advantage. However, at the same time they do strengthen human rights of workers in developing countries and may help increase the labour share of national income, which is exceedingly low in many of these countries. Providing these rights would appear to be consistent with the internationally agreed upon goal of promoting decent work. Nevertheless, developing

---

21   These are Australia, Brunei Darussalam, Canada, Chile, Malaysia, Mexico, New Zealand, Peru, Singapore, United States, and Viet Nam. Thailand will also join TPP trade talks.

Box II.4

Import tariffs and South-South trade

Many developing countries have substantially reduced effective trade tariffs starting in the 1990s. The general trend of lowering tariffs in developing countries is likely to continue, especially with regard to South-South trade (both intraregional and interregional trade). In 2011, imports by developed countries were subject to an average tariff of about 1.2 per cent (see table). Imports entering developing countries and economies in transition were subject to an average tariff ranging from about 2.2 per cent for the economies in transition to about 7.8 per cent for developing countries in South Asia. Tariffs still represent an important obstacle to South-South trade, especially in regions where the regional integration process has been slower. Intraregional trade faces relatively low tariffs within the economies in transition, Latin America and the Caribbean and East Asia largely owing to the existing preferential trade agreements. On the other hand, tariffs are still an important policy issue for most of the other regions of Asia as well as for Africa. The average tariff applied to intraregional trade in South Asia is about 4 per cent, while that of sub-Saharan Africa is 3.5 per cent. Because very few South-South RTAs span different developing country regions, interregional trade is generally subject to higher tariffs than intraregional trade. Thus, higher tariffs are imposed by countries in South Asia and sub-Saharan Africa (especially on products originating from East Asia) and by countries in the regions comprising Northern Africa, Western Asia and Central Asia (especially versus products originating from Latin America and the Caribbean).

Source: UNCTAD TRAINS database.

Effective trade-weighted tariffs by main regions and country groupings in 2011
(Changes from 2005 through 2011 are indicated in parentheses)

Percentage

Importer	Exporting region							
	High-income countries	Economies in transition	East Asia	South Asia	Northern Africa, Western Asia and Central Asia	Latin America and the Caribbean	Sub-Saharan Africa	Average tariff imposed on imports
High-income countries	0.9	0.4	2.2	2.8	0.5	0.7	0.8	1.2
	-(0.1)	-(0.4)	-(0.3)	-(0.5)	-(0.2)	-(0.4)	(0.2)	-(0.1)
Economies in transition	2.3	0.7	4.1	4.6	2.8	2.0	0.5	2.2
	(0.0)	-(1.3)	-(0.4)	-(0.9)	(0.0)	-(0.7)	-(1.4)	-(0.3)
East Asia	4.6	2.4	2.1	1.8	0.5	1.5	0.4	3.6
	-(0.7)	-(2.0)	-(2.0)	-(1.2)	-(0.6)	-(1.5)	-(1.7)	-(1.2)
South Asia	7.9	7.0	13.1	4.0	2.5	2.1	3.3	7.8
	-(5.2)	-(6.8)	-(5.0)	-(5.9)	-(9.0)	-(19.2)	-(10.6)	-(6.1)
Northern Africa, Western Asia and Central Asia	4.6	4.7	7.1	5.0	3.5	9.8	3.7	5.1
	-(0.3)	(1.4)	-(1.5)	-(0.2)	-(0.3)	-(0.4)	-(1.3)	-(0.1)
Latin America and the Caribbean	4.0	3.2	7.7	7.6	4.0	1.1	1.3	4.0
	-(0.2)	-(1.7)	-(0.9)	-(2.3)	(0.9)	-(0.8)	-(0.9)	-(0.2)
Sub-Saharan Africa	6.5	4.3	10.5	6.3	8.4	8.7	3.5	6.9
	-(0.1)	-(2.3)	-(1.5)	-(0.6)	(0.3)	-(1.0)	-(1.0)	-(0.2)
Average tariff faced by exports	2.1	1.0	3.2	3.2	1.2	1.2	1.3	
	-(0.1)	-(0.6)	-(0.1)	-(0.8)	-(0.3)	-(0.5)	-(0.5)	

countries' market access could be made less predictable under the threat of trade sanctions. It is often alleged that the linkage between trade and labour standards is a disguise for protectionism in developed countries. However, it is also alleged that the concern for developing countries' comparative advantage is a disguise for protecting the economic rents of the elites in the developing economies. Recently, provisions related to the enforcement of labour standards have been included in several bilateral preferential North-South agreements, reflecting developed countries' negotiating priorities that mostly stem from domestic concerns about losing jobs to low-wage countries.

Protectionist pressures

Existing trade restrictions are removed, but slowly

The joint WTO-OECD-UNCTAD monitoring report on G20 trade and investment measures of 31 October 2012 showed a certain slowdown of trade-restrictive measures with 71 new import restrictions taken in mid-May through mid-October of 2012, affecting around 0.4 per cent of total G20 merchandise imports, or 0.3 per cent of world imports. These involved mostly non-tariff measures, including trade remedy actions (like anti-dumping and countervailing measures), import licensing and customs controls. There are growing concerns about the proliferation of non-tariff measures implemented through technical requirements, like standards and sanitary and phytosanitary regulations. The sectors most heavily affected in terms of trade coverage were electrical machinery, mineral fuels and oils, fertilizers, chemical products, machinery and mechanical appliances, and plastics.[22] On the other hand, the number of new export restrictions had declined significantly from that reported in previous monitoring reports.

The trend of slow removal of existing measures continued, in compliance with G20 commitments. Yet, only 21 per cent of trade restrictions introduced since the start of the crisis in October 2008 have been eliminated. Those measures related to the termination of trade remedy actions and phasing out temporary tariff increases. Overall, the trade coverage of the remaining restrictive measures put in place beginning in October 2008 is about 3.5 per cent of world merchandise imports.[23]

The G20 recognizes the role of global value chains, but unchecked growth of intrafirm trade is environmentally suboptimal

With government budget cuts, persistent high unemployment and expected slowing global output growth, the threat of protectionist pressures is likely to increase. This trend is also supported by what is appearing as an escalation of trade frictions and disputes between major trading countries. To a large extent, such disputes are fuelled by traditional bilateral trade imbalance concerns and accusations of unfair trade practices that are linked to job losses in importing countries. However, these traditional arguments neither recognize the growing importance of global value and supply chains, which are increasingly shaping the flows of international trade and foreign direct investment, nor do they show awareness of the related environmental challenges. In this regard, the recognition of the role of such chains in fostering economic growth, employment and development by Leaders at the G20 Summit at Los Cabos is significant. The G20 also emphasized the

---

[22] It was estimated that if the trade restrictive measures were implemented in all advanced economies, the developing economies in Asia and the Pacific could experience an export loss of over $27 billion. In this case, least developed countries, land-locked developing countries and small island developing States could face a significant contraction in their exports to the advanced economies as compared to the baseline scenario. See Sudip Ranjan Basu and others, "Euro zone debt crisis: scenario analysis and implications for developing Asia-Pacific", MPDD Working paper, No. WP/12/03 (UNCTAD, Macroeconomic Policy and Development Division).

[23] See Organization for Economic Cooperation and Development (OECD), UNCTAD and WTO, "Reports on G20 Trade and Investment Measures (mid-May to mid-October 2012)", 31 October 2012, available from http://www.oecd.org/daf/internationalinvestment/8thG20report.pdf.

need to enhance the participation of developing countries in such chains. Measuring the precise contribution of global value chains to growth of world trade and output remains a challenge (box II.5).[24] This also hampers assessment of environmental implications of expanding trade and production through global value chains (see box II.1). Unchecked growth of trade in intermediate goods and intrafirm trade is environmentally detrimental, inter alia, because freight transport is a major contributor to global CO_2 emissions and, hence, to climate change. The prevailing sectoral policy approach to climate change mitigation further hinders a precise assessment of CO_2 emissions along global value chains. The rapid growth of global supply chains will require a different, more integral approach if policymakers are to adequately identify and address trade-offs between the economic and environmental costs and benefits associated with international trade.

Box II.5

Measuring trade in value added

Recently, economists and statisticians have been paying increasing attention to measuring the value added of international trade and the implications for economic analysis.[a] Conventional international trade statistics record trade flows between countries on the basis of the gross value of traded goods and services. However, as a result of the rapid expansion of global production chains, an exported final product usually contains a significant share of imported intermediate goods, such as parts and components, which may have crossed borders many times. Hence, conventional trade statistics likely overestimate the true contribution of international trade flows to economic activity. An iPhone exported from China to the United States, for instance, is adding $200 to the record of Chinese exports, whereas only about $10 of value added is generated in China where it is assembled. The remaining value stems from immediate parts and components imported from Japan, the Republic of Korea and other countries.

In general, along with the increasing geographical fragmentation of global manufacturing processes, intrafirm trade and trade in intermediate goods have been growing rapidly, accounting for nearly 50 per cent of total international merchandise trade. Conventional trade statistics may thus provide an inaccurate picture of actual trade linkages between countries and be a highly imperfect guide for trade, macroeconomic and development policies.

In response to these challenges, work coordinated through the United Nations Statistical Commission and various research institutes, as well a WTO-OECD joint initiative,[b] are under way to formulate a new metric that identifies trade in value added. Under this approach, trade flows across countries are measured on a net basis, that is, obtaining the domestically generated value added of exported goods by subtracting the value of imported intermediates from the total export value.

Measuring trade in terms of value added provides a substantially different picture of bilateral trade patterns. For instance, by conventional measures, China records a large bilateral trade surplus with the United States of around $200 billion per year. In value added terms, however, China's surplus with the United States would be 40 per cent smaller. In contrast, the bilateral trade surplus of the Republic of Korea and Japan with the United States would be about 40 per cent larger, because those two countries are large exporters of intermediate products. Furthermore, China's trade surplus with Japan would turn into a deficit.

a For example, World Trade Organization and Institute of Developing Economies-JETRO, "Trade patterns and global value chains in East Asia: from trade in goods to trade in tasks" (Geneva, 2011), available from http://www.wto.org/english/res_e/booksp_e/stat_tradepat_globvalchains_e.pdf; and Robert Koopman, Zhi Wang, and Shang-Jin Wei, "Estimating domestic value added in exports when processing trade is prevalent," *Journal of Development Economics*, forthcoming. Available from http://www.ecb.europa.eu/home/pdf/research/compnet/DEVEC_1670.pdf?57a5265fab96f74f6f7a2ab0464575d3.

b See OECD, "Measuring Trade in Value-Added: An OECD-WTO joint initiative", available from http://www.oecd.org/sti/industryandglobalisation/measuringtradeinvalueaddedanoecd-wtojointinitiative.htm.

---

24   See the G20 Los Cabos Summit Leaders Declaration of 19 June 2012, para. 29: "We value the discussion held by our Trade Ministers in Puerto Vallarta on the relevance of regional and global value chains to world trade, recognizing their role in fostering economic growth, employment and development and emphasizing the need to enhance the participation of developing countries in such value chains. We encourage a deepening of these discussions in the WTO, UNCTAD and OECD within their respective mandates, and we call on them to accelerate their work on analyzing the functioning of global value chains and their relationship with trade and investment flows, development and jobs, as well as on how to measure trade flows, to better understand how our actions affect our countries and others, and to report on progress under Russia's Presidency." Available from http://www.g20.utoronto.ca/2012/2012-0619-loscabos.html.

Box II.5 (cont'd)

Measuring bilateral trade in terms of value added would better identify the degree to which countries are connected through trade. If charted out through the full global value chain, such measuring would provide a more accurate basis to assess the transmission of changes in economic conditions from one country to another that occurs through trade channels. It would potentially also alter assessments of policy spillover effects, such as exchange rate adjustments. Many large-scale econometric models of the world economy, such as the United Nations World Economic Forecasting Model, contain a bilateral trade matrix linking individual country models together. The parameters of this matrix are key for the analysis of policy studies and significantly influence outcomes of the alternative scenarios simulated using the model. If this matrix is re-estimated using new data on trade in value added, the resulting policy analysis and model simulations could be significantly different, altering our understanding of the spillover effects of national policies.

New trade statistics would also affect other important measures guiding macroeconomic policymaking. The real effective exchange rate (REER), for instance, is used as a proxy measure of international competitiveness. It is measured using bilateral trade shares as weights for shifts in the value of the national currency against that of major trading partners. Using shares of trade in value added as weights could thus shed a different light on a country's competitiveness with its various trading partners, especially if its exports contain significant amounts of imported inputs. By the same token, the revealed comparative advantage of individual countries, as measured by the share of a sector in the country's total exports relative to the world average share of this sector, would also be more accurately estimated.

However, because the new trade statistics only redistributes net bilateral trade flows by adjusting both the exports and imports of individual trading partners, each country's overall current-account balance and, thus, global imbalances would remain unchanged. Nonetheless, it would not be immaterial to policymakers, however, as the effects of rebalancing policy actions can be quantitatively different from that anticipated when using conventional trade statistics. For example, a policy to stimulate consumption in China, along with a revaluation of the renminbi against the United States dollar, would be expected to lead to a substantial reduction in the current-account deficit of the United States on the basis of the large bilateral trade imbalance between these two economies (as measured conventionally). Based on the new approach, however, China has a smaller bilateral trade surplus with the United States and a deficit instead of a surplus with Japan. So the same policy action would be expected to lead to a much more muted narrowing of the trade deficit of the United States with China, while it would widen China's deficit with Japan.

Chapter 3
International finance for development

There is increasing awareness that substantial financing will be needed to meet global development challenges, such as mitigating the effects of climate change and achieving the Millennium Development Goals (MDGs). Given the scope of the financing needs, both private and public sector funds will be necessary, underscoring the importance of having sound financial sectors capable of providing stable long-term financing for sustainable development.

Four years after the crisis, the global financial system remains volatile

Yet, four years after the crisis began, the international financial system continues to be plagued by vulnerabilities. The sovereign debt crisis in Europe and the uneven global recovery have led to heightened risk aversion and increased volatility of private capital flows (see chapter I). Deleveraging of financial institutions continues, particularly in Europe, where many banks hold large amounts of sovereign bonds from debt-distressed countries on their balance sheets. In recipient countries, flows of official development assistance (ODA) also tend to be highly volatile. In 2011, total ODA flows, net of debt cancellation, fell in real terms for the first time since 1997, owing to greater fiscal austerity and sovereign debt problems in developed countries. At the same time, institutional investors appear to have become increasingly oriented to the short term, with fewer resources dedicated to long-term investments since the crisis.

The international community has taken steps to address some of these vulnerabilities by strengthening the banking system through regulatory reforms. Although these reforms represent important steps forward, they are being phased in only gradually, are not comprehensive, and are not adequately focused on the underlying goal of the financial system to effectively allocate credit for long-term sustainable development. This chapter discusses the underlying risks in the international financial system and its possible impact on financing for sustainable development.

Trends in private capital and other private flows

In 2012, net international private capital flows to developing countries and economies in transition fell by more than 50 per cent, from $425 billion in 2011 to an estimated $206 billion in 2012 (table III.1). More broadly, private capital flows have been highly volatile since 2008. Net private capital inflows collapsed during the crisis, surged in 2010 to approximately $525 billion, and declined again in the latter part of 2011. While some stability seemed to return to international currency and capital markets in early 2012, new turmoil surfaced later in the year.

International private capital flows to emerging and developing countries remain extremely volatile

This heightened volatility can be attributed to several factors. An increase in global risk aversion, caused in part by growing fears about the sustainability of public finances in Europe, is leading portfolio investors to a general flight to safety. In addition, many European banks continue to face deleveraging pressures, which has led to cutbacks in lending to developing and transition economies. There is a risk that deleveraging pressures will worsen if the European crisis accelerates, which could in turn trigger significant portfolio outflows from emerging economies. A tightening in lending standards by international banks in response to Basel III might also force further deleveraging, although such an effect is likely to be rather muted because of the long phase-in period of some of its elements. In addition, signs of an economic slowdown in some leading developing economies (like Brazil, China and India) have reduced flows to these countries.

At the same time, other factors have encouraged increased inflows into developing countries. Weaknesses in developed economies have led some investors to diversify out of troubled advanced economy markets and into developing country markets.[1] In addition, extremely high global liquidity brought on by the exceptional monetary policy measures imposed in response to the crisis—such as the third round of quantitative easing in the United States—has depressed yields in some developed countries to close to zero. As a result, a search for better yields has led to an increase in short-term investments in countries with higher interest rates (often referred to as the carry trade).

This diverse set of pressures has created increased volatility and impacted different types of flows in different ways. Overall, given that much of the positive inflows are driven by a search for short-term yields resulting from low interest rates in developed countries, fixed-income investments have experienced more positive trends than equity portfolio investment and foreign direct investment (FDI).

Table III.1
Net financial flows to developing countries and economies in transition, 1999-2013

	Average annual flow						
	1999 -2002	2003 -2008	2009	2010	2011	2012[a]	2013[b]
Developing countries							
Net private capital flows	59.1	200.2	450.2	525.4	424.7	206.1	300.0
Net direct investment	151.9	251.7	253.1	332.1	435.9	374.4	371.7
Net portfolio investment[c]	-31.7	-39.5	36.6	91.0	33.7	50.1	59.2
Other net investment[d]	-61.1	-12.0	160.5	102.4	-44.8	-218.4	-130.9
Net official flows	-9.3	-88.6	8.1	32.6	-94.3	-36.4	-64.7
Total net flows	49.8	111.6	458.3	558.0	330.4	169.7	235.3
Change in reserves[e]	-121.7	-630.2	-706.5	-914.8	-777.1	-558.8	-636.9
Africa							
Net private capital flows	7.3	16.6	31.2	0.0	14.3	36.2	47.3
Net direct investment	14.9	32.4	49.1	34.6	45.4	44.6	52.4
Net portfolio investment[c]	-1.9	-4.9	-15.7	1.8	-11.0	2.6	6.8
Other net investment[d]	-5.8	-10.9	-2.2	-36.5	-20.1	-11.0	-11.9
Net official flows	-1.4	-8.7	20.1	30.0	22.1	27.1	28.3
Total net flows	5.9	7.9	51.3	29.9	36.5	63.3	75.6
Change in reserves[e]	-8.9	-58.5	1.2	-27.4	-32.8	-35.9	-43.1
East and South Asia							
Net private capital flows	17.0	99.6	301.0	387.2	208.8	10.7	94.6
Net direct investment	62.3	123.4	79.4	193.2	224.4	171.2	158.1
Net portfolio investment[c]	-17.9	-31.3	27.2	50.9	-7.1	-10.3	2.5
Other net investment[d]	-27.5	7.5	194.5	143.0	-8.6	-150.2	-65.9
Net official flows	-1.5	-6.5	19.3	15.8	9.2	2.0	3.2
Total net flows	15.5	93.1	320.4	403.0	218.0	12.6	97.7
Change in reserves[e]	-105.1	-425.6	-664.2	-689.9	-525.5	-254.5	-373.6

---

1   International Monetary Fund (IMF), *Global Financial Stability Report: Restoring Confidence and Progressing on Reforms*, October 2012.

Table III.1 (cont'd)	Average annual flow						
	1999 -2002	2003 -2008	2009	2010	2011	2012[a]	2013[b]
Western Asia							
Net private capital flows	-5.8	53.3	96.0	74.6	52.7	45.1	55.0
Net direct investment	6.2	35.7	56.1	29.7	39.1	37.9	42.0
Net portfolio investment[c]	-5.2	6.3	42.2	39.2	37.8	56.1	47.5
Other net investment[d]	-6.9	11.4	-2.3	5.8	-24.2	-48.8	-34.5
Net official flows	-11.5	-67.3	-66.8	-56.5	-153.9	-126.1	-149.7
Total net flows	-17.3	-13.9	29.1	18.2	-101.2	-81.0	-94.7
Change in reserves[e]	-7.5	-91.1	6.5	-92.8	-99.4	-198.6	-166.1
Latin America and the Caribbean							
Net private capital flows	40.7	30.7	22.0	63.6	148.9	114.2	103.1
Net direct investment	68.4	60.3	68.5	74.6	126.9	120.7	119.3
Net portfolio investment[c]	-6.7	-9.6	-17.0	-1.0	14.0	1.9	2.5
Other net investment[d]	-21.0	-20.0	-29.5	-10.0	8.0	-8.4	-18.6
Net official flows	5.0	-6.1	35.5	43.2	28.3	60.6	53.6
Total net flows	45.7	24.6	57.5	106.9	177.1	174.8	156.7
Change in reserves[e]	-0.2	-55.0	-50.0	-104.7	-119.4	-69.8	-54.1
Economies in transition							
Net private capital flows	-2.6	38.8	-49.8	-19.9	-56.2	-55.5	-31.8
Net direct investment	5.9	29.1	23.1	13.0	19.8	9.9	13.9
Net portfolio investment[c]	0.8	0.6	-10.2	9.6	-28.9	-6.5	-3.8
Other net investment[d]	-9.3	9.0	-62.7	-42.5	-47.1	-58.9	-41.8
Net official flows	-3.5	-14.2	46.4	1.6	-17.8	-21.7	-27.8
Total net flows	-6.2	24.6	-3.4	-18.3	-74.0	-77.2	-59.6
Change in reserves[e]	-15.4	-74.8	-11.7	-51.2	-27.5	-26.6	-17.6

Source: International Monetary Fund (IMF), World Economic Outlook database, October 2012.

Note: The composition of developing countries above is based on the country classification located in the statistical annex, which differs from the classification used in the World Economic Outlook. See also footnote 5 in Chapter I.

a   Preliminary.

b   Forecasts.

c   Including portfolio debt and equity investment.

d   Including short- and long-term bank lending, and possibly including some official flows owing to data limitations.

e   Negative values denote increases in reserves.

Portfolio flows and cross-border bank lending

The recent decline in international capital inflows has been mainly on account of a collapse in cross-border interbank flows (referenced under "net private flows" in table III.1), as well as a drop in equity portfolio flows.[2] Although commercial bank lending to developing countries had been following a path of gradual recovery in many countries, deleveraging pressures continue to be felt, especially from European banks. The impact of declining cross-border bank lending has been greatest in emerging Europe and Central Asia, which

Emerging Europe and Central Asia are most affected by declining cross-border bank lending…

2   Bank for International Settlements (BIS), "International Banking and Financial Market Developments", BIS Quarterly Review, June 2012.

have the most direct exposures to banks in the European Union (EU).[3] There is evidence that deleveraging in the European banking sector has especially affected trade financing,[4] which in many countries comprises a large share of short-term borrowing. Trade-oriented small- and medium-sized enterprises (SMEs) from lower-income countries, in particular, have faced a sharp shortfall in funding.

...with trade finance in low-income countries particularly impacted

In contrast, developing country fixed-income instruments have become more attractive to investors in recent months. Sovereign bond spreads on emerging market external debt tightened in the second half of 2012 from over 400 basis points at the beginning of June to about 290 basis points in late-November, after widening for much of 2011, indicating an increase in demand (see chapter I, figure I.10). Similarly, more capital has moved towards domestic bond markets of developing countries.[5] There is also evidence that investors chose to hedge currency risk selectively rather than withdraw from the developing country bond markets—which limit portfolio bond outflows during spells of heightened risk aversion[6]—although this could reflect illiquidity in some domestic bond markets, not sustained demand for the products.

Foreign direct investment

FDI fell in 2012

FDI tends to be more stable than portfolio investment and bank lending (although the volatility of FDI flows increased somewhat in recent years, as discussed below). FDI remains a major component of private capital flows to developing countries. While FDI rose sharply in 2011, reaching approximately $436 billion, it fell in the latter part of the year, as well as in 2012. Furthermore, FDI remains concentrated in a few regions and countries. Most FDI flowing to developing countries is going to Asia and Latin America. Only 10 per cent of inward FDI goes to Africa. Furthermore, the distribution of FDI flows within Africa remains uneven, with more than 80 per cent of the capital going to natural resource-rich economies. Nonetheless, FDI comprises the dominant share of private capital flows to LDCs.

Outward FDI from developing and transition economies has become increasingly significant, with a large proportion directed towards other developing and transition economies. However, their share in global FDI outflows declined from 31 per cent in 2010 to 26 per cent in 2011, mainly owing to a significant decline in outward FDI from Latin America and the Caribbean as foreign affiliates of some Latin American transnational companies repaid loans to their parent firms. Nevertheless, the overall levels of FDI flowing from developing and transition economies remained high from a historical perspective.

Remittances

Remittances are estimated to increase by 6.5 per cent in 2012

Remittances from workers abroad have continued increasing and for many developing countries have become a critical source of foreign-exchange earnings. Income from worker remittances as recorded in balance-of-payments statistics totalled $406 billion in 2012, representing a year-on-year increase of about 6.5 per cent.[7] For some countries, it is a

---

3   World Bank, *Global Economic Prospects: Maintaining progress amid turmoil*, January 2012.

4   This could be partly owing to Basel III regulations on trade finance, as may be inferred from data presented in World Bank, *Global Economic Prospects: Managing growth in a volatile world*, June 2012, Finance annex, pp. 43-51.

5   IMF, Global Financial Stability Report, op. cit.

6   World Bank, *Global Economic Prospects: Managing growth in a volatile world*, op. cit.

7   The real size of remittances, though, is probably larger, given that many remittances are channelled through informal mechanisms that are not recorded.

main source of income. For instance, remittances were as high as 47 per cent of GDP in Tajikistan, 27 per cent in Lesotho, and around 20 per cent of gross domestic product (GDP) in the Republic of Moldova, Samoa and Kosovo.[8]

The total volume of remittance flows to developing countries moderated somewhat during the initial years of the global economic and financial crisis, but the decline was not as sharp as in the case of private capital inflows. In general, remittance flows tend to be less volatile than most forms of cross-border financial flows. Yet, the economic slowdown and rise in unemployment in Europe disproportionately affects migrant workers, especially in Italy and Spain. This in turn has had a strongly adverse impact on remittance flows to Eastern European countries, such as Bosnia and Herzegovina, Poland and Romania, as well as countries in the Middle East and North Africa,[9] and some in Latin America, like Ecuador and, to a lesser extent, Colombia.

The total volume of worker remittance flows to developing countries was more than three times the size of ODA. Remittances should not be seen as an immediate substitute for ODA, however. ODA represents financial flows in support of international development cooperation and is mainly channelled through government budgets. Remittances flow directly to private households, who mainly use the additional income for consumption. A number of Governments and international organizations have taken initiatives providing incentives for using remittance income for investment purposes. For example, the Multilateral Investment Fund of the Inter-American Development Bank offers supplementary grants if remittances are channelled towards investments in housing and other forms of capital formation, education, entrepreneurship training, and research and knowledge dissemination. This way, remittances can become an important and relatively stable form for financing development.

Shortening maturities

The high volatility of most types of cross-border capital flows is indicative of the short-term behaviour of investors. Whereas greenfield direct investment tends to have longer-term investment horizons, and be attracted by factors such as high growth rates, cheap asset prices, rule of law and strong macroeconomic fundamentals, most forms of portfolio investment and cross-border interbank lending tend to be attracted to developing countries because of high relative short-term interest rates, which often outweigh longer-term fundamentals. A range of incentives drive this investor behaviour, including the compensation packages of hedge fund managers and other investment managers, who are paid annually, based on short-term performance, as well as financial management strategies that focus on the short-term share price.[10] In addition, risk models used by the financial industry (such as the "value at risk" model) exacerbate the problem, since they are generally based on short-term indicators and do not consider longer-term factors like tail risks (that is, the risk of rare but costly events).

The recent crisis, however, appears to have strengthened this short-term behaviour. The sum of professionally managed assets across the globe totalled about $65 trillion in 2009, of which about $27 trillion was owned by institutional investors such as pension

The global financial crisis has increased short-term behaviour of investors

8   World Bank, "Remittances to developing countries will surpass $400 billion in 2012", Migration and Development Brief, No. 19 (20 November 2012).

9   Ibid.

10   Joseph E. Stiglitz, "The financial crisis of 2007-8 and its macroeconomic consequences", in *Time for a Visible Hand*, Stephany Griffith-Jones, José Antonio Ocampo and Joseph E. Stiglitz, eds. (Oxford: Oxford University Press, 2010).

funds. Constraints faced by these investors allowed only a quarter of their assets to be used for long-term ventures.[11] According to analysis undertaken by the World Economic Forum (WEF), a number of institutional investors experienced difficulty refinancing liabilities during the crisis, which led them to reassess the extent to which they should undertake long-term investments. This, in combination with other factors—including a move towards "mark-to-market" accounting, which requires that long-term illiquid portfolios be evaluated relative to a public market benchmark, stricter capital requirements and the existing structure of staff evaluation, compensation schemes and internal decision-making—is argued to have restricted the proportion of assets employed by these investors for long-term investing.[12] The WEF study foresees a continuing decline in long-term investing, which will only be partly offset by increasing activity of other investors, such as endowments and foundations, which were also under stress following margin calls on levered investment during the financial crisis.

In light of these trends, there may be a need for policymakers to reconsider the impact of regulatory actions, including mark-to-market accounting, on long-term investment decisions. It also seems important to have a regulatory framework that better manages global liquidity and is conducive to long-term investments, as discussed below. At the same time, institutional investors should develop appropriate liquidity management tools, performance measurement and staff evaluation/compensation mechanisms that provide greater incentives to taking a longer investment horizon.

Even FDI shows signs of becoming increasingly short-term oriented

A further concern is that FDI is becoming more short term-oriented and that its changing composition could be making it more volatile.[13] The shift in the composition of FDI from equity to debt components has made it easier for investors to move resources between host and home countries.[14] Where a significant portion of FDI comprises intracompany debt, as opposed to greenfield direct investments, the parent company can recall this debt on short notice. In this respect, the proportion of short-term and volatile flows in FDI has increased.[15] Part of the growth in FDI flows during the past two years may have been made for the purpose of short-term gains. It is important that policymakers are cognizant of the growing proportion of short-term investments contained within FDI, which could reverse more quickly than expected in an uncertain economic and financial climate.

Management of volatile cross-border capital flows

Macroprudential measures and capital account management have gained importance

The volatility associated with short-term capital flows has given greater attention to the issue of how countries should manage cross-border risks. Capital account management has gained greater acceptance as a prudent policy measure by the international community.

---

11   World Economic Forum, "Measurement, governance and long-term investing", available from http://www3.weforum.org/docs/WEF_IV_MeasurementGovernanceLongtermInvesting_Report_2012.pdf.

12   World Economic Forum, "The future of long-term investing", available from http://www3.weforum.org/docs/WEF_FutureLongTermInvesting_Report_2011.pdf.

13   United Nations Conference on Trade and Development (UNCTAD), *World Investment Report 2011: Non-equity Modes of International Production and Development* (United Nations publication, Sales No. E.11.II.D.2).

14   Jonathan D. Ostry and others, "Managing capital inflows: what tools to use", IMF Staff Discussion Note, No. SDN11/06 (Washington, D.C., April 2011).

15   UNCTAD, *World Investment Report 2011*, op. cit.

Indeed, over the past several years a number of developing countries (including Brazil, Indonesia, Peru, the Republic of Korea and Thailand) have introduced capital-account regulatory measures to contain volatile short-term capital flows, as reported in the *World Economic Situation and Prospects 2012*.

Conventional approaches to managing capital inflows focus on macroeconomic policies, such as the exchange-rate adjustment, manipulating policy interest rates and fiscal aggregate demand management, to enhance an economy's capacity to absorb capital inflows. However, these policies are generally not sufficiently targeted to stabilize financial flows and may have undesired side effects. Letting the exchange rate appreciate, for instance, would penalize export-oriented sectors, thus impacting growth and development. Fiscal cuts to lower aggregate demand can be costly to economic growth and the slow speed of fiscal decision-making makes it a less effective policy tool for dealing with short-term volatile capital inflows. Attempts by policymakers to counteract the expansionary impact of excessive capital inflows through tightening monetary policies could be partly self-defeating as the higher interest rates may induce additional capital inflows, thus exacerbating upward pressure on the exchange rate.

To stem capital inflows and excessive credit growth, countries can implement macroprudential measures including the maintenance of sound lending standards, countercyclical capital requirements to slow down credit expansion, and balance sheet restrictions such as limiting the foreign exchange positions of banks. While these measures appear to have lengthened the composition of capital inflows in some countries (Croatia, Peru and the Republic of Korea, for example), the effect on total net flows was limited. In Peru, where there is a large amount of dollarization in the economy mediated through the banking system, macroprudential measures, such as limits on foreign-exchange mismatches, have been relatively effective at reducing risks. In the Republic of Korea, a package of macroprudential measures was introduced during 2009-2010 that appears to have brought about the intended deceleration in banks' foreign borrowing, but it did not stem the overall level of capital inflows.

Other countries, like Brazil and Indonesia, have opted to use more direct forms of capital-account regulation. Most available studies find that capital controls have been effective in changing the composition of inflows away from short-term debt. The impact on total flows is more ambiguous, with regulations appearing to have been more successful in some cases than in others.[16] More broadly, the effectiveness of measures depends on the specific circumstances of a country, including the quality of the existing regulatory framework and regulatory capacity, the structure and persistence of inflows, and the design and implementation of capital flow management measures. In particular, capital-account regulation may be particularly difficult to implement in countries where there is a large derivatives market, since speculators can often circumvent the restrictions through this market. For this reason, some countries, like Brazil, have implemented restrictions directly in the derivatives market to test the market, albeit at an initial low rate. Overall, there is no simple recipe for effectively managing cross-border capital flows. Macroeconomic policies, macroprudential tools and capital-account regulations should probably come in a balanced package of measures and be tailored to the specific circumstances of individual countries.

As discussed above, one of the drivers of recent surges in international capital flows has been monetary easing in developed countries. Given the cross-border spillover effect of monetary policy decisions, measures that incentivize investors in developed countries to invest at home would help monetary authorities respond to slowdowns in

Macroprudential measures might be most effective in highly dollarized economies

---

16   See, for example, Jonathan D. Ostry and others, "Capital inflows: the role of controls", IMF Staff Position Note, No. SPN10/04 (Washington, D.C., February 2010).

developed countries and also help allay pressures for asset bubbles in developing countries. Thus, there is a need for capital-account management in developed as well as developing countries. To this end, central banks may need to step up their international dialogue and cooperation on managing global liquidity. Better management of global liquidity would also have the effect of helping to correct global imbalances.

International reserve accumulation and global imbalances

Reserve accumulation fell sharply in the wake of the crisis

Bouts of excessive international liquidity have been part and parcel of the build-up in global imbalances, with surges and withdrawals of international capital flows correlated with the build-up of reserves by developing countries (although trade balances also play a role in some countries). Reserve holdings of developing and emerging countries as a proportion of national output more than doubled between 1999 and 2008, a period of high global liquidity. The accumulation of vast dollar reserves over this period allowed the United States to borrow cheaply from abroad, keeping long-term interest rates low, which in turn has induced greater leverage in the system. Reserve accumulation peaked at $1.2 trillion in 2007 prior to the crisis, but fell as a percentage of GDP in the years since (with the exception of 2010), following trends in capital flows. In 2012, reserve accumulation fell to an estimated $559 billion, down from $777 billion in 2011, mirroring the decline in capital inflows (see table III.1 for the change in reserve holdings and figure III.1 for stocks as a share of GDP).

Figure III.1
Ratio of reserves to GDP, 1991-2012[a]

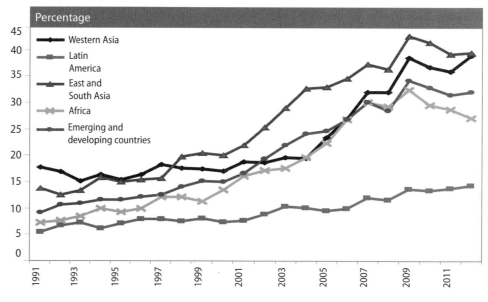

Source: IMF, World Economic Outlook database, April 2012. Data not available on WEO October 2012 database.

Notes: Regional groupings are based on UN/DESA country classification. No data from 1980–1989 on reserves for newly industrialized economies (Hong Kong SAR, Rep. of Korea, Singapore, Taiwan POC).

a Data for 2012 are WEO forecasts.

Reserve accumulation by developing countries has fallen along with the moderation in global imbalances, although as pointed out in Chapter I, this trend is related to overall weakness in global demand rather than to long-term structural adjustments (see chapter I, figure I.13). Nonetheless, accumulated reserve holdings remain significant, particularly in South-East Asia, where they amount to almost 40 per cent of GDP (figure III.1).

The massive build-up of reserves by emerging and developing countries and its effect on global stability has raised questions regarding the appropriate size of reserves. The build-up has been attributed to several factors. First, reserves serve as a form of "self-insurance" against potential external shocks. Second, they facilitate interventions in foreign-exchange markets to smooth exchange-rate or commodity price volatility and mitigate bubbles associated with excessive inflows. Third, reserves can be a by-product of export-led growth strategies that rely on interventions in the currency market to maintain an undervalued currency—actions sometimes considered to be mercantilist.[17]

Perspectives on determining the adequate size of international reserves have changed over time. In the 1980s and 1990s, reserves were insurance against trade shocks. At that time, the International Monetary Fund (IMF) advised countries to hold reserves large enough to cover three months of imports. However, the emerging market crises in the mid-1990s, such as the Mexican "tequila crisis", were triggered by difficulties in refinancing short-term dollar-denominated debt, not unexpected trade account deficits. This led to the view that reserves would need to be large enough to cover a country's short-term external debt refinancing needs. This approach did not consider, however, the fact that the emerging market crises of the1990s were also triggered by reversals in short-term capital portfolio flows and the unwinding of carry trades. By the end of the 1990s, countries realized the importance of fuller self-insurance, not just against refinancing risks of external debt, but also against volatility associated with international capital flows and open capital accounts.

Empirical studies suggest that no single explanation can account for the behaviour of all countries at all times. A recent IMF study found that precautionary demand and self-insurance motives both played a prominent role in the increase in international reserves following the East Asian crisis, although mercantilism, in the form of an undervalued real exchange rate, appears to have contributed in some cases.[18] The study also found a positive unexplained residual in more recent years, implying that reserves were higher than what would be predicted by precautionary or mercantilist motives. This is in keeping with the role of exchange-rate management in smoothing volatility in reserve accumulation. There is some evidence of this, in that central banks have been using capital management techniques to limit capital inflows rather than solely buying the inflows to build reserves in cases when the currency is not undervalued. The goal is not to keep an undervalued currency, but to stop the continued appreciation of an overvalued one while limiting the build-up in reserves.

Clearly, holding large international reserves can be costly, and for a host of reasons. First, most international reserves are held in United States treasuries, which are considered safe but are low-yielding. Foreign-exchange reserves represent a form of constrained saving, since national savings that are allocated to reserves withhold funds that could be invested elsewhere, possibly with greater social benefit. Second, accumulation of foreign-exchange reserves tends to increase the domestic money supply because the central bank buys foreign currency and sells local currency. Attempts to sterilize this increase in the money supply generally involve issuing government bonds to absorb the excess liquidity,

Holding reserves is costly, and can harm long-term investments

---

17 Atish R. Ghosh, Jonathan D. Ostry and Charalambos G. Tsangarides, "Shifting motives: explaining the build-up in official reserves in emerging markets since the 1980s", IMF Working Paper, No. WP/12/34 (Washington, D.C., January 2012).

18 Ibid.

which leads to higher domestic interest rates and thereby raises borrowing costs. Further, the increased bond issuance can lead to a worsening in the domestic public debt burden. The result is that foreign currency inflows end up being held as reserves which in turn are invested in United States Treasury bonds, while the developing country increases its debt burden to finance domestic investment, counteracting the benefit of foreign investment.

That a large share of international reserves is invested in government bonds and similar assets abroad implies a net transfer of resources from poorer countries to wealthier ones. Accumulation of major reserve currencies in developing countries is a major element in the net transfer of financial resources from developing countries to the major economies issuing the reserve currencies (table III.2 and figure III.2). Although net transfers decreased somewhat in 2012 in line with the lower accumulation of reserves, they remained negative, with the exception of the LDCs, which continue to receive net positive transfers.

Figure III.2
Net transfers of financial resources to developing economies and economies in transition, 2000-2012

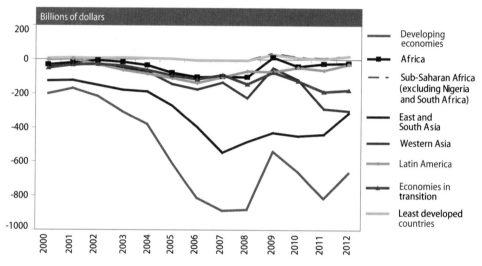

Source: UN/DESA, based on IMF, World Economic Outlook Database, October 2012; and IMF, Balance of Payments Statistics.
a Cape Verde graduated in December 2007, hence excluded from the calculations.
b Partly estimated.

Constrained investment induced by reserve accumulation could be reduced by the greater use of SDRs

Finally, precautionary reserve accumulation, while sensible at the national level, generates fallacy of composition effects at the global level, further adding to global imbalances and a less stable international financial architecture as discussed above. The Commission of Experts of the President of the United Nations General Assembly has recommended that the international reserve system make greater use of IMF Special Drawing Rights (SDRs) as these provide a low-cost alternative to accumulation of international reserves.[19] SDRs could reduce the need for precautionary reserve accumulation by providing access to foreign currency liquidity when a country's capital account is under pressure. In other words, the greater use of SDRs could reduce the need for self-insurance by many developing countries.

There have also been recommendations for mechanisms to use SDR allocations as a potential source of innovative financing for development, although care needs to be taken to preserve the role of SDRs as a monetary instrument, as discussed further below.

---

[19]   United Nations, "Report of the Commission of Experts of the President of the United Nations General Assembly on Reforms of the International Monetary and Financial System", 21 September 2009.

The Group of Twenty (G20) is considering enhancing the SDR basket to include additional currencies and possibly increasing allocations of SDRs. There is, however, political resistance and legal barrier to broadening the scope of SDRs. For example, the IMF Articles would need to be amended to change the way SDRs are allocated, and an 85 per cent majority is needed for agreement regarding new allocations. Instead, international reforms have been more narrowly focused on reducing systemic risks created by the banking sector.

International financial reform

There are several regulatory reforms underway, which are designed to reduce the risk of future financial sector crises (table III.2). The current approach to international financial reform has been focused on ensuring the safety and soundness of the financial system, focused primarily on the banking sector through Basel III. This is supplemented by national rule-setting (such as, the "Volcker rule" in the United States of America and the Vickers Commission proposals in the United Kingdom of Great Britain and Northern Ireland) that partially separate the banking sector from shadow banking (box III.2). In addition, the Financial Stability Board (FSB) has proposed a number of measures: reforms for oversight of the shadow banking system; recovery and resolution planning for systemically important institutions; reform of the over-the-counter derivatives market; uniform global accounting standards; reduction in the reliance on credit rating agencies; improved consumer protection; reform of some compensation practices; and the establishment of macroprudential regulatory frameworks. Taken together, these reforms are steps in the right direction. However, significant gaps remain. Indeed, a recent study by the IMF found that the structure of financial intermediation remains more or less the same as it was before the crisis, with excessive reliance on wholesale funding (which tends to be riskier than financing through deposits), and on trading, commission and fee income rather than on lending and credit intermediation.[20]

The current approach to international financial reform remains primarily focused on enhancing the stability of the banking sector

Broadly speaking, the objectives of financial sector regulation are fivefold: (i) to secure the safety and soundness of financial institutions and the financial system at large; (ii) to ensure competition; (iii) to protect consumers; (iv) to promote access to finance and financial services for all; and (v) to make certain that the financial sector promotes macroeconomic stability and long-term sustainable growth.[21] In addition, a key lesson from the crisis is that rules need to address systemically important institutions and should be comprehensive—in other words, incorporate all facets of credit intermediation.

To date, the reform agenda has not focused sufficiently on all of the objectives. The primary focus has been on safety and soundness. There have been some efforts to improve consumer protection by the FSB, in addition to steps taken on the national level, such as the Consumer Protection Agency in the United States, although these efforts are facing some implementation difficulties. However, the new regulatory framework might have the effect of weakening some of the other principal objectives. For example, the global crisis led to increased consolidation of commercial banks. There is some concern that the new regulatory framework will lead to even greater consolidation to accommodate the need for economies of scale, further limiting competition in the sector as well as exacerbating problems inherent in having "too big to fail" institutions. Furthermore, by raising the cost of riskier lending, capital adequacy rules might have the effect of limiting

Regulatory reform should take a more integral approach

---

20   IMF, *Global Financial Stability Report*, op. cit.

21   Presentation given by Joseph E. Stiglitz at the Initiative for Policy Dialogue, Financial Markets Reform Task Force Meeting, 25-27 July 2006, Manchester, United Kingdom.

Table III.2
A snapshot of the new regulatory initiatives

Key reforms	Elements	Timeline
Banks		
Global reforms		
Basel III capital standards	Changes to the definition of capital	Completion 2019
Basel III capital charges	Better valuation of risk	Completion 2019
	Incremental risk charge for trading-book activity	Completion 2019
	Higher capital charges for counterparty exposures in derivatives, repo trading	Completion 2019
	Additional capital conservation and countercyclical buffers	Completion 2019
	Additional capital surcharge for G-SIFIs	Completion 2019
	Capital charge assessed on (clearing member) banks' central counterparty default fund exposures	Completion 2019
G-SIFI surcharge	Additional amount of common equity for systemically important banks	Completion 2019
Basel III liquidity requirements	Liquidity coverage ratio: requires high-quality liquid assets sufficient to meet 30 days' outflows	Completion 2019
	Net stable funding ratio: requires better maturity matching of assets and liabilities	Completion 2018
Basel III leverage ratio	Sets a ceiling on the measure of exposures (regardless of risk weighting) against capital (3 percent Tier 1 capital over total exposures)	Completion 2019
FSB compensation guidelines	Responsibility of boards for compensation policies	Implemented
	Compensation should be aligned with risks and time horizons	
	Supervisors should monitor compensation policies	
Corporate governance	Emphasis on robust corporate governance, including the role of banks' boards	
Resolution of G-SIFIs	Reduce the likelihood that institutions will need to use public funds when they fail	
National reforms		
Volcker rule (Dodd-Frank Act)	Deposit-taking institutions restricted from trading activities, ownership of private equity and hedge funds	Law passed, implementation pending
Vickers report	Ring-fencing of United Kingdom retail banks from investment banking activities; additional capital for ring-fenced entity	Completion 2019
Markets		
Global reforms		
OTC derivatives	Standardization of derivatives contracts	Varied
	Clearing of standardized derivatives contracts through central counterparties (CCPs)	
	Trading of standardized derivatives contracts on exchanges or electronic trading platforms where appropriate	
	Reporting of contracts to trade repositories	
	Higher capital and margin requirements for derivatives that are not centrally cleared	

Table III.2 (cont'd)		
Key reforms	*Elements*	*Timeline*
Nonbanks		
Global reforms		
Shadow banking	Monitoring of shadow banking and evaluation of risks	
	Registration of hedge funds; improved standards for securitization	
	Future regulatory reforms include enhancements to indirect regulation (regulation of shadow banks through their interaction with banks); increased liquidity and valuation rules for money market funds; rules governing repos and securities lending	
Other initiatives		
Credit ratings	Registration and regulation of credit rating agencies; regulation includes further transparency on rating methodologies, on the performance of ratings, and raw data	Implementation ongoing
	Reduction of regulatory reliance on ratings; in the United States, this has triggered removal of references to credit ratings in laws and regulations	Implementation ongoing

Source: IMF, *Global Financial Stability Report*, October 2012, table 3.2.

Note: No entry for timeline means that the reforms are still being developed. FSB = Financial Stability Board; G-SIFIs = global systemically important financial institutions.

Box III.1

What is shadow banking?

The Financial Stability Board defines shadow banking as "credit intermediation involving entities and activities outside the regular banking system." [a] Shadow banking entities are those that create leverage or that engage in maturity and liquidity transformation.

The shadow banking sector is markedly different in developed than in developing countries. In developed countries, non-bank financial intermediation is mainly conducted by money market funds, structured finance vehicles, other investment funds including hedge, investment, and exchange-traded funds, finance companies, insurance companies, and securities brokers and dealers. These entities engage in credit intermediation through activities and instruments including securitization, securities lending, derivatives, repurchase agreements and loans, thus partly competing with banks that are relatively more strictly regulated and supervised.

The share of the United States in global shadow banking declined from 44 per cent in 2005 to 35 per cent in 2011, but its shadow banking sector remains the largest worldwide, at over 50 per cent of credit intermediation. [b] In the euro area, shadow banking represented less than 30 per cent of credit intermediation in 2010. [c] Important differences remain across countries, however. The Netherlands, Luxembourg, France and Ireland account for around three quarters of shadow banking activity in the euro area. [d]

Currently, shadow banking is of much less concern in developing economies, though it could become more of an issue if it continues to grow or engages in products without proper regulations. In developing countries, funding is currently channelled from investors to creditors, bypassing banks through entities such as finance, leasing and factoring companies, investment and equity funds, insurance companies, pawn shops and other entities such as text and mobile phone banking.

These market participants engage in diverse credit intermediation activities that involve certain risks, including credit, counterparty or collateral risks, but do not as yet involve long, complex, opaque intermediation chains that create linkages between the banking and shadow

a Financial Stability Board, "Shadow banking: strengthening oversight and regulation", 27 October 2011, available from http://www.financialstabilityboard.org/publications/r_111027a.pdf.
b Tobias Adrian and Adam B. Ashcraft, "Shadow banking: a review of literature", Federal Reserve Bank of New York Staff Reports, No. 580 (October 2012), available from http://www.newyorkfed.org/research/staff_reports/sr580.pdf.
c Klára Bakk-Simon and others, "Shadow banking in the Euro area: an overview", European Central Bank Occasional Paper, No. 133 (April 2012), available from http://www.ecb.europa.eu/pub/pdf/scpops/ecbocp133.pdf.
d Ibid.

Box III.1 (cont'd)

e Landon Thomas, "Turkey spends freely again, and some analysts worry", *The New York Times*, 25 April 2011.

f Swati Ghosh, Ines Gonzalez del Mazo and İnci Ötker-Robe, "Chasing the shadows: how significant is shadow banking in emerging markets?", The World Bank Economic Premise, No. 88 (September 2012), available from http://siteresources.worldbank.org/EXTPREMNET/Resources/EP88.pdf.

g Ibid.

banking sectors. One of the primary risks from shadow banking in developing countries appears to be from finance companies feeding credit booms without thorough credit screening. For example, in Turkey, inappropriately regulated and aggressive commercial practices by finance companies offering quick loan approval via text message or automated teller machine[e] nurtured an unsustainable credit boom in 2011, which had to be curbed by interventions of the central bank and regulators. Non-bank credit intermediation for corporations and financial institutions can take on many different and less predatory forms, but it relies on the same fragile funding model. Nonetheless, the financial markets of many developing countries are only partially integrated with global financial markets. As a consequence, shadow banking in developing countries poses risks that are more traditional and local than systemic.[f]

As in the developed world, the share of shadow banking in credit intermediation varies by country. According to some estimates, shadow banking may represent between 35 per cent and 40 per cent of the financial sector in the Philippines or Thailand, but only about 20 per cent in Indonesia and Croatia, and only slightly above 10 per cent in China.[g]

access to finance, since smaller entities, such as micro-enterprises and SMEs, have higher capital costs. The role of regulatory regimes in macroeconomic stability and long-term sustainable growth has not been sufficiently addressed. Basel III includes a countercyclical buffer, although it is limited.

Achieving these goals presents a complex challenge for policymakers since there can be trade-offs between ensuring stability and providing necessary access to credit. However, finding an appropriate balance is imperative if the financial sector is to fulfill its role of allocating credit effectively for long-term sustainable growth.

Progress in implementing Basel III

Implementation of Basel III will be phased in through 2019

The agreed deadline for initiating implementation of Basel III is 1 January 2013. According to the Basel Committee, the adoption of the Basel III rules under national law was planned or under way in all 27 member jurisdictions of the Basel Committee in 2012, with some members facing significant challenges to meeting the deadline. The framework is also expected to be implemented to some extent in many non-member countries of the Basel Committee. Judging from past experience, implementing the framework within the agreed schedule indeed represents a challenge. As of 2012, the previous frameworks of Basel II and Basel II.5 (expected to come into force in end-2006 and end-2011, respectively) have not been implemented as yet by all Basel Committee Members.[22] Moreover, some elements of Basel III will be fully phased in as late as 2018 or 2019.[23] Monetary and financial supervision authorities might consider accelerating regulatory reforms, or at least ensuring that critical elements of the reform package can enter into force sooner.

Basel III reforms—which include higher and better quality capital requirements, liquidity buffers and leverage rules—are designed to impose higher costs on risky

---

22   Basel Committee on Banking Supervision, "Report to G20 Leaders on Basel III implementation" (Bank for International Settlements, June 2012).

23   The capital conservation and countercyclical buffers will be gradually phased in from January 2016 to January 2019; the leverage ratio is intended to be implemented in January 2018, following a parallel run; the liquidity buffers will be implemented in January 2015 (30 day liquidity) and January 2018 (longer-term liquidity).

activities of banks to internalize the costs of risky behaviour, in an attempt to incentivize banks to reduce risky activities. As such, it should enhance the resilience of banks towards future shocks. Nonetheless, it has been suggested that the measures may not be sufficient to create a stable and well-capitalized financial system. Several studies have concluded that capital requirements should be significantly higher than those envisaged by Basel III.[24] Indeed, several countries, notably some with outsized financial sectors such as Switzerland and the United Kingdom, have already phased in higher capital requirements for important banks in their jurisdictions. It is also argued that the leverage ratio had been met before the financial crisis by many banks that later faced distress.[25]

There are also concerns that tighter bank regulations, in conjunction with the complexity of the Basel III framework, might trigger a new wave of regulatory arbitrage. It is reported that new products are already being created to circumvent the new rules (box III.3).[26] In most countries the regulatory supervisory capacity is limited, making it difficult for regulators to keep pace with these kinds of developments. It is thus crucial to improve regulatory supervisory capacity through programmes geared towards education of regulators as well as more competitive compensation. Nonetheless, financial markets have been characterized by innovations and change, making it difficult for even well-trained supervisors to be able to effectively oversee a complex regulatory system. More generally, complex regulations can be difficult to administer and costly. This argues for broad-based simple regulations, such as high capital ratios and low leverage ratios, with simple countercyclical rules built in.[27] Indeed, there are calls for greater regulatory simplicity and transparency as a way to enhance accountability, avoid regulatory loopholes and arbitrage, and facilitate implementation.[28]

There are trade-offs between safety and allocation of credit to risky, albeit productive, activities. Basel rules, which have higher capital charges for riskier investments, could result in less lending to SMEs. The tighter capital and liquidity standards in Basel III could also reduce the availability of long-term financing, with a particularly negative impact on green investments, as well as on developing countries that have large infrastructure needs. Overall lending to some developing countries (particularly to those with sub-investment-grade credit ratings) is likely to be impacted, as the capital requirements under Basel III would imply higher borrowing costs and scarcity of credit in these markets. In particular, and despite amendments to the Basel III framework,[29] there are continuing concerns over the implications of the new rules for trade finance (box III.2). Similarly, very safe financial systems might also tend not to be inclusive in terms of offering financial services to the poor.

Discrepancies in financial reform between the banking and shadow banking sectors is likely to induce more regulatory arbitrage

Basel rules could result in less lending to SMEs and reduce availability of long-term financing, particularly in developing countries.

---

24   See *World Economic Situation and Prospects 2012* (United Nations publication, Sales No. E.12. II.C.2).

25   Stephany Griffith-Jones, Shari Spiegel and Matthias Thiemann, "Recent developments in regulation in the light of the global financial crisis: implications for developing countries", IPD Working Paper (Initiative for Policy Dialogue, Columbia University, 2011).

26   IMF, *Global Financial Stability Report*, op. cit.

27   It may still be appropriate to have some specific regulations in particular areas, but only when they are areas that are relatively self-contained and for which regulators have access to full information.

28   See "The dog and the frisbee", speech by Andrew G. Haldane, Executive Director, Bank of England, at the Federal Reserve Bank of Kansas City's 366th economic policy symposium, Jackson Hole, Wyoming, 31 August 2012; and World Bank, *Global Financial Development Report 2013: Rethinking the Role of the State in Finance* (Washington, D.C., September 2012).

29   Basel Committee on Banking Supervision, "Treatment of trade finance under the Basel capital framework" (Bank for International Settlements, 2011).

Box III.2

Capital arbitrage since the crisis: trade finance securitization

a IMF, *Global Financial Stability Report: Restoring Confidence and Progressing on Reforms*, October 2012.

Despite a decline in securitization following the financial crisis, new financial products that appear to circumvent regulatory rules are being created.[a] It has, however, been argued that not all of what has come to be known as "regulatory arbitrage" (that is, using off-balance-sheet structures to circumvent capital requirements) necessarily increases systemic risks. To the extent that regulators with limited market information misprice risk, it is argued that these trades might have the effect of making the market more efficient. An example where this might be the case is in trade financing. Many trade finance instruments, such as letters of credit, are held off balance sheet. The leverage rule in Basel III requires banks to set aside the capital equivalent of the value of off-balance-sheet items using a credit-conversion factor that reflects the likelihood of a contingent off-balance sheet risk becoming an on-balance sheet item. The Basel III credit conversion factor for trade finance is 100 per cent, five times the 20 per cent figure generally used in Basel II. The implication is that the collateral used in trade financing is not counted in the evaluation of the risk of the loan.

Aside from raising questions on whether such items should be held off balance sheet to begin with, the underlying question is how to value the collateral in trade finance. The problem is based on an informational asymmetry. From the regulator's perspective, there is not enough data on trade finance defaults available to reduce the risk weighting.[b] Banks, which believe they have a better idea of the risks in the loan portfolios, argue that trade finance is less likely to default and that many, although not all, trade finance deals are backed by strong collateral. Nonetheless, the regulatory capital costs of the loans devalue the collateral. As a result, banks have created products to securitize pools of trade financing loans, which are then sold to investors.

b Basel Committee on Banking Supervision, "Treatment of trade finance under the Basel capital framework (Bank for International Settlements, 2011).

This securitization has allowed some banks to continue trade financing in developing countries, and underscores the potential benefits that securitizations can have for financing for development. There are, however, real risks associated with these products that need to be addressed. Many structures incorporate bank guarantees that are not necessarily fully reported, despite the fact that the banks still maintain some exposure to the underlying risks. At present this does not pose systemic risks since the market is small and limited to investors with expertise in this area. However, if it were to grow in size it would likely bring in investors with limited knowledge of trade finance, which could result in severe mispricing, similar to what happened in the mortgage markets (although most likely on a smaller scale). In addition, there is a risk associated with the loans being originated for the purpose of securitization (referred to as the "originate to distribute" model), which often implies reduced credit monitoring and screening. Ironically, this then justifies the higher risk ratings, but also leads to increased risks for both borrowers and investors, as well as systemic risks created by credit bubbles.

There is a need to keep exposures, such as those implicit in guarantees or other mechanisms, on balance sheet, transparent, and within the regulatory monitoring framework. In addition, there is a need for regulators to monitor the growth of securitizations in different sectors across the system in order to better track the build-up that creates bubbles with systemic implications.

Global systemically important financial institutions

Global systemically important financial institutions will have to raise their loss-absorbing capacity

During the global financial crisis, large financial institutions, in particular, were found to have spread systemic risks. In response, G20 leaders agreed to strengthen the oversight and regulation of global systemically important financial institutions (G-SIFIs), focused on minimizing the adverse impacts their distress or failure might have on the financial sector as well as on the broader economy. In 2011, the FSB identified an initial group of 29 G-SIFIs, nine of which are headquartered in jurisdictions that have not yet fully implemented Basel II or II.5. A key element of the measures put forward by the FSB to address the phenomenon of "too big to fail" is that G-SIFIs should have a loss-absorbing capacity beyond the general standards of Basel III (that is, an additional capital requirement of between 1.0 per cent and 3.5 per cent, to be phased in by 2019), although it is not clear that this will be sufficient. A further concern is that the new regulations might exacerbate this concentration of the financial sector in a few big banks, since absorbing the higher costs may require economies of scale.[30]

The FSB has also recommended that G-SIFIs develop recovery and resolution plans (also known as living wills), and that countries prioritize this in national regulatory frameworks. Other related FSB recommendations include the establishment of crisis management groups for G-SIFIs, which would include regulators, supervisors, central banks, and other authorities, as well as cross-border cooperation. The FSB is currently developing standards for domestic regulators to follow in supervising G-SIFIs, and is working to extend the resolution planning framework to systemically important insurers and non-bank G-SIFIs.

Most countries have been slow to implement the FSB recommendations. There are some exceptions, however, such as the Dodd-Frank Wall Street Reform and Consumer Protection Act in the United States, which incorporates living wills into its framework. Altogether, the "too big to fail" problem remains largely unresolved. Measures to decrease financial concentration should be explored, including steps to reduce the size of financial conglomerates by separating different business lines and creating a more diversified banking system, with a greater role for cooperative and savings banks, for instance.

The "too big to fail" problem continues to be unresolved

Reforms in compensation and incentives

Compensation practices encouraging excessive risk-taking were a key contributing factor to the global financial crisis. Many financial market participants are compensated on the basis of annual performance, which can incentivize excessive short-term risk-taking, without factoring in medium- or long-term risks. According to FSB surveys of market participants, more than 80 per cent of respondents believe that compensation packages contributed to the accumulation of risks that led to the crisis, with general agreement that without changes in such incentives, other reforms are likely to be less effective.[31]

The dominant view among policymakers as represented by the FSB is that "executive compensation is not simply a market wage, but an incentive system".[32] The implication is that because compensation structures and incentive structures have an effect on risk-taking within financial institutions, they should fall under the regulatory framework, whereas compensation levels, as such, need not. To this end, in 2009 the FSB defined "principles and guidelines for sound compensation", aimed at curbing excessive risk-taking by financial institutions by improving the alignment of compensation with risk-taking, as well as the governance and supervision of compensation practices. Many countries have since taken steps to incorporate compensation structures into their supervisory frameworks, but in general it is not clear that these will be strong enough to fully alter incentives. In particular, the FSB rules define broad guidelines only and do not set clear parameters on how they should be implemented. For example, in the United States, banks with a global presence are required to identify employees whose incentive compensation can influence risk-taking and to incorporate features into their compensation packages that promote balanced risk-taking. The details vary, however, across jobs and businesses.

Efforts to improve compensation practices in the financial sector remain minimal

---

30   IMF, *Global Financial Stability Report*, op. cit.

31   Financial Stability Board (FSB), "Principles for sound compensation practices: Implementation standards", 25 September 2009, available from http://www.financialstabilityboard.org/publications/r_090925c.pdf.

32   FSB, "Principles for sound compensation practices", 2 April 2009, available from http://www.financialstabilityboard.org/publications/r_0904b.pdf.

In 2012, JP Morgan Chase's unexpected multibillion dollar loss in a group that was meant to be hedging the bank's positions—not engaged in risk-taking—shows how difficult such identification and monitoring can be. Furthermore, the proposed measures apply to only the banking sector, and in particular to G-SIFIs, and do not address shadow banking, where risk-taking and compensation are highest.

Global risks of shadow banking

Shadow banking assets amount to 24 per cent of the global financial system

Another side effect of the new regulations is that risky activities that require higher capital might shift from the regulated banking system to shadow banking practices. The value of shadow banking assets rose from an estimated $26 trillion in 2002 to $62 trillion in 2007. Although shadow banking as a percentage of GDP declined after the crisis, assets in the shadow banking sector remain significant, at $67 trillion in 2011 (figure III.3), or 24 per cent of assets held by the global financial system (figure III.4). Shadow banking activities are particularly important in certain countries, such as the United States where the sector harbours assets worth around $23 trillion[33] and represents 53 per cent of credit intermediation (down from 60 per cent in 2007).[34]

Figure III.3
Assets of shadow banking entities worldwide, 2002-2011

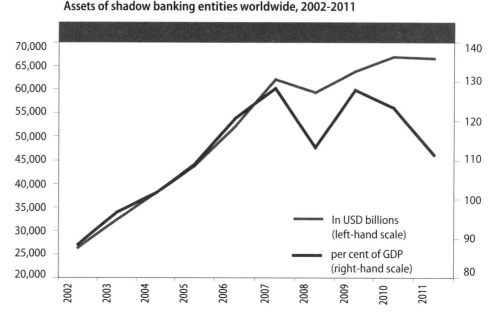

Source: Financial Stability Board, based on national flow-of-funds data.
Note: Includes 20 jurisdictions and the euro area.

Credit intermediation in the shadow banking sector is performed by a wide range of disparate entities with very different characteristics (box III.2) However, two common elements exist among them: they are not subject to the banking sector regulatory framework and, as such, they lack direct access to a liquidity backstop through a public lender of last resort (although central banks have provided shadow banking entities with

---

33   FSB, "Shadow banking: strengthening oversight and regulation: recommendations of the Financial Stability Board", 27 October 2011, available from http://www.financialstabilityboard.org/publications/r_111027a.pdf.

34   Tobias Adrian and Adam B. Ashcraft, "Shadow banking: a review of literature", Federal Reserve Bank of New York Staff Reports, No. 580 (October 2012), available from http://www.newyorkfed.org/research/staff_reports/sr580.pdf.

liquidity in crisis situations with systemic implications, as was the case with money market funds in the United States, discussed below).[35] As a result, shadow banking allows greater risk-taking than traditional banking, as well as opportunities for capital, tax and accounting arbitrage.

Figure III.4
Share of total financial assets, 2002-2011

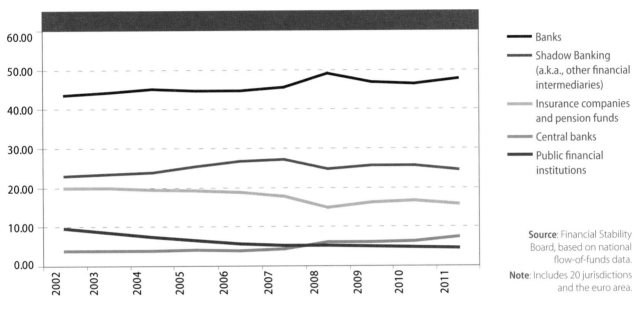

Banks

Shadow Banking (a.k.a., other financial intermediaries)

Insurance companies and pension funds

Central banks

Public financial institutions

Source: Financial Stability Board, based on national flow-of-funds data.
Note: Includes 20 jurisdictions and the euro area.

Weakly regulated shadow banking magnifies leverage, maturity and liquidity mismatches, procyclicality and lack of transparency

Both banking and non-banking credit intermediation involve risks, including leverage, maturity and liquidity mismatches, procyclicality, and lack of transparency. These risks become magnified in shadow banking entities, in large part because they are outside of the banking regulatory framework. In addition, many shadow banking entities have compensation schemes based on short-term performance that can lead to excessive risk-taking, as discussed earlier.

Leverage ratios in shadow banking entities are often much higher than in banks. Leverage ratios were close to 30 in many investment banks prior to the financial crisis.[36] Some hedge fund strategies are based on leveraging more than 50 to 100 times the fund equity, and structured vehicles, or at least certain tranches, tend to be highly leveraged by design. Shadow banking entities, such as hedge funds, pose systemic risks through interlinkages with the banking system, such as leverage provided to hedge funds by regulated banks and counterparty risks from trading activities. In the absence of clear ring-fencing between banks and shadow banks, many leveraged shadow banking entities remain affiliated with banks or directly owned by them. While moving activities off banks' balance sheets may be consistent with the regulatory framework, the build-up of leverage in shadow banking entities with linkages to banks jeopardizes financial stability. Although some regulation, like the Dodd-Frank Wall Street Reform and Consumer Protection Act in the United States, attempts to limit these linkages, many of the measures that may have ensured a more solid ring-fencing were left out or diluted in the final agreement.

---

35   Ibid.

36   William Wright, "Investment banks and the death of leverage", *Financial News*, 26 April 2011, available from http://www.efinancialnews.com/story/2011-04-26/investment-banks-and-the-death-of-leverage.

Shadow banking's excessive
reliance on short-term and
secured funding heightens
systemic risk

In addition, many shadow banking entities use short-term wholesale funding to finance long-term and illiquid assets, such as borrowing from money market funds or by issuing short-term securities, which entail greater refinancing risks than traditional deposits. At the same time, shadow banking entities generally lack official access to a lender of last resort, and are also outside government deposit insurance programmes, making them more vulnerable to bank runs.[37] For example, money market funds (MMFs) in the United States experienced such a run during the crisis. MMFs hold short-term securities, and pass the interest on to their investors. Consumers and investors often use these funds as alternatives to bank accounts, and do not expect to lose their principal investment. However, during the crisis, the value of the short-term securities held by the funds fell, so that the net asset value of at least one MMF fell below 100 per cent. Within two days of the announcement of "breaking the buck", investors had withdrawn approximately $200 billion or 10 per cent of assets from the MMF market. The redemptions contributed to a freezing of the United States commercial paper market, so that top-rated United States firms were unable to refinance working capital loans, and to a spike in short-term United States interest rates. Ultimately, the Government provided a guarantee and liquidity backstop to stop the run.[38]

Most shadow banking entities are also subject to mark-to-market accounting, which amplifies procyclicality, especially in combination with secured (or collateralized) financing. When asset values fall, additional collateral must be posted, which can force entities into sell positions in order to meet collateral calls, further depressing asset prices. This amplifies deleveraging during crises and, conversely, money creation in good times, potentially weakening the countercyclical effectiveness of monetary policy.

These risks are compounded by the lack of transparency in many shadow banking activities. Hedge funds are notoriously secretive about their strategies and positions, and many structured products are opaque. For example, prior to the crisis, banks provided guarantees to off-balance-sheet structured investment vehicles (SIVs). In the event of defaults above a specified threshold on the underlying loans, the SIVs would transfer the non-performing loans to the bank's balance sheet. These guarantees, which were generally hidden from both regulators and shareholders, substantially increased the riskiness of the banks.

Many shadow banking
entities are prone to
mispricing securities
and misleading risk
management practices

In addition, many shadow banking entities are extremely complex and difficult to understand, leading to systemic mispricing of securities, which can amplify boom and bust cycles. This was particularly evident prior to the crisis with respect to securitization and structured products, especially those that securitized sub-prime mortgages. Although the sub-prime mortgage market was introduced in the United States in the 1980s, it did not become sizeable until the late 1990s, growing from 83,000 mortgages in 1995 to more than 1,600,000 in 2006.[39] As such, there were only limited data on how these mortgages

---

37   Whereas deposits in banks are guaranteed by official insurance funds, such as the Federal Insurance Deposit Corporation (FDIC) in the United States, shadow banking at best relies on private guarantees, which often become unreliable in difficult times.

38   The direct extension of public guarantees to several shadow banking entities and markets contributed to restoring some financial stability, but it also opened a debate about the legality and legitimacy of using public funds to assist parts of the financial sector that were not entitled to such assistance as well as shortcomings of existing governance mechanisms. See Levy Economics Institute of Bard College, "Improving governance of the government safety net in financial crisis", April 2012, available from http://www.levyinstitute.org/pubs/rpr_gov_12_04.pdf.

39   Souphala Chomsisengphet and Anthony Pennington-Cross, "The evolution of the subprime mortgage market", Federal Reserve Bank of St. Louis *Review*, vol. 88, No. 1 (January/February 2006), pp. 31-56.

would perform in a severe economic slowdown. Given the limited historical data, rating agencies used dubious assumptions about default rates and correlations that were plugged into models designed to be overoptimistic. As a result, risks were systematically ignored and not captured in available data. Ultimately, investors' blind reliance on ratings led many in the financial community to trade products they did not understand. While securitized products can have benefits for lending, especially to underserved groups (box III.3 above), it is crucial that they be effectively regulated in order to identify and reduce systemic risks.

Progress in regulating shadow banking

The build-up of systemic risk that occurred in shadow banking entities in the run-up to the crisis highlights the need for a new approach to financial sector regulation—one that encompasses monitoring and regulation of all mechanisms that intermediate credit. Most efforts to reform shadow banking are being coordinated at the international level, but progress has been slower than expected. At the November 2010 Seoul Summit, in view of the completion of the agreement on new capital standards for banks in Basel III, the G20 leaders requested that the FSB, in collaboration with other international standard-setting bodies, develop recommendations to strengthen the oversight and regulation of the shadow banking system by mid-2011.[40]

> Progress in coordinating reform efforts to reduce systemic risk in shadow banking has been slow

In October 2011, the FSB proposed an overall approach and formulated some general principles and recommendations,[41] focused on banks' interactions with shadow banking entities, MMFs, other shadow banking entities, securitization, and securities lending and repos.[42] The proposed approach and possible regulatory measures were further refined and open for public consultation in November 2012.[43] Those measures include imposing concentration and exposure limits as well as stricter consolidation rules to limit the vulnerability of banks to risks in the shadow banking sector, and to ensure that bank guarantees are included on bank balance sheets. In the case of MMFs, the rules being considered would require that MMFs move from constant to variable net asset value accounting and accept the imposition of bank-like capital buffers. Proposed measures to reduce risks in relation to securitization include improving information disclosure and imposing retention requirements, which require banks to maintain a portion of the security on their balance sheet in order to increase their stake in credit evaluation and monitoring of the portfolios. Proposed rules to temper the procyclicality of collateralized lending include providing better guidelines on collateral management, valuation and reuse. Finally, the role of credit rating agencies should be reduced and the transparency and reporting of information continually improved.

---

40   FSB, "Shadow banking: scoping the issues", 12 April 2011, available from http://www. financialstabilityboard.org/publications/r_110412a.pdf.

41   FSB, "Shadow banking: strengthening oversight and regulation", op. cit.

42   FSB, "Strengthening the oversight and regulation of shadow banking: progress report to G20 Ministers and Governors, 16 April 2012, available from http://www.financialstabilityboard.org/ publications/r_120420c.pdf and "Progress of financial regulatory reforms", 31 October 2012, available from http://www.financialstabilityboard.org/publications/r_121105.pdf.

43   FSB, "Strengthening the oversight and regulation of shadow banking: an integrated overview of policy recommendations", 18 November 2012, available from http://www.financialstabilityboard. org/publications/r_121118.pdf and "Strengthening the oversight and regulation of shadow banking:a policy framework for strengthening oversight and regulation of shadow banking entities", 18 November 2012, available from http://www.financialstabilityboard.org/publications/ r_121118a.pdf.

To reduce risks in the derivatives market, the G20 has also agreed that OTC derivatives that can be standardized should be traded on formal exchanges or electronic platforms by the end of 2012. The United States, the EU and Japan have made progress in implementing these reforms and are expected to have them fully implemented by the end of 2012. The regulation and transparency of the over-the-counter derivatives market should be improved through requirements for the reporting and central clearing of transactions. Despite slow implementation, it is expected that the progress in terms of infrastructure and legislation will allow at least the jurisdictions with the largest markets in over-the-counter derivatives to comply with the deadline.[44]

Opportunities for capital, tax and accounting arbitrage remain abundant

At the domestic level, initiatives have been taken in some countries to improve regulation in a limited number of areas.[45] Information disclosure standards in debt securitization, for instance, have been strengthened in several countries. However, recent setbacks of regulatory proposals in the United States and slow progress in other developed countries cast doubt over the possibility of reaching an international consensus that would significantly reform and contain systemic risk generated in shadow banking. The continued existence of opportunities for capital, tax and accounting arbitrage, and the exclusion of shadow banking from the debate on perverse compensation incentives and excessive risk-taking, further hinder the possibility of decisively tackling systemic risks generated by shadow banking.

At the global level, it is crucial to ensure that the implementation of regulations is internationally coordinated and consistent. Although a regulatory framework needs to ultimately be designed for the needs of the domestic economy, which can differ across countries, regulatory arbitrage needs to be limited so that high-risk activities will not be merely shifted from more to less strictly regulated sectors or jurisdictions. The establishment of frameworks for monitoring implementation by the FSB and the Basel Committee for Banking Supervision, which involve peer reviews, is a step in the right direction in this regard. Nonetheless, the complexity of the proposed regulations could present new costs. Ultimately, a simple, comprehensive regulatory structure might be more efficient.

Other international financial stability issues

Global financial safety net

IMF resources were sharply increased in 2012

The multilateral capacity to provide liquidity represents a crucial factor in safeguarding global financial stability. A reliable global financial safety net would also reduce the incentive for countries to accumulate reserves in order to cope with adverse shocks. In the wake of the financial crisis, steps have been taken to strengthen the global financial safety net.

In 2012, resources available to the IMF for crisis prevention and resolution were significantly reinforced. A number of countries committed themselves to provide an additional $461 billion for this purpose, almost doubling the Fund's lending capacity. These resources will be in addition to quota increases under the IMF 2010 quota review and previously enhanced borrowing arrangements of the Fund with member countries

---

44 FSB, "Overview of progress in the implementation of the G20 recommendations for strengthening financial stability", 19 June 2012, available from http://www.financialstabilityboard.org/publications/r_120619a.pdf.

45 For a snapshot of the status of various financial reform initiatives, see IMF, *Global Financial Stability Report*, op. cit., table 3.8.

and central banks. The IMF also continued to reform its liquidity and emergency lending facilities. In 2011, the Precautionary Credit Line was replaced by the Precautionary and Liquidity Line, which is designed to more flexibly meet the liquidity needs of member countries with sound economic fundamentals. In addition, the Fund's instruments for emergency assistance were consolidated under the new Rapid Financing Instrument, which may be used to support a range of urgent balance-of-payments needs.

Altogether, the international financial safety net has continued to evolve towards a multilayered structure comprising global, regional and bilateral components.[46] The overall size of the collective safety net, however, remains small in comparison to reserves accumulated by national central banks. Moreover, there continues to be a lack of a global mechanism ensuring the swift and sufficient availability of substantial resources to stabilize market conditions in times of systemic liquidity crises. Efforts to further strengthen crisis-lending facilities should therefore focus on enhancing the different layers of the financial safety net as well as strengthening the coordination and consistency between the mechanisms at different levels.

More efforts are needed for improving global safety nets

The G20 Principles for Cooperation between the IMF and Regional Financing Arrangements, endorsed at the Cannes Summit, recognized that enhanced cooperation between IMF and regional financial arrangements would be a step towards better crisis prevention and resolution. The financial and operational capacity of mechanisms in some regions has been reinforced, as in Europe or in East Asia. In the euro area, the European Stability Mechanism was introduced, which provides rescue funds of €500 billion (about $628 billion). In May 2012, the members of the Association of Southeast Asian Nations plus China, Japan and the Republic of Korea under the Chiang Mai Initiative agreed to double the size of their emergency liquidity programme to $240 billion and make it more readily available.[47] In Latin America, the Inter-American Development Bank and the Andean Development Bank are playing increasingly important roles, but these act as development banks rather than as monetary funds. In Africa, there is no appropriate institution that can step in to provide regional liquidity.

In terms of the relative size of the different components of the global financial safety net, it is important to note that the bulk of liquidity needed to ease funding pressures has been provided by key central banks. For instance, the volume of Long-Term Refinancing Operations offered by the European Central Bank in late 2011 and early 2012 alone amounted to over €1 trillion. The involvement of major central banks will therefore remain pivotal for a functioning and sufficient global financial safety net. The creation of a more permanent framework of liquidity lines between key central banks should be given consideration. The existence of such agreements, even in times of limited usage, is considered to have a stabilizing effect on markets.

Multilateral and financial sector surveillance

Surveillance of the global economy for early warnings on economic and financial risks is another key element in taming the boom-bust cycles of international finance. In the run-up to the global crisis, the build-up of such risks was not properly captured by IMF

Comprehensive and timely risk identification should be the priority for multilateral financial surveillance

---

46 See, for instance, Pradumna B. Rana, "The evolving multi-layered global financial safety net: role of Asia", RSIS Working Paper, No. 238 (S. Rajaratnam School of International Studies, Singapore, 16 May 2012).

47 See "Reforming international financial safety nets", statement by Naoyuki Shinohara, IMF Deputy Managing Director, to the Asian Development Bank 45th Annual Meeting, Manila, Philippines, 5 May 2012, available from imf.org/external/np/speeches/2012/050512.htm.

surveillance. In particular, shortcomings in the surveillance approach were identified with regard to cross-border and cross-sectoral linkages. The ability to assess the impact of policies and shocks in major economies on other countries and regions and determine the linkages between the financial sector and the real economy are central to effective surveillance. Efforts of the IMF have continued to strengthen the capacity of multilateral surveillance to identify risks to global financial and economic stability in a timely and comprehensive manner. It has also taken a number of steps to strengthen the quality and coverage of its surveillance activities.

In 2011, the Fund prepared its first spillover reports for the world's five largest economies (China, Japan, the United Kingdom, the United States, and the euro area) to better reflect interconnections between the world's economies. The reports assessed the impact of policies in those economies on partner economies and stressed the importance of financial channels for transmitting global shocks. Implementing the recommendations of its 2011 Triennial Surveillance Review and the related Managing Director's Action Plan, the Fund has furthermore continued to reform and broaden its surveillance approach, through better integration of bilateral and multilateral surveillance, for instance. The monitoring of global stability risks emanating from financial sectors has been strengthened by the decision to make financial stability assessments at five-year intervals a mandatory part of surveillance for the 25 jurisdictions with systemically important financial sectors. Under the revamped IMF/World Bank Financial Sector Assessment Programme, several systemically important financial sectors have been assessed in 2012. Furthermore, a new IMF Financial Surveillance Strategy was adopted in September 2012, which aims to strengthen the analytical underpinnings of risk assessments and policy advice, upgrade the instruments and products of financial surveillance, and engage more actively with stakeholders in order to improve the traction and impact of financial surveillance.

International development cooperation and official flows

Official development assistance

In 2011, ODA fell for the first time in fifteen years

International public financing represents a form of global collective action for financing of global social, economic and environmental goals, which are often not financed by the private sector. In addition, official financing can be used to leverage private finance in areas that promote social goals, such as climate financing. However, similar to private finance, official financing to countries has been subject to instability and unpredictability. After reaching a peak in 2010, ODA from member countries of the Development Assistance Committee (DAC) of the Organization for Economic Cooperation and Development (OECD) fell 2.7 per cent in real terms to $25 billion in 2011, equivalent to 0.31 of gross national income (GNI) of DAC members. This represents the first significant fall in ODA, excluding years of exceptional debt relief, since 1997 (figure III.5). Net ODA fell in 16 countries, including the largest donors, such as the United States and the EU countries, which reduced their shares of ODA in GNI from 0.21 per cent to 0.20 per cent and from 0.44 per cent to 0.42 per cent, respectively. Steep declines were observed in Greece and Spain (more than 33 per cent) and Austria, Belgium and Japan (more than 10 per cent). Moreover, expected tight aid budgets in DAC member countries are expected in the coming years.

Figure III.5
ODA from Development Assistance Committee (DAC) countries as a percentage of donor-country gross national income and in United States dollars, 1960-2011

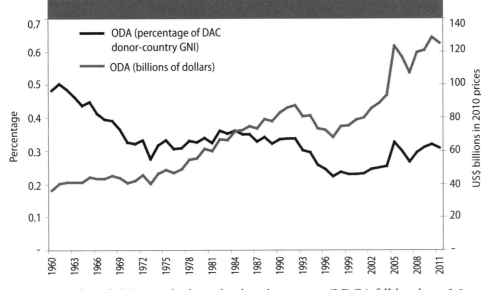

Source: OECD online database, available at http://www.oecd-ilibrary.org/statistics (accessed 16 November 2012).

Bilateral ODA to the least developed countries (LDCs) fell by about 2.0 per cent in real terms in 2011, even though donors renewed their commitment to provide at least 0.15 per cent of their GNI as aid to LDCs by 2015 at the Fourth United Nations Conference on the Least Developed Countries (LDC IV) in May 2011. The Programme of Action for the Least Developed Countries for the Decade 2011-2020 set a target that at least half of the LDCs should be eligible for graduation from the category by 2020.

The fall in ODA widens the gap on aid delivery between global aid and the 0.7 per cent agreed United Nations target by $4 billion, from 0.38 per cent of donor GNI in 2010 to 0.39 per cent. Total ODA would have to more than double to about $300 billion in 2011 dollars to reach the target.[48] As of 2011, only Denmark, Luxembourg, the Netherlands, Norway and Sweden exceeded the United Nations ODA target. More recently, however, the Netherlands announced plans to cut its aid budget by €1 billion by 2017, which will bring its contribution well below 0.7 per cent.

Declining ODA thus endangers the prospect of achieving the international targets adopted by donors at major international fora[49] during the past decade. This was already apparent in 2010 in the failure to reach the G20 Gleneagles summit pledge of reaching 0.36 percent level of the combined GNI of the DAC members, which was, in turn, regarded as an intermediate objective toward meeting the long-standing United Nations ODA target of 0.7 per cent. In addition, the commitment made in Gleneagles to increase aid to Africa by $25 billion in 2010 was not met either.

An OECD Development Centre Study, published in April 2012,[50] estimates a $120 billion additional resources gap to achieving the MDGs, while the current flows of

---

48   See *MDG Gap Task Force Report 2012: The Global Partnership for Development—Making Rhetoric a Reality* (United Nations publication, Sales No. E.12.I.5), p 9.

49   Including the Monterrey (2002) and Doha (2008) conferences on financing for development, the Millennium Development Goals (MDG) and the Fourth United Nations Conference on the Least Developed Countries in Istanbul (2011), in particular, the G20 Gleneagles summit pledges.

50   Organization for Economic Cooperation and Development (OECD), "Achieving the Millennium Development Goals: more money or better policies (or both)?", Issue Paper, available from http://www.oecd.org/social/povertyreductionandsocialdevelopment/50463407.pdf.

country-programmable aid from OECD countries stand at roughly half this figure. More than half of it is needed in 20 low-income countries with per capita income lower than $1,000 and, in the absence of expeditious action, about 35 countries will fall short of the goal of halving the number of people living in absolute poverty. Urgent action is required for these pledges to regain credibility and the necessary political traction.

Following the shortfall in the EU target for ODA delivery, the Foreign Affairs Council of the European Union took a decision on the proposed "Agenda for Change" by the EU Commission, in which it reaffirmed its commitment to achieve all their development aid targets—including the collective 0.7 per cent ODA to GNI target—by 2015.[51] Furthermore, the Council reiterated its commitment to policy coherence for development and identified key strategic priorities. The Council's focus is on governance and inclusive sustainable growth as the two over-arching pillars of development cooperation, and it will follow a more differentiated approach to countries at varying levels of development and concentrate on a maximum of three sectors per country. The mix and level of aid would be adapted according to needs, capacity and impact, as well as the progress made in commitments to—and the record on—human rights, democracy and rule of law, reforms implementation and meeting the needs of the people.

Before the Council approved the "Agenda for Change", the April 2012 DAC Review of the Development Cooperation Policies and Programmes of the European Union noted that more progress was needed. The Review made a number of recommendations,[52] including strengthening its differentiated international cooperation strategy with appropriate funding within the 2014-2020 financial framework, simplifying its complex budgetary and administrative processes, while aligning with member country policies and devolving more authority to its staff in the field.

Recently, the European Parliament development committee adopted a set of amendments that will be the basis of the negotiations with the Council on the new Development Cooperation Instrument regulation that will come into effect when the current one expires (after December 2013). The September 2012 proposed amendments[53] include a renewed focus on inequality, since the proposed Agenda for Change selection implied that middle-income countries would lose EU bilateral aid, based mostly on per capita income. Other important aspects are the call for a smoother transition when phasing out aid, more democratic oversight, and making climate change-related aid additional to the 0.7 per cent contribution that member states have to provide as ODA.

DAC members approved a Recommendation on Good Pledging Practice to ensure credible and feasible pledges with enhanced accountability and transparency in 2011. Now, donor countries, who are in a position to do so, need to set progressive quantitative aid targets based on recipients' needs assessments. Furthermore, LDCs need more access to highly concessional funds and grants if they are to meet their essential spending needs and also respond in a countercyclical way to the global economic crisis without falling back into debt distress. This is particularly true for those LDCs facing fragile situations resulting from institutions being weakened by the risk that their share of ODA allocation will be lowered based on performance.

---

51   Council of the European Union, "Council conclusions: increasing the impact of EU development policy—an agenda for change", issued at the 3166th Foreign Affairs Council meeting in Brussels, 14 May 2012.

52   OECD, "EU development co-operation: improving but still cumbersome", available from http://www.oecd.org/newsroom/eudevelopmentco-operationimprovingbutstillcumbersome.htm.

53   See, "EU development aid must take social inequalities into account, say MEPs", European Parliament News, 18 September 2012, available from http://www.europarl.europa.eu/news/en/pressroom/content/20120917IPR51498/html/EU-development-aid-must-take-social-inequalities-into-account-say-MEPs.

There is also evidence that along with the drop in ODA, the profile of ODA has shifted, particularly for low-income country recipients. As shown in figure III.6, budget support has fallen and project support has grown, along with the decline in aid. This could be indicative of an effort by donors to make aid allocation more results orientated, believing that this increases aid efficiency. "Measurable outputs" are important from the donors' perspective, as programmes that have a clear results focus tend to more readily receive parliamentary approval in donor countries. Nonetheless, the explosion in the number of individual aid projects by multiple donors has been widely criticized for not only exacerbating the fragmentation of aid architecture, but also imposing high transaction costs on recipient governments with scarce resources, failing to align with countries' national priorities and development strategies, and undermining country ownership—which is at the core of the Paris Principles of on Aid Effectiveness. Recognition that the role of aid lies in encouraging and supplementing national resource mobilization to meet national development goals, including the MDGs, has led to calls for aid to be increasingly used for budget support.

ODA is becoming more fragmented

Figure III.6
Low-income countries: concessional financing, 2003-2016

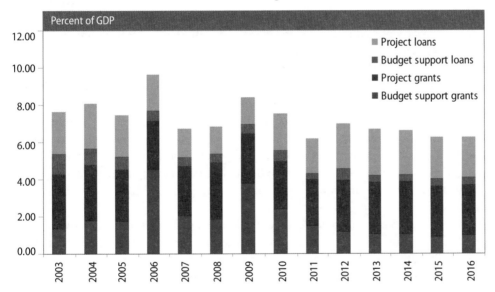

Source: IMF, World Economic Outlook database, October 2012; and IMF, "Fiscal Monitor: Taking stock—progress report on fiscal adjustment", October 2012, p.32.

Note: Average for low-income countries and fragile states of Africa, with oil producers excluded.

As a whole, the objectives of the 2005 Paris Declaration on Aid Effectiveness set for 2010 have not been fully implemented, with only one out of 13 targets met. Establishing mutual accountability mechanisms has been the indicator with the least progress so far. While recipients have, in general, complied with this framework, donors have not.[54] As recognized in the Accra Agenda of Action, aid distribution across countries remains insufficiently coordinated and the problem of aid "darlings" and "orphans", as well as "herding" behaviour by donors persists, with donor self-interest and geopolitical factors often outweighing recipients' needs and their ability to use aid effectively.

Although the proportion of official aid in total financing flows to developing countries is diminishing, ODA remains critical for many countries. Many countries are in need of increased assistance to meet emerging additional challenges such as climate change and food price increases. The Global Partnership for Effective Development was launched

ODA remains a key financing source for low-income countries

---

54 Ibid.

at the Fourth High Level Forum on Aid Effectiveness in Busan, Korea in November-December 2011. The principles of the Global Partnership for inclusive development need to be translated into balanced, effective arrangements benefitting all.

There is scope to further improve collaboration and coordination among donors and between donor and recipients at both global and national levels. Together with fostering the Global Partnership, the Development Cooperation Forum of the United Nations Economic and Social Council could be strengthened to ensure that the concept of aid effectiveness—broadened to capture all aspects of development effectiveness—goes beyond strengthening country ownership by aligning ODA with recipient country's development strategies and plans, and increasing the use of their own systems for procurement and financial management.

South-South cooperation

South-South cooperation continues to grow, mirroring the increasing global relevance of these economies

The dynamism of South-South trade and financing is part of the explanation for the relative resilience of developing countries in the recent crisis. The estimated volume of South-South cooperation financial flows was calculated to have reached 20 billion in 2010,[55] and is expected to grow further. However, the full size of South-South cooperation is not known, as many of the transactions are not fully reported. The knowledge gaps in South-South cooperation need to be acknowledged and addressed by creating proper reporting procedures that can solve the problem of fragmented and incomplete data.

Most of the resources in South-South flows are in the form of bilateral programmes of project funding. Unlike traditional aid, South-South cooperation tends to use a multi-pronged development strategy, incorporating trade and investment along with aid to support necessary infrastructure for the broader investment, generally without conditionalities.[56] South-South cooperation also extends to areas of knowledge-sharing, as a tool for facilitating capacity development and innovation. Much South-South cooperation, particularly from China, appears to be market driven (using market interest rates) in the area of natural resources, with much of the lending collateralized.[57] As such, it is not an alternative to existing aid.

The Busan outcome document acknowledged the difference between South-South cooperation and North-South cooperation in terms of nature, modalities and responsibilities.[58] At Busan, countries agreed to form an integral part of a new and more inclusive development agenda, in which actors participate on the basis of common goals, shared principles and differential commitments. South-South cooperation can work in concert with traditional forms of development aid which, in recent years, have tended to focus more on humanitarian and social interventions, and increasingly, on climate adaptation and mitigation.[59] The complementarity of South-South flows, traditional ODA, and other flows should be integrated to enhance the overall development architecture.

---

55   Sachin Chaturvedi, Thomas Fues and Elizabeth Sidiropoulos, *Development Cooperation and Emerging Powers: New partners or Old Patterns?* (Zed Books, 2012), p. 255.

56   See United Nations, General Assembly, "Report of the Secretary-General on the state of South-South cooperation" (A/66/229), para. 15.

57   Kevin P. Gallagher and Roberto Porzecanski, *The Dragon in the Room: China and the Future of Latin American Industrialization* (Stanford University Press, 2010).

58   See "Busan Partnership for Effective Development Cooperation", Outcome document at the Fourth High Level Forum on Aid Effectiveness held in Busan, Republic Of Korea from 29 November-1 December 2011, paras. 2 and 14.

59   United Nations, General Assembly, "Report of the Secretary-General on the state of South-South cooperation", op. cit., para. 53.

Innovative sources of international financing for development

Nonetheless, shortfalls in traditional ODA and the need for additional and more predictable international public financing has led to a search for new funding sources in addition to South-South cooperation and other flows— not as a substitute for aid, but as a complement to it. The G20 at the Cannes Summit on 4 November 2011 acknowledged the need to tap new sources of funds for development and global public goods. The outcome document of the United Nations Conference on Sustainable Development (Rio+20), entitled "The future we want", also states: "We consider that innovative financing mechanisms can make a positive contribution in assisting developing countries to mobilize additional resources ... (s)uch financing should supplement and not be a substitute for traditional sources of financing."[60]

Estimating the amounts raised through innovative financing mechanisms is a true challenge. There is no internationally agreed definition of innovative financing and as a consequence there are no standardized reporting systems to monitor these flows. As a result, estimates differ according to the mechanisms and sectors deemed as innovative financing. Classification schemes such as those by the OECD and the World Bank differ in their coverage, and so their estimates are not strictly comparable. The 2011 Report of the Secretary-General on Innovative mechanisms of financing for development[61] estimated that funds raised through innovative financing mechanisms for the period 2002-2011 ranged between $37 billion and $60 billion.

A recent comprehensive study by the United Nations estimates that when restricting the concept of innovative financing for development to include only mechanisms involving public sector involvement linked to international development cooperation, about $8.4 billion in resources are being channelled through innovative financing mechanisms, at best, with only a few hundred million dollars in new, additional funding raised annually.[62] The innovative initiatives that have been launched during the past decade,[63] such as the solidarity levy on airline tickets, Norway's tax on CO_2 emission from aviation fuel, the Affordable Medicines Facility - malaria, the International Finance Facility for Immunisation (IFFIm), and Debt2Health, share of proceeds from issuing new certified emissions reduction units (CERs) have in large part been used to fund global health programmes and to finance climate change mitigation and adaptation. While these initiatives have successfully provided immunizations and AIDS and tuberculosis treatments to millions of people in the developing world, they have not yielded significant additional funding on top of traditional development assistance. Most of the new mechanisms are not designed to raise additional resources. Instead, they are designed to restructure existing ODA to better match sources with needs. For example, the IFFIm brings forward future ODA for present expenditure, without providing a net increase in funds. Initiatives such as the GAVI Alliance, are designed to disburse financing.

So far, only limited resources have been raised from existing innovative sources of financing

---

60   See General Assembly resolution 66/288 of 27 July 2012, annex, para. 267.

61   The report concluded that in order to correctly record the scale of revenues raised, an international agreement is needed on the precise definition and scope of the term. Such an agreed definition would then provide the appropriate reference point for standardized reporting and accounting frameworks, which can be set up for recording reliable and coherent data over time.

62   See *World Economic and Social Survey 2012: In Search of New Development Finance* (United Nations publication, Sales No. E.12.II.C.1).

63   *World Economic and Social Survey 2012*, op. cit.

As discussed in the *World Economic and Social Survey 2012*,[64] concentrating external resources on particular diseases may skew health sector policies away from national health priorities. There is a risk that the global focus on communicable diseases does not coincide with national concerns about other diseases, the development of effective and equitable health systems, and efforts to deal with broader determinants of health (such as food security, nutrition and diet, water and sanitation, and living and working environments). The Leading Group Task Force on Innovative Financing for Health[65] recommended following aid effectiveness principles of country ownership in identifying health priorities within comprehensive national health strategies and plans, as well as investigating on possibilities to support comprehensive national health strategies and plans through resources raised by innovative financing mechanisms, channelled through country systems where the conditions are in place.

The Finnish Presidency of the Leading Group on Innovative Financing for Development announced in September 2012 that it is planning to work on clarifying and seeking common understanding of the concept of innovative financing mechanisms and its relationship to official development assistance, as part of the financing for development agenda.[66] An internationally agreed definition will be an important step towards a consistent reporting system that will deliver reliable data on the volume and scale of innovative finance. An agreed definition will also be key in future evaluations of the total volume of resources for development in terms of judging whether new funds are in fact additional to existing ODA, and determining the contribution and effectiveness of innovative financing to meet development objectives.

International taxes on financial transactions and carbon, and the use of Special Drawing Rights, have large potential

Innovative mechanisms with larger fundraising potential include international taxes on financial transactions and on carbon emissions, and the use of IMF's Special Drawing Rights (SDRs). Around $400 billion to $450 billion per year could be raised through a combination of mechanisms. For instance, the *World Economic and Social Survey 2012* estimates that a tiny tax of 0.005 per cent on major currency foreign-exchange transactions (dollar, euro, yen and sterling) would generate $40 billion in additional development resources annually, while broader taxes on financial transactions such as trades, bonds and derivatives could yield between $15 billion and $75 billion. The proposed EU financial transaction tax is estimated to raise $75 billion per year, although little, if any, would be for development purposes. A tax of $25 per ton of CO_2 emissions by developed countries could raise $250 billion in revenues for international climate financing. Proposals for annual issuance of additional SDRs and/or leveraging idle SDRs could yield at least $100 billion (Box III.4).[67]

Each of these options is technically feasible and economically sensible. Realizing their potential, however, will require international agreement and political will. As with existing mechanisms, efforts are needed to ensure that resources raised through new mechanisms are stable, aligned to recipient countries' development strategies, and that delivery is consistent with recipient countries' priorities and systems.

---

64   *World Economic and Social Survey 2012*, op. cit.

65   Leading Group, "Recommendations task force on innovative financing for health", available from http://leadinggroup.org/IMG/pdf/Recommendations_TFFIS_for_Madrid_En_.pdf.

66   Message of the Finnish Presidency to the Leading Group members, 28 September 2012, available from http://leadinggroup.org/article1112.html (accessed on 9 October 2012).

67   *World Economic and Social Survey 2012: In Search of New Development Finance*, op. cit., table O.1.

Box III.3

SDRs for development finance?

One potential innovative source of development finance is through the Special Drawing Rights (SDRs) of the IMF. It is important to separate the possible development financing functions of SDRs allocated to developed countries from their role in increasing the reserves of developing countries. There are two types of proposals for using SDRs for development purposes, as presented in the *World Economic and Social Survey 2012*.[a] The first is based on new annual issues, with the SDR allocations favouring developing countries. The proposed additional collective insurance would reduce the need for developing countries to accumulate reserves from their own resources, thus potentially freeing up space for enhanced developmental investments. Note that while this mechanism should help increase global stability, it only indirectly contributes to enhancing existing pools of development finance.

The second proposal leverages developed country allocations for development financing by floating bonds backed by SDRs, rather than by spending the SDRs directly. This more direct channel would leverage the "idle" SDR allocations held by developed and emerging economies with abundant official reserves. Idle SDRs jumped from approximately SDR13 billion to almost SDR200 billion ($320 billion) after the issuance of SDR250 billion in 2009 (figure). Using a conservative estimate, around $150 billion of existing idle reserves could be utilized to purchase bonds.[b] If combined with new allocations of between 150 billion and 250 billion in SDRs every year, amounts in that order may be usable for financing long-term development on an annual basis.

An alternative would be to create "trust funds" to leverage SDRs. In this proposal, $100 billion in "SDR equity" could be used to back issuance of $1 trillion in bonds, using a leverage ratio of 10 to 1. Assuming a 10-year maturity, this would provide $100 billion for development financing per year. This could, for instance, meet the initially agreed needs for climate financing for the Green Climate Fund. A high leverage ratio, however, exposes bond holders to greater risk, thus raising the cost of borrowing. An additional argument against the use of such leverage is that it breaches the original purpose of SDRs, which were created solely for transactions of a purely monetary nature. Leveraging SDRs in such a way as to expose their holders to risks of illiquidity distorts the purpose for which they were created. The viability of the proposal thus depends on how much risk would be involved, and on designing the financial instrument for leveraging SDRs carefully enough to maintain its function as a reserve mechanism. The risks are further limited to the extent that the proposal is restricted to using idle SDRs, which is similar to the existing practice by a fair number of countries of moving excess foreign currency reserves into sovereign wealth funds. These proposals are technically feasible, but international agreements and political will are necessary.

a *World Economic and Social Survey 2012: In Search of New Development Finance* (United Nations publication, Sales No. E.12.II.C.1), pp. 31-35.

b Bilge Erten and José Antonio Ocampo, "Building a stable and equitable global monetary system", DESA Working Paper, No. ST/ESA/2012/DWP/118 (Department of Economic and Social Affairs of the United Nations Secretariat, August 2012).

Total net undrawn SDRs

Millions of SDRs

Source: IMF International Financial Statistics.

Debt relief and sustainability

The debt situation
has improved in
developing countries, but
vulnerabilities remain

The current debt situation in developing countries does not pose a systemic problem, although vulnerabilities remain in some regions and countries,[68] particularly the Caribbean, where two countries (Grenada and Haiti) were classified as in high risk of debt distress, and four (Dominica, Guyana, St. Lucia and St. Vincent and the Grenadines) were in moderate risk of debt distress as of 9 August 2012.[69] Six countries which had received irrevocable debt relief under the Heavily Indebted Poor Countries (HIPC) Initiative are still in high risk of debt distress, and there is a risk that continued global weakness will worsen debt sustainability in additional countries. As HIPC and multilateral debt relief initiatives are coming to a close, a new international framework for addressing future sovereign debt crises needs to be on the policy agenda.

Gaps in the financial architecture for debt restructuring were manifested in earlier sovereign debt crises in emerging markets and developing countries. For debtors, solutions have often been accompanied by undue lags and, for the most part, have provided too little relief, often leading to future debt restructurings, jeopardizing the resumption of growth and prospects for keeping debt sustainable. Concerns remain that efforts to reform the architecture have been insufficient and inadequate.

The euro area sovereign debt crisis has brought many of these issues to the fore even more forcefully. The rescue packages by the official sector, including the IMF, are unprecedented in history, putting considerable strains on the balance sheets of the public sector. The incremental policy response has yet to ensure a definite and timely end for the crisis, endangering the global economic recovery and the stability of the global financial sector. Moreover, there are concerns that such actions may also generate moral hazard. In debt restructurings this has been shown to lead to sovereign debtors deferring adjustments, to international lenders inadequately pricing risk, and to negotiations leading to lower debt write-offs, thereby postponing rather than solving the underlying problems of the sovereign debtor.

New forms of managing
sovereign debt crises
should be considered

Given these and related issues, it is time to consider alternatives to ad hoc resolutions to sovereign debt crises. There are several options going forward with proposals ranging from those under the voluntary and contractual approach, such as ex ante structures and frameworks for creditor committees, to a statutory approach, or in-between solutions such as the setting up of a Sovereign Debt Forum, which would be a neutral organization with broad participation from debtors, private creditors and multilateral institutions. The lack of a mechanism to restructure sovereign debt in a fair and efficient manner contributes to global risks, threatening financing for development and adding to pressures on countries to build reserves, and thereby contributing to global imbalances.[70]

Financing for long-term sustainable global development

In summary, the international financial system continues to be plagued by volatility and incentives to short-term behaviour. Volatile capital flows may result in higher volatility of

---

68   *MDG Gap Task Force Report 2012*, op. cit.

69   IMF, "List of LIC DSAs for PGRT-Eligible Countries, as of 9 August 2012".

70   See "Principles on sovereign lending and borrowing: UNCTAD kick starts endorsement process", UNCTAD Information Note, 23 April 2012, available from http://unctad.org/en/pages/InformationNoteDetails.aspx?OriginalVersionID=20.

consumption and boom and bust cycles, and the associated uncertainty may reduce investment and economic growth. In addition, capital account volatility has led to reserve accumulation as a form of self-insurance, exacerbating global imbalances, and holding back resources for long-term development investment. The lack of coordination of monetary policies among developed countries compounds this problem, as evident from continued stop-and-go capital flows to emerging markets, which also has the effect of weakening monetary policy responses in developed countries.

Proposals and reforms to financial regulation have been insufficient to address the problems of volatility and short-termism, including insufficient attention to incentives for excessive risk-taking in the banking and the shadow banking systems. Existing proposals and reforms have been mostly focused on the safety and stability of the banking system, with some attention to risks in the shadow banking system and risks associated with G-SIFIs (although these have been insufficient).

While a focus on stability is important, the ultimate goal of the global financial system should be to effectively allocate finance to long-term sustainable development in a stable manner. In particular, reforms to banking regulation need to take into account any impact they may have on growth and access to credit, as well as on stability. This is particularly important in developing countries, where access to credit for productive investment may be more limited. Policymakers in developing countries can choose to implement elements of Basel III and other regulations that best suit their needs, rather than necessarily implementing the full package. For example, it might make sense to integrate several of the ideas underlying Basel III—such as countercyclical buffers, liquidity ratios, increase in the quantity and, especially, the quality of core capital, adapted to local circumstances—into national regulatory frameworks. Policymakers should also engage in emergency planning to address the failure of large international banks operating in the country. Requiring banks to have subsidiaries, rather than branches, in the local market can help in this area. Alternative measures such as public development banks and directed credit could also be employed to improve access to credit.

Reforms to the international financial system need to emphasize both stability and effective allocation of credit for sustainable growth. To that end, reducing global risks through a mechanism for resolving sovereign debt and strengthening the global safety net are also key. Reforming and improving financial regulation in emerging economies and developing countries is an important part of the global reform agenda to promote the mobilization of resources, reduce risks and promote sustainable financing for development.

Global financial reform still has significant challenges ahead in promoting adequate and stable financing for long-term sustainable development

Chapter IV
Regional developments and outlook

Developed market economies

The economies of the developed countries still face strong headwinds in their struggle to return to sustained growth. The Great Recession left a host of troublesome legacies: continued deleveraging by households and firms, which is holding back consumption and investment demand; still fragile banking sectors whose lending to the private sector is not yet normalized; depressed housing markets that put additional strains on the banking system and hold back consumer spending and construction investment; and substantially deteriorated fiscal balances and rising public indebtedness that Governments are trying to redress through fiscal austerity, but which, in already depressed economic situations, is further pushing up unemployment rates and slowing economic recovery. Unemployment rates remain high in most developed economies and in some cases have reached disturbing levels, affecting a quarter or more of the work force. A large share of workers remains without having had a job for a year or longer, a major social concern that threatens to lower long-run economic growth. Slower growth in emerging market economies, which had proved a strong support to global growth since the end of the Great Recession, started to compound these difficulties in the course of 2012. Many of these factors have also led to a tremendous drop in confidence by both firms and consumers, leading to postponed investment and consumption decisions.

Most developed countries are responding to these problems by combining a mix of highly accommodative monetary policy (keeping policy interest rates near zero coupled with a wide variety of unconventional policies) with very tight fiscal policy in an attempt to bring down budget deficits. Thus far, however, this policy mix has proven insufficient to reinvigorate the recovery and bring down unemployment. Gross domestic product (GDP) of developed economies as a group is expected to grow by a meagre 1.1 per cent in 2012 and 2013 and 2.0 per cent in 2014, well below the pace needed to recover the jobs lost during the Great Recession.

North America

United States: protracted and anaemic growth

The economy of the United States continues to struggle to overcome the deep-rooted problems that surfaced with the sub-prime mortgage crisis of six years ago. Per capita income and employment levels are still below those reached before the crisis. In early 2012, there were signs of a more robust recovery. Business investment and exports were on the rise and job creation was stronger than expected. However, those promising signs faded later in the year with the further deepening of the sovereign debt crisis in the euro area and the worldwide slowdown of economic activity. At home, increasing concerns over the looming fiscal cliff cast a darkening shadow over the domestic economy (see chapter I). As these factors continue to linger, growth prospects for the United States economy remain sluggish for 2013. Nascent signs of recovery of the beleaguered housing sector form a bright spot between the darkening clouds. Also, additional policy support is expected to come in the form of the new round of quantitative easing launched by the United States Federal Reserve (Fed), which committed to continue purchasing mortgage-backed securities until the employment situation improves substantially. In the United Nations baseline outlook, GDP growth is forecast to be 1.7 per cent in 2013, lower than the already anaemic pace of 2.1 per cent estimated for 2012 (see table I.1 and annex table A.1). Risks remain for an even worse scenario in the short run, emanating from the possibilities of a fiscal cliff, further eruption in the euro area debt crisis and a hard landing in large developing economies.

Assuming these downside risks can be averted, the economy of the United States is expected to gain some strength in the medium term. The process of deleveraging seen in the household and financial sectors over the past four years is expected to ease in 2014. This would help improved lending conditions and could underpin stronger investment and consumption spending.

Business investment is hindered by heightened risk factors

Business investment was a key driver of the moderate recovery of the past two years, growing at about 8.6 per cent for 2011 and 7.5 per cent for the first quarter of 2012. However, as firms have become more risk averse amid the heightened economic uncertainties at home and abroad, investment demand has weakened notably. Growth of investments in business equipment and software is expected to slow from 11 per cent in 2011 to 7 per cent in 2012 and further to 6 per cent in 2013, while investment in business structures is expected to slow to below 4 per cent in 2013.

The housing sector is recovering slowly and residential investment is picking up

After five years of slump, the housing sector is showing signs of recovery. According to the Federal Housing Finance Agency (FHFA) price index, house prices are estimated to increase by more than 4 per cent in 2012. Inventories of unsold homes are falling and housing permits and starts are on an upward trend. Residential investment has been on the rise in 2012 and is expected to continue growing in the following years, driven by population growth and very low interest rates.

Poor job market restrains consumption

Nonetheless, consumer demand is expected to remain subdued in the short run as households continue to face constraints, including the lingering need to reduce debt burdens, persistent high unemployment, and uncertainties about possible shifts in tax policy in the coming years. Payroll employment increased by slightly more than 1 per cent in 2012, exceeding labour force growth, but not enough to make up much of the job loss from the Great Recession (figure IV.1). The unemployment rate stayed above 8 per cent for most of 2012, but dropped below 8 per cent in the final months of the year. The participation rate remains at a low of about 63 per cent, while the share of long-term unemployed (those unemployed for more than six months) is at a historic high of about 40 percent, well above the peak of 25 per cent observed in previous post-war recessions. In the outlook, employment is expected to continue growing at a moderate pace, keeping the unemployment rate above 7 per cent by the end of 2013 (see annex table A.7).

Inflation, as measured by the headline consumer price index (CPI), moderated in 2012 to about 2.0 per cent from 3.1 per cent in 2011 and is expected to retreat further in 2013 to 1.3 per cent (see annex table A.4).

Exports were another driver of output growth over the past two years, reaching about 11.0 per cent in 2010 and 6.7 per cent in 2011. However, it has moderated

Figure IV.1
United States: Post-recession recovery of employment[a] over five decades

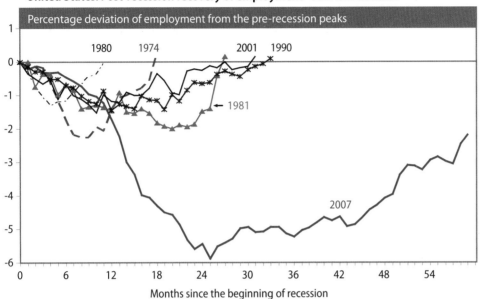

Percentage deviation of employment from the pre-recession peaks

Months since the beginning of recession

Source: UN/DESA, based on data from the United States Bureau of Labor Statistics.
a Monthly seasonally adjusted level of civilian employment.

significantly in 2012, slowing to 3.6 per cent for the year as a whole. Demand for United States exports declined in Europe and slowed markedly in large developing countries. Import growth has also decelerated at a similar pace. In the outlook for 2013, exports and imports are both expected to grow by around 3.5 per cent. The current-account deficit in the balance of payments fell to about 3 per cent of GDP in 2012 and is forecast to narrow slightly in 2013.

The monetary policy stance remains very accommodative in the United States. In September 2012, the Fed announced that it would keep the target range for the federal funds rate between 0.0 and 0.25 per cent through mid-2015, providing an anchor for the expectations of businesses and households. The Fed also decided to extend the average maturity of its holdings of securities through 2012 and to maintain its existing policy of reinvesting principal payments from its holdings of agency debt and agency mortgage-backed securities. In addition, the Fed launched a new round of quantitative easing to purchase agency mortgage-backed securities at a pace of $40 billion per month until the labour market has improved substantially—meaning, technically, that such purchases will most likely continue through mid-2014.

Monetary policy continues to aggressively support growth

Fiscal policy, in contrast, is expected to tighten further in the outlook. Real federal government spending on goods and services is expected to fall by about 3 per cent in 2013 and 2014. Spending had already been curtailed by 2.5 per cent in the previous two years. More importantly, significant uncertainty remains about how Congress will decide on the key components of the stimulus measures of the past years, including the expiration of the payroll tax cut and emergency unemployment insurance benefits. There is equal uncertainty about the fate of the Bush tax cuts and the automatic spending cuts that would come into effect in the absence of Congressional agreement (see the "Uncertainties and risks" section in chapter I). In the baseline, it is assumed that the 2 per cent payroll tax cut and emergency unemployment insurance benefits are extended for 2013, and then phased out gradually in subsequent years. It is also assumed that the automatic spending

The risk of a fiscal cliff was a major cause of enhanced uncertainty during 2012

cuts now scheduled to begin in January 2013 will be delayed, giving more time for the new Congress and re-elected president to produce a package of spending cuts and tax increases, including a combination of cuts in Medicare, Medicaid and Social Security and increases in income taxes, effective in 2014. The Bush tax cuts are assumed to be extended during 2013-2014.

Canada: economy losing momentum

The Canadian economy started 2012 on a positive note, but lost momentum during the year, as its two drivers of growth, business investment and exports, weakened visibly. In the outlook, declining government spending and residential construction investment will continue to be a drag on economic activity in the short run. Weaker global economic prospects will lower demand for Canadian exports. GDP is forecast to grow by 1.5 per cent in 2013, down from an estimate of 1.8 per cent in 2012. Some strengthening is expected in 2014, as GDP is forecast to increase by 2.8 per cent. The rate of unemployment is expected to stagnate at 7.4 per cent in 2013, the same level as in 2012. Inflation is forecast to stay below 2 per cent.

The Bank of Canada is expected to maintain its interest-rate target at the current level and only allow for a gradual increase from mid-2014. Government spending is expected to be retrenched further as part of fiscal consolidation efforts that aim to yield a budget surplus by 2015. Budget plans implemented in 2012 also include incentives for investments in research and development and capital equipment, in efforts to buttress productivity growth over the medium and long run.

Developed Asia and the Pacific

Japan: economy back in recession

In 2012, Japan's economy made a rugged recovery from the 0.7 per cent decline in the previous year. Growth was strong in the first quarter of 2012, but the momentum was lost shortly thereafter and the economy fell back into recession, in the second half of the year. GDP growth for 2012 as a whole is estimated at a meagre 1.5 per cent. In the outlook, Japan's economy is expected to climb out of the recession, but GDP growth will remain very weak at 0.6 per cent in 2013 and 0.8 per cent in 2014 (see table I.1 and annex table A.1). At this pace, it will likely be 2015 before Japan's economy returns to its size preceding the Great Recession in 2007.

Deteriorating trade seriously impacts the entire economy

A much weaker trade performance has had a strong, economy-wide impact. Since 2011, GDP shrank during all four quarters against the backdrop of steep declines in net exports (figure IV.2). The interruptions to industrial production caused by the earthquake and tsunami in March 2011 and the flooding in Thailand during the fourth quarter critically influenced these trends. These adverse factors were compounded by weaker external demand, the appreciation of the Japanese yen, and increased fuel imports for electricity generation after the stoppage of nuclear power plants. In 2011, Japan's trade balance showed a deficit for the first time in 20 years. It is expected to remain in deficit in 2012 and the outlook period. The current account of the balance of payments continued recording a surplus, however, as a result of positive investment income earned on the country's large stock of foreign assets. The external surplus stood at 1.5 per cent of GDP in 2012 and is expected to remain at this level during 2013 and 2014, much smaller than the surpluses recorded before the global economic crisis.

Figure IV.2
Japan: Contribution of major expenditure categories to the growth of GDP

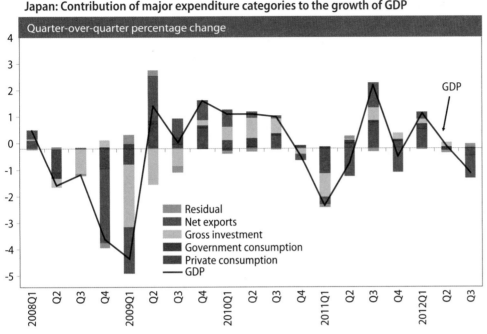

Source: UN/DESA, based on data from Japan Economic and Social Research Institute, available from http://www.esri.go.jp/index-e.html (accessed on 13 November 2012).

Private consumption grew by 1.9 per cent in 2012, helped by the post-disaster reconstruction and boosted by government incentives to encourage the purchase of energy-efficient automobiles. Consumer demand is expected to slow considerably, however, with the broader economic slowdown, the end of the automobile subsidy programme, scheduled cuts in pension benefits,[1] and the planned increase in the consumption tax rate. Private consumption is expected to grow at a meagre 0.1 per cent in 2013 and 0.2 per cent in 2014.

During 2012, reconstruction in the disaster-affected areas generated the strongest investment growth in 15 years. In 2013 and 2014, however, fixed investment is expected to decelerate sharply to 1.7 per cent and 1.5 per cent, respectively. After growing by 1.3 per cent in 2012, government consumption is expected to decelerate to 0.4 per cent in 2013 and 0.1 per cent in 2014. The fiscal tightening is the result of policymakers' concerns over the budget deficit and the phasing out of post-disaster reconstruction spending.

Although Japan was in recession in 2011, the open unemployment actually declined to 4.6 per cent, down from 5.1 per cent in the previous year. A shrinking labour force—now a long-term trend—is the main factor explaining the decline. Employment is expected to grow only slowly over the forecast period and the unemployment rate is expected to stay around 5.0 per cent over the outlook horizon (see annex table IV.7).

Nominal wages increased in 2010, but declined by 0.2 per cent in 2011 and still further in 2012. After two years of continuous increase, real wages declined in 2012 as a result of the lower nominal wage and weakened deflation. Deflationary conditions still prevail, although the decline in consumer prices moderated in both 2011 and 2012 as energy prices rose. Given the projections of tepid growth in the outlook, deflationary pressure on core consumer price is expected to persist in 2013 and 2014, although it will be

Despite the weak growth outlook, unemployment rates are expected to remain stable

Deflation continues

---

1   Beginning in April 2013, the pension age in Japan will increase gradually from 60 to 65.

less pronounced than during the 2000s as the output gap has narrowed with post-disaster reconstruction. In 2014, headline consumer price inflation is expected to accelerate to 1.8 per cent, owing to the planned increase in the consumption tax rate (see annex table A.4).

Fiscal policy is targeted to reduce deficit

In 2012, the Japanese parliament ratified a package of reforms of the social security and tax systems. The tax reforms include a change in the tax code that will enhance the tax base, and the consumption tax rate will be increased from the current level of 5 per cent to 8 per cent in April 2014, and further to 10 per cent in October 2015. The social security reforms involve extension of the retirement age, requirements for firms to hire workers older than 60, and cuts in pension benefits. According to Government estimates, the tax increase and the other elements of the package would reduce the budget deficit by more than 4 per cent of GDP over the medium run.

Bank of Japan adopts inflation targeting and continues monetary easing

The Bank of Japan (BoJ) has kept its policy interest rate near zero for several years already and is expected to continue to do so throughout the forecast period. It also adopted the practice of inflation targeting on 14 February 2012, with the target currently set at an annual change of 1 per cent in the CPI. In the baseline outlook, it is assumed that the predicted acceleration in inflation resulting from the consumption tax increase during 2014 will not induce the BoJ to raise its policy rate. During the first ten months of 2012, the BoJ further expanded its Asset Purchase Programme to ¥91 trillion and extended the time frame for implementation from mid- to end-2013. The quantitative easing is expected to lower long-term interest rates further. The BoJ also introduced a new element of monetary easing. Under the new framework, depository institutions can ask the BoJ to provide the full amount of the net increase in lending to the private sector. The cost of this funding is initially set to the level of the overnight call rate, which is assumed to remain between of 0.0-0.1 per cent for a few years.

Australia: recovering from the worst flooding in history

Australia suffered from devastating floods in 2010 and early 2011, which led to a sharp decline in exports in 2011. Nevertheless, the gradual recovery of coal production and investment for reconstruction and new production capacity more than compensated for these losses, such that GDP increased by 2.3 per cent. Driven by a solid expansion in exports and robust private consumption spending, and given the trend of continuing population growth, GDP growth rebounded further to 3.0 per cent in 2012 and is forecast to sustain this pace at 2.6 per cent and 3.3 per cent for 2013 and 2014, respectively. In 2012, exports grew by 5.4 per cent, facilitated by new production capacity in the mining sector. However, with the global economic slowdown, export growth is expected to decelerate to 3.4 per cent and 3.6 per cent in the coming two years. Investment in the mining sector is likely to expand at a robust pace, but will most likely remain tepid in other sectors.

In July 2012, a carbon tax was introduced in Australia, which temporarily lifted inflation to an annualized rate of 2 per cent, the lower bound of the inflation target zone set by the Reserve Bank of Australia. In November 2011, the central bank eased monetary policies by lowering policy interest rates after two years of policy tightening. Low inflation, the weak external environment and declining housing prices motivated the policy shift.

New Zealand: earthquake reconstruction boosts growth

In 2011, New Zealand suffered from a severe earthquake in the Canterbury region for the second time in recent years. The delayed reconstruction activity is expected to push the average investment growth rate to around 7 per cent during 2012-2014. In mid-2012, the Government was aiming to balance the budget by mid-2015, but was also expected to allocate more funds for reconstruction in the short run. Exports from New Zealand to developing Asia and Australia (mainly food and live animals) are expected to see moderate growth in 2013 and 2014. Overall, GDP is expected to grow by 2.1 per cent in 2012 and by 2.1 per cent and 2.7 per cent for 2013 and 2014, respectively.

Europe

Western Europe: the debt crisis and its reverberations continue to depress the region

The euro area sovereign debt crisis and attendant fiscal austerity programmes remain the dominant forces depressing growth in the region. Coupled with slowing external demand and high oil prices, this portends bleak prospects in the outlook. The first quarter of 2012 saw a stabilization of economic activity in the euro area as a whole after the sharp drop in activity experienced at the end of the previous year. In the remainder of 2012, however, the euro area economy witnessed continuous deterioration, with negative quarterly rates of growth in the second and third quarters—a technical recession—and an expected sharp drop in GDP in the fourth quarter. For the year as a whole, GDP is expected to decline by 0.5 per cent in 2012 and, given the weak starting point and continuing negative pressures, growth is expected to reach only 0.3 per cent in 2013 and strengthen marginally to 1.4 per cent in 2014 (annex table A.1).

Business, consumer and financial market confidence has closely followed the perceived policy successes and failures in moving the euro area sovereign debt crisis towards resolution (figure IV.3). At the end of 2011 and in February 2012, the European Central Bank (ECB) conducted two large-scale long-term refinancing operations (LTRO). These operations were successful in halting the liquidity crisis in the banking system and, for a few months, tensions abated and confidence improved. But tensions returned not long after, with bond yields for the crisis countries surging upwards, and confidence resumed its downward trend. Two policy initiatives were announced later in the year: the Outright Monetary Transactions (OMT) of the ECB, under which it would make unlimited purchases of the sovereign bonds of countries under stress, but with the stipulation that the country formally request assistance; and an agreement by Heads of State that would allow the use of the new rescue facility, the European Stability Mechanism (ESM), to directly recapitalize banks, thus breaking the link between bank recapitalization and government debt—again, with the condition that a new banking supervision entity be created first. These initiatives were successful at cooling tensions as bond yields for Italy and Spain dropped significantly. The efforts have been undermined, however: in the case of OMT, by reluctance to request formal assistance; and with the use of ESM for bank recapitalizations, by subsequent clarifications that legacy bank problems would not be covered, which then meant that the link between banking problems and sovereign debt was not broken.

Confidence is severely hit by the continuing sovereign debt crisis

These issues, coupled with the increasing realization that an agreement on a banking union may take a considerable period of time (exacerbated by a dismal economic situation with many countries in recession and unemployment rates in some cases at record highs), have been further reasons for continued concerns.

Figure IV.3
Confidence in the euro area and selected 10-year bond yields

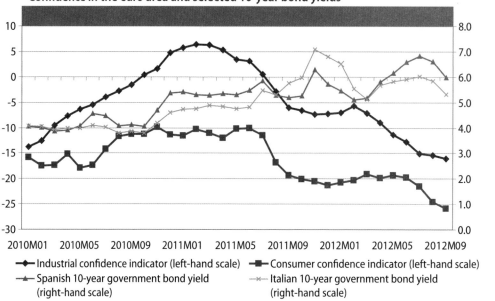

Source: European Commission and JPMorgan Chase.

Industrial confidence indicator (left-hand scale)   Consumer confidence indicator (left-hand scale)
Spanish 10-year government bond yield (right-hand scale)   Italian 10-year government bond yield (right-hand scale)

Other measures taken during the year include agreement on a new Fiscal Compact—essentially a beefed-up version of the Stability and Growth Pact—and the final approval by all member states of the new rescue fund, the ESM, which is now operational. Taken together, these policies address many of the defects in the original design of the EMU by adding a lender of last resort, a banking union and a more credible Fiscal Compact. But they do not address the key short-term issues of restoring growth in the region or how to put the crisis countries on a more probable path to fiscal sustainability.

Depressed confidence provides another route for crisis contagion across Western Europe

The confidence crisis has affected all countries in Western Europe and together with trade effects and financial market contagion, it has reduced the growth divergence previously in evidence. At least five economies are now in technical recession. Italy's GDP is expected to decline by 2.4 per cent in 2012 and 0.3 per cent in 2013 and Spain's by 1.6 per cent and 1.4 per cent, respectively. The other countries in recession are Cyprus, Greece and Portugal. Not all economies are equally affected. Germany's economy has slowed substantially and is expected to grow by only 0.8 per cent in 2012 after 3.0 per cent in 2011, with only a marginal rise to 1.0 per cent in 2013. France narrowly averted recession with a slight up-tick in GDP growth in the third quarter. Output growth is expected to reach only 0.1 per cent for 2012 as a whole and 0.3 per cent in 2013. Outside of the euro area, the economy of the United Kingdom of Great Britain and Northern Ireland exited recession in the third quarter, boosted by the Olympic games, but nonetheless GDP is expected to contract by 0.3 per cent for 2012. In the baseline forecast, only a slight rebound to 1.2 per cent is expected for 2013, as exports pick up (aided by a depreciation of the currency) and domestic demand solidifies.

Consumption is expected to remain weak in the outlook, but with significant differences across the region. Austerity programmes depress consumption but vary in intensity across countries. The strength of labour markets is another key factor, in terms of both employment and wages, and also varies significantly. The level of uncertainty stemming from the ebbs and flows of the euro area crisis is having a more uniform impact across the region, as consumer confidence, which had been improving earlier in the year, has since declined sharply. For the euro area, consumption is expected to decline in both 2012 and 2013, but this is dominated by the large declines in only some countries, particularly those in crisis, while other countries are expected to see some support from consumer spending.

Consumption is held back by low confidence and harsh fiscal austerity

Investment spending also remains weak in the region with little prospect for a sustained upturn given weak demand, elevated uncertainty from the sovereign debt crisis, and funding difficulties, particularly in the crisis countries. Fixed investment declined sharply in the euro area in 2012, with only a slight rebound expected in 2013 and 2014. Both domestic and foreign demand remains anaemic. Industrial confidence has been hit badly by the sovereign debt crisis. Although rising in the early part of 2012, renewed tensions from the crisis led to further sharp declines throughout the year. Capacity utilization picked up slightly in the first quarter of 2012, but then dropped in the subsequent quarters and remains low by historical standards. Bank lending to non-financial corporations continued to decline in the third quarter, owing both to declining demand, as firms cut back on investment spending, and to supply conditions. Despite better access to retail and wholesale funding, banks tightened credit standards further in the third quarter and are expected to do so again in the final quarter of the year, owing to a perceived increase in risk.[2] Funding conditions do vary across the region, however. In the crisis countries, conditions are extremely tight as their banking systems remain under tremendous pressure, but conditions are much easier in other countries. Housing investment remains a major drag on activity in some countries, particularly those that experienced a housing bubble and subsequent collapse, such as Spain and the United Kingdom.

Investment spending stymied by a lack of demand and heightened uncertainty

Exports slowed noticeably during the year, given the extremely weak intraregional import demand, compounded by weaker extraregional demand, particularly from East Asia. The latter had been an important source of export growth for countries specializing in capital goods. In the euro area, some support to export performance (and muting of imports) is coming from the depreciation of the euro, but lackluster demand is currently the dominant force.

Meagre growth in some countries and recession in others has wreaked havoc on labour markets. In the euro area the rate of unemployment climbed to 11.6 per cent in September, up 1.3 percentage points from one year ago and another record for the EMU era. Significant regional differences remain. In Greece and Spain, unemployment is above 25 per cent and in Portugal above 15.7 per cent—countries which have all been subject to harsh austerity programmes. At the other extreme are Austria, Germany, Luxembourg and the Netherlands where rates of unemployment are nearer to 5 per cent. Yet, given the only marginal pick up in activity expected from mid-2013 and into 2014, all countries are expected to see at least some increase in unemployment in 2013 before gradually coming down, with an estimated average of 11.3 per cent in the euro area in 2012, 11.8 per cent in 2013 and 11.6 in 2014 (see annex table A.7).

Unemployment continues to rise, in some cases to EMU record levels

Headline inflation, as measured by the Harmonized Index of Consumer Prices (HICP), has been above 2 per cent since December 2010 (the upper bound of the targeted

---

2   European Central Bank, "The Euro area bank lending survey: 3rd Quarter of 2012" (October).

inflation rate set by ECB). It reached 2.5 per cent in October 2012, boosted in part by high energy and other commodity prices as well as by administered prices (including rises in VAT rates). Core inflation, which abstracts from energy, food, alcohol and tobacco to measure underlying inflationary pressures, has been much lower, at about 1.5 per cent, with no evidence of upward creep. In the outlook, headline inflation is expected to drift down slowly, averaging 2.2 per cent in 2012, 2.0 per cent in 2013 and 1.9 per cent in 2014 (see annex table A.4). Given the poor outlook for growth, the output gap will remain large, wage growth, while picking up modestly, will remain contained, and the assumptions on oil and other commodity prices will yield little impact from these sources.

Fiscal austerity dominates
the macroeconomic
policy stance

Fiscal policy in the region continues to be focused on reducing fiscal imbalances. Government budget deficits of euro area members declined on average from 6.0 per cent of GDP in 2010 to 4.1 per cent of GDP in 2011, and further in 2012 to near 3.0 per cent. Most countries have been subject to Excessive Deficit Procedures (EDP) since the end of the Great Recession, which typically requires a minimum of 0.5 per cent correction in the deficit-to-GDP ratio per annum with a specified time frame for return to balance. The situation in the crisis-affected countries is far more severe, with significantly higher targeted annual consolidations and longer time periods of austerity necessary. Given that these targets are established in terms of ratios to GDP, growth shortfalls have required additional austerity measures, thereby adding pressure to the continued downward spiral, especially in the debt-ridden crisis countries. In the outlook, it is assumed that existing fiscal plans are implemented so that growth shortfalls will not be made up; rather, the time periods for consolidation are lengthened.

The ECB continues to
be active in attempts to
combat the sovereign
debt crisis

Since the crisis erupted, the ECB has relied on unconventional policies, leaving its main policy interest rate at 1 per cent. These policies included: refinancing operations conducted at fixed rates with unlimited supplies of liquidity, at increasingly long maturities and with reduced collateral requirements; provision of foreign currency liquidity; purchases of covered bonds; and, more controversially, purchases of sovereign debt in secondary markets under the Securities Markets Programme (SMP). At the end of 2011 and in February 2012, the ECB introduced a bold new policy, two large-scale LTROs. In July, it returned to conventional policy, lowering all three of its policy rates by 25 basis points, bringing its main refinancing rate to 0.75 per cent and the deposit rate to 0 per cent. In September, the ECB announced a new policy initiative dubbed "Outright Monetary Transactions" (OMT), whereby it would make potentially unlimited purchases of selected country bonds and hold them for a potentially unlimited duration in order to reduce the yields, but with the stipulation that the country must first formally request assistance and accept conditionality (this now supersedes the SMP, which has ended).

In the outlook, given the backdrop of recessionary conditions throughout the rest of 2012 and only very minor pick-up expected in 2013 and 2014, policy is expected to remain highly accommodative. For conventional policy, it is assumed that the ECB will cut the minimum bid rate by another 25 basis points, but hold the deposit rate at 0 per cent. It is also assumed that the new OMT will remain in place throughout the forecast period, and will be activated if necessary to maintain appropriate bounds to selected country bond yields.

Key risks to the forecast continue to be weighted to the downside. The sovereign debt crisis could flare up significantly, impacting on bank solvency and depressing confidence. Governments may be forced to make up for growth shortfalls by introducing new austerity measures. Oil prices could surge again. On the positive side, external demand, particularly from East Asia and perhaps the United States, may pick up earlier and with more vigour than anticipated, giving a boost to exports and investment. Tensions may subside in the region following more convincing implementation of already announced packages of policy measures, which would boost confidence.

The new EU members: "muddling through" continues

The tenuous economic recovery that emerged in the new European Union (EU) member States in 2010 has continued to weaken throughout 2012. Although some countries of the region, such as the Baltic States and Poland, started the year with solid first quarter economic results, the ongoing troubles in the euro area, which still remains the major export market for the region and the biggest source of foreign direct investment (FDI), has led to a visible deterioration of the region's current economic prospects. Some of the new EU members, such as the Czech Republic, Hungary and Slovenia, saw negative annual economic growth.

The impact of the unfavourable trade environment in 2012 has been further aggravated by the ongoing fiscal austerity measures and, consequently, by suppressed domestic demand and weak labour markets. Most of the fiscal space the new EU members possessed has been exhausted and some countries, such as Poland, face constitutional limits on the size of public debt. The search for alternative markets by portfolio investors has led to more favourable borrowing terms for the new EU members in 2012. However, the commitment to fiscal discipline remains one of the prerequisites for the low sovereign debt yields of those countries and further squeezes fiscal policy space.

Both external and internal demand remain weak

New EU banking regulations compelled the parent EU-15 banks operating in the region to improve their capital adequacy ratios. This led to continued deleveraging in the new EU member States in 2012, partially mitigated by the actions of the ECB. A serious distress in those parent banks could still lead to a severe credit crunch in Eastern Europe. The new Vienna Initiative, agreed in early 2012 to prevent such a development, does not contain the same commitments as the earlier initiative by the same name adopted in 2009.

The persistent weakness in external and domestic demand led to a slowdown in GDP growth in 2012. Aggregate GDP of the new EU members expanded by 1.2 per cent in 2012 and growth will accelerate to a still moderate rate of 2.0 per cent in 2013 amid numerous uncertainties and risks.

Economic performance varied in the region in 2012. The biggest economy, Poland, is relatively sheltered from the euro area troubles, having a smaller export-to-GDP ratio compared with its regional peers and exhibiting extensive trade ties with the Russian Federation. In 2012, the country benefited from the massive infrastructure spending related to the Euro 2012 Football Championship. However, cooling domestic demand and the need for fiscal consolidation slowed the economy in the second half of the year, with annual growth expected to be below 3 per cent in 2012 and in 2013. For other countries in Central Europe, industrial output in 2012 was held back by faltering external demand. The automotive industry slowed in the second half of 2012. Economic growth prospects for those exporters in 2013 will largely depend on the developments in the euro area. The economies of the Baltic States may grow at about 3 per cent in 2013. Bulgaria and Romania may face additional risks as they have stronger trade, finance and investment links with Greece and Italy.

The region exhibits divergent trends in 2012

Price pressures in the region that resurfaced in mid-2012, triggered by higher oil and food prices, subsided later in the year. Although headline inflation rates in a number of cases overshot the respective central banks' targets, this was mostly driven by external shocks and increases in indirect taxes to meet fiscal revenue targets. Core inflation remained weak, with the exception of the Baltic States and Poland. Provided that economic activity picks up in 2013, inflationary pressures may strengthen, but headline inflation in 2013 is likely to be lower because of the base effect of one-off price increases in 2012.

The impact of fiscal policy
is contractionary

Fiscal policies have been following a consolidation path to reduce the budget deficits in the medium term to the required benchmark of 3 per cent of GDP, as stipulated by the EU Stability and Growth Pact. Lower than projected economic growth forced fiscal authorities to revise their budgets in mid-2012, resorting to new revenue-enhancing measures, such as additional increases in indirect and other taxes. Those policies improved sentiment in international capital markets but are contractionary, at least in the short term.

By contrast, monetary policies remained expansionary during 2012. Benchmark interest rates were cut in the Czech Republic, Hungary (where the central bank prioritized growth over inflation), Latvia and Poland. Nevertheless, credit markets remain stagnant, although banking sectors in some of the new EU members recorded profits in 2012 (figure IV.4). Both demand for credit and credit supply remain weak, as households continue to repay their debt, businesses are cautious, and banks, facing reduced access to cross-border funding, clearly refrain from risky lending. Accommodative monetary policy may, however, support the region's exports through weaker exchange rates.

Figure IV.4
Net domestic credit in selected new EU member States, 2008-2011

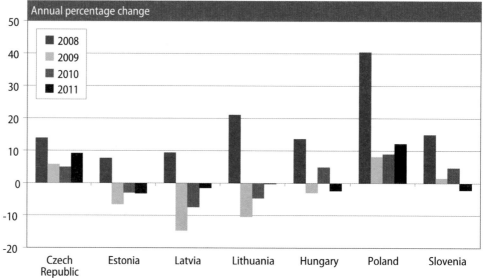

Source: World Bank.

Labour markets require
policy action

Labour markets, which recovered in 2011 most notably in the Baltic States, suffered some setbacks in 2012 as the unemployment rates slightly increased, partly reflecting reductions in the size of the public sector. The ongoing fiscal consolidation is complicating Governments' efforts to address labour market issues, although public works programmes in some countries, such as Hungary, created some employment for low-skilled workers. Much of the unemployment in the region is long term, requiring much stronger policy action.

In line with the deceleration in global trade growth, the expansion in exports and imports of the new EU members weakened in 2012. External demand for manufactured goods softened most notably, which in turn weakened demand for imported inputs by export industries. Import demand slowed further as a result of weaker domestic demand. Nonetheless, volume growth rates of both exports and imports remained mostly positive. Most export gains came from trade with non-EU partners such as the Russian Federation and Ukraine. In 2012, the current account was in surplus in Hungary and Slovakia and in deficit in other countries in the region, with a similar situation being expected in 2013.

Trade of new EU members weakened in 2012

A protracted recession in the EU-15, which would delay the recovery of FDI, remains the biggest risk faced by new EU members. Other downside risks include the inability to prevent a sharp cut in cross-border lending and an excessively contractionary impact of fiscal tightening.

Economies in transition

In the difficult global environment of 2012, the economies of the Commonwealth of Independent States (CIS) and South-Eastern Europe exhibited divergent trends. The aggregate GDP of both regions expanded by 3.5 per cent in 2012, but this figure masks significant variations. While the economies of the CIS continued to grow, although at a lower rate as compared with 2011, South-Eastern Europe saw another year of economic stagnation with declining output in Croatia and Serbia. Commodity exports and robust domestic demand supported growth in the key economies of the CIS, while worker remittances, mainly from the Russian Federation, played an important role for the smaller economies of that area. For the countries of South-Eastern Europe, both external demand, hit by the crisis in the euro area, and internal demand, undermined by fiscal austerity policies and stagnant labour markets, remained weak. Both country groups continue to face serious economic challenges, such as diversification of output in the CIS and reindustrialization of South-Eastern Europe. In line with the expected mild recovery in the global economy, growth in the aggregate GDP of transition economies is projected to accelerate to 3.6 per cent in 2013, as economic activity in South-Eastern Europe improves.

South-Eastern Europe: countries face another year of economic stagnation

Real economic activity in South-Eastern Europe in 2012 remained below that achieved in 2008 before the onset of the global financial crisis. After a very weak recovery in 2010 and 2011, the region's growth turned negative in 2012 and is forecast to remain below trend in 2013 owing to weakness in both external and internal demand. As a result, exceedingly high rates of unemployment that plagued the region even before the global crisis are expected to continue for at least several more years, if not longer. In 2012, spring floods, summer droughts and forest fires destroyed crops, especially corn and potatoes, and physical infrastructure throughout the region. The major risks to the forecast are to the downside as the region's strong financial, trade and remittance linkages with some of the most troubled countries of the EU, such as Greece and Italy, make it quite vulnerable should there be a further deterioration in the euro area. FDI inflows into these economies remain depressed at about half their levels prior to the crisis. This decline in investment is an important factor in explaining not only the currently low growth and high unemployment rates, but also the fairly weak medium- to long-run growth prospects. The aggregate GDP of South-Eastern Europe declined by 0.6 per cent in 2012 and is forecast to recover only modestly to 1.2 per cent in 2013. In 2013, Croatia is set to join the EU. The country's admission to the Union should bring certain economic benefits, through the removal of the last trade barriers and stronger FDI inflows, as well as larger financial assistance.

There has been considerable variation in the economic performance of the South-Eastern European economies. Albania and the former Yugoslav Republic of Macedonia have both experienced solid growth since 2010, although it moderated significantly in 2012 as growth in the EU declined. Among the other four economies, Bosnia and Herzegovina and Montenegro recorded growth near 0 per cent in 2012, while Croatia and Serbia experienced a recession.

Unemployment is expected to remain elevated

Although the economies of South-Eastern Europe were quite negatively impacted by the global crisis of 2008-2009, their unemployment rates did not increase initially as much as might have been expected. Likewise, their unemployment rates have not declined appreciably with the recovery and are expected to stay elevated for many years. In Bosnia and Herzegovina and the former Yugoslav Republic of Macedonia, unemployment is above 30 per cent, while in Serbia, it is above 25 per cent.[3] The unemployment in South-Eastern Europe is mostly structural; active labour market policies, improved education and training facilities, and more incentives for investment would be required—in addition to aggregate demand policies—to reduce it.

Inflation has been moderate in the region, with rates in the 2 to 4 per cent range, although in mid-2012, inflationary pressures intensified following a spike in food and energy prices, or some one-off effects such as rises in VAT rates or increases in administratively controlled utility prices. As the impact of one-off factors tapers off, inflation in the region in 2013 should be one half of a percentage point weaker.

Fiscal stimulus is unlikely

Fiscal policies in 2013 will hardly be able to support growth, as most Governments aim to consolidate public finances. Faced with lower-than-projected economic growth in the first half of 2012 and lower-than-anticipated revenue intake, some Governments in the region had to revise their annual budgets and introduce additional measures to meet fiscal targets. For Bosnia and Herzegovina, which obtained a new standby loan from the International Monetary Fund (IMF), fiscal policy should also meet the conditions set by the Fund.

The conduct of monetary policy in South-Eastern Europe is constrained by unilateral "euroization", which is the case in Montenegro, or by formal or informal currency pegs. In the countries with flexible currencies, monetary easing continued in 2012 in Albania, but interest rates in Serbia, where inflation moved beyond the central bank's tolerance band, were raised several times. Monetary conditions in the region should remain mostly accommodative in 2013, however, as private credit growth remains slow to pick up.

Current-account deficits remain a risk for the region

All South-Eastern European countries have run trade deficits in goods in 2012 and this is expected to continue in 2013. The tourism sector, on the other hand, performed well in Croatia and in Montenegro. The current-account deficits in the region, despite the inflows of workers remittances, again started to expand in 2010, as recovering domestic demand spurred imports. Albania, Bosnia and Herzegovina, Montenegro and Serbia have relatively large current-account deficits, approaching or exceeding 10 per cent of GDP.

---

3   In some countries, there are substantial differences between monthly registered unemployment rates and labour force surveys, which are only conducted on a yearly basis.

The Commonwealth of Independent States: growth slows down

Economic growth slowed down across the region in 2012.[4] A tepid global recovery dampened economic activity and constrained access to external financing. Economic performance has weakened in most countries, including in the largest economy, the Russian Federation, which remains a major influence on the others. Aggregate GDP in the region rose by around 3.8 per cent in 2012. Growth is expected to remain at a similar level next year, well below potential, as the world economy continues to provide a difficult background for the economies of the region. The recent accession of the Russian Federation to the World Trade Organization (WTO) may generate some additional positive growth impulses in the long term (box IV.1).

Box IV.1

The economic effects of the Russian Federation's accession to the World Trade Organization

In August 2012, after 18 years of protracted negotiations, the Russian Federation eventually joined the World Trade Organization (WTO). Following the accession of China in 2001, the Russian Federation was the largest economy outside of the WTO framework. By joining the organization, the country undertook a number of serious commitments: to gradually reduce its average tariff bound to about 8 per cent; to bring its national regulation of market access for services in line with the General Agreement on Trade in Services (GATS); to soften its barriers on foreign direct investment; and to reduce state interference into the economy. The country's negotiating team, however, refused to accept the commitment to allow foreign banks to establish their presence in the economy, except as subsidiaries or representative offices.

On the global scale, the economic implications of the country's WTO membership will be very modest, compared with China's accession in 2001. The admission of China to the WTO has eventually led to a significant decline in the prices of manufactured goods, but in the case of the Russian Federation, most of the exports currently consist of primary commodities, which are generally not subject to tariff barriers. For the Russian Federation itself, however, the membership and its potential impact on economic diversification will have significant macroeconomic implications.

The Russian economy remains in dire need of diversification. Most of its exports (about 69 per cent in 2010) consist of oil, fuels and natural gas, and the economy is dependent on imports of manufactured goods. The high volatility of global energy prices and the country's dependence on this sector has resulted in considerable macroeconomic volatility. As productivity growth in commodity sectors is generally below those in manufactures, this production structure has contributed to slower long-term economic growth. Given population ageing and projected shortfalls in the pension system in the coming decades, this has significant implications for fiscal sustainability.

Despite limited manufactured exports, the Russian economy is currently running a comfortable trade surplus and is diverting part of its hydrocarbon revenues to a national wealth fund. However, in the longer run, the country may face serious challenges when it is eventually confronted with significant declines in oil production and a tighter market for natural gas. Still, the Russian economy contains certain industrial sectors, such as aviation and engine production, which may find a niche in global markets, if managed efficiently, and has a well-educated and professional labour force. The Russian automotive sector, which attracted a significant amount of FDI and is benefiting from booming car sales, is an example of a successfully upgraded industry, although it may need further modernization to withstand the post-transition competitive environment.

---

4   Georgia's performance is also discussed in the context of this region for reasons of geographic proximity and similarities in economic structure.

Box IV.1 (cont'd)

Prior to the WTO accession, Russian policies aimed at industrial diversification were not always friendly to the concept of free trade. To achieve import substitution, the Government resorted to introducing export taxes, increasing import tariffs and requiring local content for manufactured products. Direct state intervention was quite common and the country routinely resorted to protectionist policies. FDI into the Russian Federation was at least partially restricted in 42 sectors designated to be "strategic". Consequently, FDI flows into the Russian economy were more modest compared with other emerging markets (see figure). Since domestic businesses, on the other hand, often did not have adequate access to financing, investment rates remained low.

The immediate economic impact of the country's WTO membership is expected to be limited. Only about one third of tariff reductions will be applied immediately; for most other product groups, a transition period of several years has been agreed upon. Some sectors, such as pig farming, dairy production and pharmaceuticals, as well as production of trucks and buses, will come under stiffer competition. The federal budget may lose about $6 billion in 2013 alone through reduced import duties.

The long-run impact matters more though. Assessments of potential longer-term gains or losses for the Russian economy vary, with both optimistic and pessimistic views. According to the optimistic views,[a] which are contingent on much higher investment rates, significant inflows of FDI (including into the services sector) and further financial deepening, the Russian economy will gain about 10 per cent of GDP in the long term. Private consumption in the medium run will gain several percentage points, improving the livelihoods of many households. As the Russian Federation already enjoys a most favoured nation status with virtually all of its trading partners, most of those advantages will not come from market access terms; rather, benefits will derive from the drastic increase in productivity in the most competitive exporting sectors, a higher variety of imported inputs, a serious technological upgrade, and the ability to use the WTO dispute settlement framework for resolving anti-dumping cases. The Russian services sector (including finance, telecommunication and transportation) is expected to gain in size and efficiency following strong FDI inflows.

The more pessimistic view, however, assumes low FDI inflows and little progress in domestic modernization that will lead to negative effects on the economy at large, as many weak industries would lose market shares and the Russian Federation could lose out in any trade dispute because of inexperience in using WTO's dispute settlement framework. Significantly reduced support for the agricultural sector will make it uncompetitive, while lower customs revenues will affect the budget. The closing of unprofitable enterprises and loss of corporate income tax payments will impact regional budgets. Some economists fear that agriculture and manufacturing sectors for construction materials, consumer goods, food industries and machine building could lose as many as 2 million jobs or more in less than ten years, and that the accession will induce output losses, affect household consumption and worsen income inequality.

Which one of those scenarios will materialize? Following China's accession to the WTO, which led to a more predictable business and dispute resolution environment, FDI inflows into China's manufacturing sector, with its abundant labour resources, surged, and export growth accelerated further, to about 20 per cent a year. Such a scenario is unlikely in the case of the Russian Federation. Therefore, the proponents of both views agree that the transition period should be used efficiently. Since currently protected manufacturing sectors, oriented towards the domestic market, are likely to shrink, the key to success would be to expand export-intensive industries and services. It will be important, to the extent allowed by the WTO framework, to create incentives for exporters and to attract FDI into those industries and services. Attracting FDI into high value-added sectors where the entire vertical integration chain can be developed domestically will improve the access to know-how and technology, and increase employment and the quality of human capital. Potential investors into the Russian economy would benefit not only from exporting opportunities, but also from the sheer size of the Russian domestic market and the free trade agreements in the CIS area.

According to the World Bank's *Doing Business 2013* report, the Russian Federation ranked 112 out of 185 economies on ease of doing business. The Government aims to achieve a much better ranking within several years, and drafted several road maps outlining ways to improve the investment

a See, for example, Thomas Rutherford and David Tarr, "Russia's WTO accession: What are the macroeconomic, sector, labor market and household effects?" available from http://siteresources.worldbank.org/INTRANETTRADE/Resources/Topics/Accession/Rutherford-Tarr_russia-macro-effects.pdf, accessed on 4 December 2012.

Box IV.1 (cont'd)

climate both for domestic and foreign businesses, including reducing bureaucracy, achieving serious progress in investor protection and fighting corruption. The quality of the business environment will be an important factor influencing the eventual impact of WTO membership. The Government has also to improve the institutional capacity to utilize the WTO dispute settlement mechanism.

The proponents of both views also agree that an efficient government-sponsored policy of mitigating the social costs of WTO membership, especially for unskilled workers, will be needed for the transition period. Therefore, strengthening the social safety net and investing in retraining should remain the focus of economic policymakers.

Annual average FDI flows as a share of GDP, 1996–2010

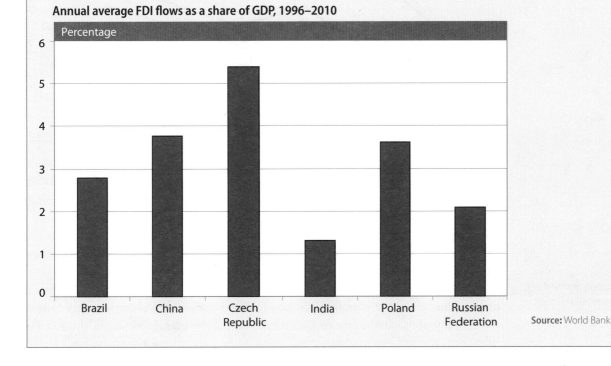

Percentage

Source: World Bank.

Continued income growth, favourable labour market dynamics and declining inflation have provided impetus to domestic demand through the region. However, persistent uncertainty regarding economic prospects and difficult international financing conditions contributed to a slowdown in investment. While growth of retail lending supported private consumption in the Russian Federation, high shares of non-performing loans in the banking system constrained new lending and thereby the expansion of domestic demand in Kazakhstan. In Azerbaijan, the oil sector stabilized after last year's large fall in output, although the non-hydrocarbons economy remained the main source of economic dynamism. In Ukraine, the poor performance of export-oriented industrial branches was compounded by the problems of the agricultural sector. For the smaller, low-income countries, the Russian economy provides an important source of revenue through the remittances sent back home by workers from these countries (figure IV.5). Problems in the gold sector, including a drastic fall in output caused by social protests and strikes, resulted in a sharp economy-wide slowdown in the Kyrgyz Republic.

Domestic demand offsets external weakness

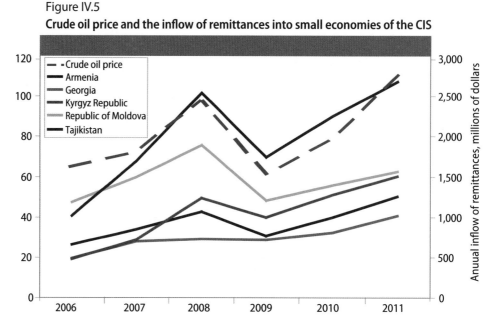

Figure IV.5
Crude oil price and the inflow of remittances into small economies of the CIS

Source: World Bank.

Sustained economic expansion has brought a reduction in unemployment in the region, although there are some marked differences in the performance of labour markets across countries. The unemployment rate reached historic lows in the Russian Federation, as jobs growth was accompanied by a shrinking active population. By contrast, the economy of Kazakhstan continued to generate employment at a rapid pace, but this was in line with the growth of the labour force. For low-income countries, migration and remittances remained a channel to alleviate labour market tensions and support domestic demand.

Inflation declines, but tensions re-emerge

Inflation fell throughout the region in 2012. Following sharp increases in food and fuel prices last year, inflation slowed down markedly in the non-energy exporters. Inflation accelerated again in the second half of the year, however. In the Russian Federation, the implementation of postponed administrative price increases and a poor grain harvest resulted in growing inflationary pressure in the last months of the year and annual inflation is estimated to exceed 5 per cent. In other CIS economies, inflation rates varied in 2012 from about 0.5 per cent in Georgia to over 60.0 per cent in Belarus, where the currency drastically depreciated in the aftermath of a balance-of-payments crisis. Except for Belarus, inflation is expected to stay up during 2013 as the disinflation process will be counteracted by further increases in regulated prices across the CIS. Other factors pushing prices up include expected nominal wage increases in energy-exporters and higher foreign-exchange earnings pushing up money supply and domestic demand.

Monetary policy loosening comes to a standstill

Despite the continued strength of domestic demand and, in some countries, accelerating credit growth, benign inflationary trends created room for some monetary loosening early in the year. However, renewed inflationary pressures put an end to the monetary easing. In the Russian Federation, capital outflows tightened monetary conditions, obviating the need for further increasing the policy interest rate. In Belarus, the improvement of financial indicators after last year's devaluation led to large cuts in the refinancing rate, which were accompanied by rapid monetary growth in the presence of still significant inflationary expectations. Despite low inflation, there was no strong move towards monetary easing in Ukraine, because of concerns regarding the stability of the national currency. Monetary authorities moved to support the currency by limiting domestic and import demand through limits on the supply of credit after imposing stricter reserve requirements for commercial banks. Despite a more complicated inflationary outlook, further weakening of the CIS economies may require further monetary easing.

Sustained economic growth has boosted revenues, although non-energy exporters have continued to face difficult fiscal positions. By contrast, the Russian Federation and other oil- and natural gas-rich countries continue to enjoy the fiscal space required to support their recoveries in the face of a difficult global environment. In Ukraine, after a large adjustment in 2011, fiscal consolidation was undermined by rapid expenditure growth in the run-up to the parliamentary elections and the negative impact of a slowing economy on revenues. Delays in rising gas tariffs resulted in continued large financial transfers to the state-owned oil and gas company Naftogaz. Oil funds of several CIS countries, which were partially depleted during the financial crisis, have been quickly rebuilt, such as in Kazakhstan and the Russian Federation, in particular. By contrast, the non-energy exporting countries continue to face fiscal tensions. In the Kyrgyz Republic, for instance, slowing GDP growth owing to the problems in the gold sector and growing pressures to increase agricultural subsidies sharply widened the fiscal deficit.

Economic growth has boosted government revenue

Export growth moderated throughout the region as a result of lower global demand. While oil prices remained elevated, current-account surpluses shrank in most energy-producing countries, including the Russian Federation, which makes the largest contribution to the aggregate surplus balance in the region. By contrast, Belarus made some progress in reducing its large current-account deficit, partly thanks to reduced energy import bills from the Russian Federation. The deficit also fell in most small non-energy exporters, but the gap is still very large and a major source of economic fragility in Armenia, Georgia and the Republic of Moldova, in particular. Lower cotton prices contributed to a shrinking surplus in Uzbekistan. The high cost of energy imports and falling steel prices kept the deficit large in Ukraine, despite sharply declining growth.

The fragility of the world economy continues to weigh on the economic prospects of the region, which remains exposed to a worsening of the global situation, particularly in Europe, the main economic partner. Any further deterioration in the external environment will result in falling export demand, lower commodity prices and difficulties in accessing finance. Growing expenditures in the Russian Federation have increased the region's vulnerability to a decline in oil prices, but the implementation of fiscal consolidation plans and a lower dependence on capital inflows are expected to increase resilience. In Ukraine, fragile fiscal and international reserve positions reduce the policy space for addressing a further deterioration in the global environment. Other medium-term risks emerge from a weak banking sector and a high share of non-performing loans, especially in Kazakhstan and in a number of smaller CIS economies.

Risks for CIS economies remain elevated

Developing economies

Developing economies saw a slowdown in their aggregate growth rate in 2012 to 4.7 per cent, compared with 5.7 per cent in 2011. There were two major outliers from this performance: Africa, which registered a sharp increase in growth to 5.0 per cent in 2012 after a more pronounced slowdown in 2011 caused by the political changes in North Africa; and Western Asia, where growth decreased markedly, mainly owing to the weaker performance of the oil-importing countries in the subregion.

In the outlook, developing economies will register a moderate acceleration in economic growth to 5.1 per cent in 2013 and 5.6 per cent in 2014. An outlier will again be Africa, which will experience a modest slowdown in growth in 2013 stemming from the vanishing base effect of the rebound in growth in North Africa. While these rates remain below those achieved in the years before the economic crisis, they still set developing economies apart from the much lower growth rates of developed economies. The reasons for this include relatively greater policy space in a number of developing economies to address weakening demand, expanding trade and finance ties between developing economies, as well as the still solid price levels for a number of export commodities.

Africa: solid growth expected with a more favourable risk profile

Despite the global slowdown, Africa's economic growth rate (excluding Libya) will see a visible rebound to 4.5 per cent in 2013 compared to 3.4 per cent in 2012 (figure IV.6). The upward trend is expected to continue in 2014, with growth reaching 5.0 per cent. Key factors underpinning Africa's strong growth prospects include solid growth in oil-exporting countries, supported by increased oil production, and still elevated oil prices (box IV.2), as well as increased fiscal expenditure, especially on infrastructure. At the same time, Africa's increasing trade and investment ties with emerging and developing economies are likely to mitigate the impact of negative shocks emanating from the recession in Europe. Similarly, other growth factors, such as increasing domestic demand associated with rising incomes and urbanization, will help reduce vulnerability to external shocks. Increasing diversification into services, such as telecommunication, construction and other non-primary commodity sectors, including manufacturing, also contribute to Africa's positive growth outlook in the medium term.

Figure IV.6
GDP growth rates for selected African economies, 2012–2013

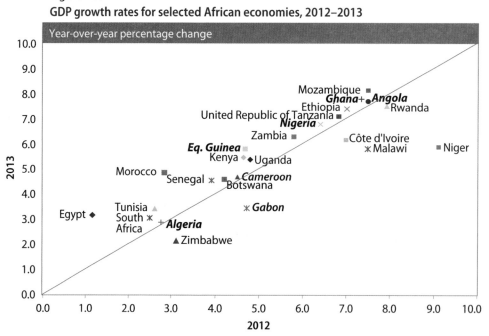

Source: UN/DESA.
Note: Oil exporters in bold.

Box IV.2

New oil discoveries and the implications for growth in Africa

Recent discoveries and key features

In 2012, Kenya became the latest frontier for new oil discoveries in Africa, following a series of previously announced discoveries, notably in Ghana, Sierra Leone and Uganda. Ghana's Jubilee field, with an estimated total reserve of 490 million barrels of high quality oil, is expected to yield government revenues of $1 billion on average per year between 2011 and 2029, based on a long-run price assumption of $75 per barrel. In Uganda, the Lake Albert Rift Basin is estimated to have oil reserves of 1.1 billion barrels, translating into 100,000 to 300,000 barrels of oil per day.[a] Oil production started in Ghana in 2010 and there are plans to begin production in Uganda in the coming years. These discoveries potentially add to the nine existing major oil-exporting countries (Algeria, Angola, Cameroon, Chad, Congo, Equatorial Guinea, Gabon, Libya and Nigeria).[b]

Past performance of oil-exporting African countries

Examining the economic performance of the African countries already exporting oil shows that, in general, oil exporters have tended to fare better in terms of average income growth than non-oil exporters. However, one of the major issues is that the relatively high overall growth of oil exporters has not delivered the expected benefits. The enormous revenues from oil have not measurably boosted per capita incomes in many countries, and where they have, it has been unequally distributed. For example, Nigeria has exported over $700 billion in oil between 1980 and 2010[c] (which breaks down to almost 40 per cent of per capita income on a yearly basis), and yet the country's per capita income is barely above the average for Africa. As well, despite having one of the highest GDP per capita in Africa, Equatorial Guinea is still only ranked 136 in the United Nations Human Development Index, whereas Kenya, with a per capita income less than one tenth that of Equatorial Guinea, is ranked 143. This points to either severe mismanagement of the revenue or significant concentration of the oil wealth.

Natural resource dependence of selected oil-exporting African countries, 2010

	Resource exports (percentage of non-resource GDP)	Resource revenue (percentage of total revenue)	GDP per capita (United States dollars)
Angola	110.6	75.9	4,423
Cameroon	10.5	26.6	1,143
Chad	60.2	67.6	676
Congo	224.1	79.0	2,943
Equatorial Guinea	171.6	88.1	19,998
Gabon	116.3	53.9	8,643
Nigeria	54.3	72.2	1,222

Source: IMF, *Regional Economic Outlook: Sub-Saharan Africa*, October 2012.

As a result of the oil wealth, the economies of a number of these oil-rich countries have been distorted and they are now heavily dependent on the revenues from oil production (table). The size of the oil revenues relative to the rest of the economy has resulted in real exchange-rate appreciation and lack of economic diversification. The reliance on and ample availability of those revenues has weakened governance and become a source of rent-seeking behaviour.[d] Evidence suggests that countries that are fiscally dependent on oil experienced significantly higher volatility in exports, revenue and non-oil GDP growth.[e] This is largely attributed to the high volatility in world market prices of natural resources compared to other goods, which leads to higher volatility of budget revenues and risks macroeconomic stability in fiscally dependent countries. In addition, the net barter terms of trade have depended heavily on changes in oil prices, which declined in the 1980s, remained flat

a Ernest Aryeetey and others, "Foresight Africa: The Continent's Greatest Challenges and Opportunities for 2011" (Africa Growth Initiative at Brookings, January 2011), pp. 22-24.

b Prior to the breakup, Sudan would have been included in this list. Given recent conflicts between Sudan and South Sudan, it is difficult to estimate what combined exports for the two countries are likely to be going forward.

c International Monetary Fund, World Economic Outlook database, October 2012.

d Pedro Conceição, Ricardo Fuentes and Sebastian Levine, "Managing natural resources for human development in low-income countries", Working Paper, No. 2011-002 (UNDP Regional Bureau for Africa, December 2011).

e International Monetary Fund, *Regional Economic Outlook: Sub-Saharan Africa—Sustaining Growth amid Global Uncertainty* (Washington, D.C., October 2012).

Box IV.2 (cont'd)

in the 1990s and jumped up significantly in the last decade, particularly between 2004 and 2008 (figure). This implies that the countries with new oil discoveries will have to be well served by countercyclical macroeconomic policies, including through the use of oil stabilization funds, to smooth use of the newly acquired wealth over time.

Net barter terms of trade for selected African oil exporters

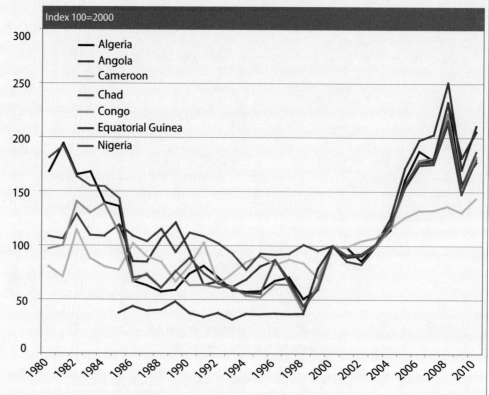

Index 100=2000

- Algeria
- Angola
- Cameroon
- Chad
- Congo
- Equatorial Guinea
- Nigeria

Source: World Bank.

Policy options for African countries

The recent discoveries have occurred in countries with low levels of income per capita and high economic and social inequalities. It is natural that expectations of their citizens would be raised and hopes for improved conditions voiced. The track record of managing and redistributing oil wealth has been less than stellar among most of the existing oil exporters in the region. Yet, if well-managed, new oil discoveries could present unique opportunities for accelerated growth and development in Africa. While it seems likely that the new oil discoveries will boost the GDP of these countries, the real questions are whether those gains are sustainable and how they are distributed. Achieving sustainability and equitable distribution requires a mix of policy options that addresses short-term fiscal issues and long-term investments and sustainability concerns. There are a few primary-exporting countries in the region that have been moderately successful in meeting these goals, such as Botswana, through its Community Based Natural Resource Management (CBNRM). While CBNRM in Botswana was not based on management of oil revenues, it is nonetheless a good example of establishing the appropriate relationships between the communities directly affected by the extraction operations, the Government and the resource extractors (or end users). There have also been relatively recent efforts by Angola to establish an oil-financed sovereign wealth fund to aid in diversification of the economy through investments in domestic agriculture, water, power and transportation projects. The planned creation of Stabilization and Heritage Funds outlined in Ghana's Petroleum Revenue Management Bill would utilize oil revenues both to cushion against oil price volatility and to support future social programmes.

Economic growth in North Africa is forecast to rebound strongly in 2013 and 2014 in the aftermath of the Arab Spring, despite continued uncertainty. Egypt is expected to grow at 3.2 per cent in 2013 as concerns over stability dissipate with increased external support. Libya's economy is expected to recover to its pre-crisis level, while growth in Algeria, Mauritania, Morocco and Sudan will benefit from the end of the drought. However, the protracted and unresolved euro area sovereign debt crisis still threatens the economies of the subregion through the trade and tourism channels.

North Africa is forecast to see a strong recovery in the wake of the Arab Spring

Central, Eastern, Southern and West Africa's economies continue to see a generally vibrant development in domestic demand, based on strong investment in view of the shortfall in infrastructure and the expansion of service sectors such as telecommunications and construction. This applies, for example, to Kenya, which is expected to maintain relatively robust growth of 5.4 per cent in 2013, with a rebound in domestic investment helped further by lower interest rates.

In the rest of Africa, infrastructure investment and expanding service sectors drive domestic demand

South Africa will register accelerating growth of 3.1 per cent in 2013 in view of a stabilizing international economic environment that is particularly relevant for its resources and manufacturing sector. On the domestic side, however, growth will be held back by continued high unemployment. In addition, further labour unrest and social tensions emanating from pervasive inequalities continue to form a significant downside risk to economic growth.

South Africa will see solid growth that is tempered by high unemployment and inequality

The oil-producing economies in Central, Southern and West Africa will benefit from sustained strong demand for oil and elevated export prices. In Nigeria, growth is forecast to accelerate to 6.8 per cent in 2013, with non-oil sectors such as telecommunications and construction providing significant impetus to economic activity. The positive impact of the oil and services sectors on growth is similar in Ghana, where solid agricultural output and increasing production by gold mines are forecast to lend additional support to the economic performance. Other economies that will benefit from conditions in the oil market include Angola, Cameroon, Chad, Equatorial Guinea and Gabon. However, this exposure to the international oil market also implies a major downside risk in the case of a significant fall in oil prices that could be triggered, for example, by a more pronounced global slowdown. Capacity-increasing investments in their mining sectors will be important drivers of GDP growth in countries like United Republic of Tanzania and Zambia, even though these mineral and metal exporting countries will also be vulnerable to volatile commodity prices and slowing international demand, especially from China.

Despite the positive growth picture, the employment situation remains a major problem across the region, both in terms of the level of employment as well as the quality of jobs that are generated, especially in North Africa. Wide gender disparities in employment and earnings remain a major concern. Women face unemployment rates at least double that of men in countries such as Algeria and Egypt. High youth unemployment is a further concern. With the fast growth of the labour force, the solid rates of GDP growth have proven far from sufficient to absorb all new labour market entrants, given the current pattern of production and employment generation. The lack of economic diversification away from the heavy dependence on resource extraction or agriculture is a key reason why labour demand is not more dynamic. Continued growth in other sectors like telecommunications and construction in countries such as Ghana, Kenya and Nigeria is helping to change this situation, however. At the same time, labour conflicts and social unrest constitute a major downside risk to the economic performance of the region. In South Africa, for example, a labour conflict in the mining sector caused the loss of numerous

Unemployment remains a pressing problem

lives and major disruptions in a crucial sector of the economy in 2012. Strikes by public sector workers also occurred in Kenya and the United Republic of Tanzania, causing major disruptions in the health and education sectors.

Inflation is moderating, but remains high in some countries

On average, inflation rates will recede moderately across the region in view of the weakening international environment and the fading one-off impact of drought conditions on harvest yields and domestic food prices. In South Africa, upward inflation pressure from wage growth and higher regulated prices will increasingly be offset by weakening commodity prices, resulting in an expected inflation rate of 4.2 per cent in 2013. Côte d'Ivoire will register one of the lowest inflation rates in the region; a more stable political situation and the normalization of trading activities on local markets will keep price increases limited to 2.1 per cent in 2013. By contrast, some of the oil-exporting economies are expected to see high inflation. In the case of Nigeria, government spending, especially at the state level, will keep inflation above 10 per cent in 2013, while strong domestic consumption will keep inflation in Angola and Ghana at about 10 per cent and 8 per cent, respectively, in 2013. A number of countries will see a continuation of a pronounced downward trend in inflation rates. In Kenya and Uganda, for example, the high inflation rates of late 2011 and early 2012 have been brought down mainly through decreases in food price inflation and by aggressive interest-rate policies which contained currency depreciation in these countries. Barring a return of significant drought conditions, inflation will continue to moderate and remain in single digits in 2013.

Fiscal budgets will have to address multiple policy challenges

Fiscal budgets will remain under pressure on a number of fronts. The lack of adequate infrastructure will require significant investments, while extremely low coverage of social security and high unemployment levels will create continuing pressure to initiate new spending to address at least some of the urgent welfare problems. At the same time, generating sufficient revenues will remain challenging for a host of reasons: many countries have only limited tax collection capabilities; oil prices will provide no additional boost to fiscal revenues for oil-exporting countries; and official development assistance (ODA) is also expected to remain under pressure, given the fiscal austerity measures among many of the donor countries. In the forecast, fiscal policies will remain relatively loose in 2013, with many economies running budget deficits, while some move towards consolidation is expected in 2014.

Although Africa's average current-account deficit narrowed to just 0.6 per cent of GDP in 2012, oil-exporting countries recorded a surplus of 3.7 per cent compared to a deficit of 6.9 per cent for oil-importing countries. Current-account deficits widened in many countries because of large food and energy imports and dependence on imported services. With increased pressure exerted by widening current-account deficits, domestic currencies depreciated against the United States dollar in several oil-importing countries. The pressure is forecast to continue in the medium term owing to increased demand for imported capital goods in many countries and the knock-on effect of the recession in Europe on demand for African exports.

The global economic picture will put pressure on ODA

Aid flows to Africa are expected to stabilize or even decline in 2013 and 2014 following the global economic slowdown and fiscal difficulties in many donor countries. Africa's external debt is expected to rise because of increased external financing needs of some of the Arab Spring countries, such as Egypt and Tunisia, and borrowing in private capital markets by countries such as Ghana, Senegal and South Africa.

The outlook is subject to a number of risks and uncertainties. A more severe and broader global economic slowdown encompassing emerging economies would hold the potential to inflict significant damage on the region's performance through a contraction in trade, tourism and remittances. Moreover, the fiscal problems in developed economies continue to create uncertainty regarding future ODA flows. In addition, unexpected adverse weather conditions that would negatively affect harvest yields pose another downside risk, given the significant role of the agricultural sector in many economies.

East Asia: slowdown in China and recession in Europe weigh on regional growth

Sluggish demand in developed economies and a sharper-than-expected slowdown in China have weighed on economic growth in East Asia over the past year. The region's aggregate gross domestic product expanded by 5.8 per cent in 2012, down from 7.1 per cent in 2011 and 9.2 per cent in 2010 as export growth faltered and investment spending in many economies slowed. Household consumption continued to grow at a robust pace in most countries, supported by resilient labour markets and a decline in inflation. In the outlook, GDP growth in the region is forecast to pick up to an average of 6.2 per cent in 2013 and 6.5 per cent in 2014, supported by a modest recovery in external demand and more expansionary monetary and fiscal policy.

In China, the pace of economic expansion declined from 9.2 per cent in 2011 to 7.7 per cent in 2012, the lowest rate in more than a decade. Weaker export demand and a sharp decline in investment growth, especially in the real estate sector, dampened overall output growth. Because of more structural problems, there is a risk of a possible hard landing of the Chinese economy (see chapter I), but it is not considered very high in the immediate outlook. In 2013, consumption and investment demand in China will be supported by the loosening of monetary and fiscal policy, with full-year growth projected to pick up slightly to 7.9 per cent. Weaker domestic demand in China, along with the recession in the euro area and subdued demand in Japan and the United States, weighed heavily on activity in East Asia's higher-income and export-dependent economies. Hong Kong Special Administrative Region of China, the Republic of Korea, Singapore and Taiwan Province of China saw a sharp drop-off in growth in 2012 as subdued demand for exports led to lower capital spending. Along with a modest expected improvement in global conditions, these economies are likely to see moderate recovery in 2013 and 2014, but growth is projected to remain well below potential.

The slowdown in China and the higher-income economies of East Asia contrasts with the solid growth momentum in Indonesia, Malaysia, the Philippines and Thailand, where buoyant consumption and investment demand largely offset lower net exports. The strong growth performance in the Philippines and Thailand was supported by significant rises in public investment spending, but also reflects a base effect following weak growth in 2011. Growth in this group of countries is forecast to remain fairly stable in 2013.

Labour markets in East Asia have so far remained resilient to the slowdown in growth, although unemployment rates edged up in some of the region's export-dependent economies in the course of 2012. In several countries, including Malaysia, the Republic of Korea and Singapore, the unemployment rate continues to be close to historic lows as robust domestic demand helped offset the impact of weaker exports and manufacturing activity. In Indonesia, unemployment declined to 6.3 per cent in the first quarter of 2012, about half the rate of 2006. As in other East Asian countries, most of the new jobs in Indonesia have been created in the service sector, where productivity continues to be much lower than in the manufacturing sector. As a result, the share of workers in vulnerable

Export-dependent economies have seen the largest drop-off in growth

Labour market conditions have so far remained fairly resilient to the slowdown

employment conditions remains high, ranging from about 20 per cent in Malaysia according to International Labour Organization (ILO) estimates to 50 per cent in Thailand and 60 per cent in Indonesia. Since labour markets tend to react with a lag to weakening economic activity, employment growth in many countries is likely to slow in the quarters ahead. Unemployment rates are expected to show little change in 2013 and 2014.

Inflationary pressures are projected to remain low

Inflation has declined significantly in East Asia over the past year as domestic demand softened and many international commodity prices eased. For the region as a whole, consumer price inflation averaged 2.9 per cent in 2012, well below the rate of 4.9 per cent recorded in 2011. In most economies, including China, Indonesia and the Republic of Korea, the current rate of inflation is firmly within the target ranges set by central banks. The recent hikes in the international prices of several food commodities, notably corn, soybeans and wheat, have not led to a significant increase in food price inflation across the region. This can be attributed to the relatively small weight of these grains in consumer price index baskets and the fact that prices of rice, East Asia's staple food, have remained stable. Looking forward, consumer price inflation across the region is projected to remain relatively low as more moderate economic growth will not lead to significant demand-pull pressures. In addition, the strength of regional currencies against the dollar and the euro is expected to contain imported inflation. Regional inflation is projected to average 3.1 per cent in 2013 and 3.5 per cent in 2014, in line with an expected gradual recovery in growth. Upside risks to inflation include the re-emergence of strong capital inflows following the new round of quantitative easing (QE) policies in developed economies, the impact of planned subsidy reductions (for instance, in Indonesia and Malaysia) and strong nominal wage growth, especially in China, Thailand and Viet Nam.

Central banks have shifted focus from inflation to growth

Against the backdrop of slowing economic activity and reduced inflationary pressures, East Asia's monetary authorities have shifted focus from containing inflation to stimulating growth. After tightening monetary policy in 2010/11, many central banks have cut interest rates over the past year to support domestic demand. The People's Bank of China (PBC) reduced the one-year benchmark deposit rate by a total of 50 basis points to 3 per cent and the one-year benchmark loan rate by 56 basis points to 6 per cent. The PBC also lowered the reserve requirement ratio for deposit-taking institutions and used open-market operations to inject liquidity into the banking sector. Similarly, the central banks in Indonesia, the Philippines, the Republic of Korea and Thailand eased monetary policy in the course of 2012. In contrast to the cautious approach taken by other monetary authorities in the region, the State Bank of Viet Nam cut interest rates aggressively in the first half of 2012 amid rapidly declining inflation and weakening growth. However, the re-emergence of inflationary pressures in the third quarter reduced the scope for further monetary easing in Viet Nam. The monetary authorities in Hong Kong Special Administrative Region of China, Singapore and Taiwan Province of China have so far refrained from loosening monetary policy despite markedly lower growth. In the quarters ahead, some further monetary easing in East Asia may take place. However, unless the regional outlook deteriorates significantly, most central banks will maintain their cautious approach.

Fiscal policy has become more expansionary to counter the slowdown

Across East Asia, Governments adopted a more expansionary fiscal policy in the course of 2012 as the economic slowdown became increasingly apparent. In Indonesia, Malaysia, the Republic of Korea, Thailand and Viet Nam, the authorities introduced low-interest loans, cash transfers to low-income households, lower tax rates and tax breaks to fuel private sector demand and mitigate the social impact of the slowdown. The Governments in China, Indonesia and the Philippines also announced increases in public infrastructure spending. The size of these fiscal injections is, however, small relative to the unprecedented policy responses in the wake of the global financial crisis. As a result of rising expenditures and weaker revenue growth, fiscal balances deteriorated in 2012. Still, budget deficits remained below 3 per cent of GDP in all East Asian economies, except Malaysia and Viet Nam. Going forward, fiscal deficits are projected to narrow as a share of GDP in most countries, as income growth and government revenues are expected to recover gradually and authorities remain committed to long-term fiscal sustainability. While low deficit and debt levels imply that most Governments have ample room for additional fiscal stimulus measures, they are only expected to do so if growth prospects deteriorate more sharply.

Trade and current-account surpluses in most East Asian economies narrowed in 2012 (figure IV.7) as exports decelerated more rapidly than imports. The weakness in export earnings across the region reflects subdued import demand in developed economies, slowing demand in China and a decline in the prices of many export commodities, such as rubber and copper. The region was particularly affected by the fall in EU demand for machinery, transport equipment and other manufactures. Compared to 2011, the dollar value of merchandise exports remained flat or declined slightly in most East Asian economies, including Indonesia, Malaysia, the Republic of Korea and Taiwan Province of China. At the same time, import bills continued to grow in most countries, although much more slowly than in the past two years. In Indonesia, however, import growth remained robust owing to strong domestic demand, resulting in a sharp contraction of the trade surplus and the first annual current-account deficit in 15 years. China's external surplus, in contrast, did not decline, as export earnings continued to grow in 2012. Although export growth was weaker than in 2011, it outpaced import growth. In 2013, East Asia's exports and imports are projected to grow at a subdued pace given the continuing weakness in global conditions. Trade and current-account balances are expected to improve slightly.

Current-account surpluses decline owing to a slump in exports

Figure IV.7
Current-account balances of selected East Asian economies, 2000-2012

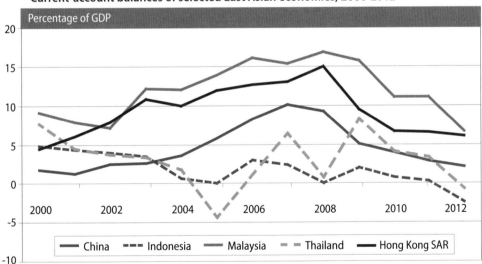

Source: UN/DESA based on data from EIU and national sources.
Note: Figures for 2012 are partly estimated.

Even though economic fundamentals remain strong, risks to the region's economic outlook remain tilted to the downside. A further deterioration of the sovereign debt crisis in Europe remains a major risk for East Asia's economies since it would likely lead to renewed turmoil on financial markets and a sharp contraction in global trade activity.

Euro area crisis and a possible hard landing of China's economy remain key risks

A sharp deceleration in the pace of growth in China would have a severe impact on economic activity in the region, with Hong Kong Special Administrative Region of China, Singapore and Taiwan likely to suffer most from lower demand for their exports. Fiscal policy uncertainty in the United States and continued geopolitical risks in oil-producing areas represent additional risk factors for regional growth.

South Asia: internal and external headwinds further weaken economic activity

Economic activity in South Asia slowed further in 2012 as internal and external headwinds persisted. After growing by 5.8 per cent in 2011, the region's gross domestic product expanded by 4.4 per cent in 2012, the slowest pace in a decade. Persistent high inflation, political uncertainties, and transport and energy constraints have weighed on household consumption and business investment. At the same time, the exports of most countries in the region have been affected by weakening global demand. In most countries, the scope for macroeconomic policies to support growth is limited. Central banks are trying to walk a fine line between supporting demand and curbing inflation, while Governments face pressures to bring down budget deficits. Going forward, economic growth in the region is projected to accelerate moderately to 5.0 per cent on average in 2013 and 5.7 per cent in 2014, led by a gradual recovery in India.

India's economic growth slows to a ten-year low

India's economy, which accounts for almost three quarters of the region's GDP, has slowed markedly over the past two years. Annual growth declined from more than 9 per cent in 2010 to 5.5 per cent in 2012, the slowest pace in 10 years. The slowdown primarily reflects weaker consumption and investment demand as a result of persistent inflation, high nominal interest rates, large fiscal deficits and political gridlock. These factors will likely remain a drag on economic growth in the outlook period. Nonetheless, GDP growth is forecast to accelerate moderately to 6.1 per cent in 2013, as a result of stronger growth of exports and capital investment. Investment demand is expected to respond to the more accommodative monetary policy stance and slightly improved business confidence.

Nepal and Pakistan continue to experience subdued growth as ongoing political instability and security concerns weigh on domestic demand. In Pakistan, investment has been in decline for four consecutive years, down to only 12.5 per cent of GDP in 2011/12. Economic activity in the Islamic Republic of Iran contracted in 2012 as international sanctions led to a sharp decline in oil exports and a sharp fall in the value of the rial. Economic prospects for Bangladesh and Sri Lanka, in contrast, remain largely favourable despite a moderate slowdown in 2012. In both countries, the economic expansion is based on strong growth in private investment and consumption, which is supported by a steady increase in worker's remittances.

South Asia continues to struggle with deep-rooted structural challenges in its labour market

Given the lack of sufficiently up-to-date labour market data in South Asia, the employment impact of the recent economic slowdown is not yet clear. The fourteenth report on employment changes in selected sectors, published by India's Labour Bureau in May 2012, indicates that employment growth in the country's manufacturing sector had slowed considerably during 2011/12. According to the survey, employment continued to increase in India's exporting firms, but declined in the non-exporting sector amid weakening domestic demand. Although open unemployment rates in the region are low—the ILO projects an average unemployment rate for the region of only 3.8 per cent in 2012—there are deep-rooted structural challenges in the labour market. These challenges include the dominance of low-productivity jobs in the large informal sector, high shares of working poor, low female participation rates and high youth unemployment. Recent labour market reports for India and Pakistan illustrate the magnitude of these challenges. In India, less than 20 per cent of persons are classified as wage earners, whereas about 80 per cent are either self-employed or temporary workers. The female labour force participation rate in India is estimated at 25.4 per cent, compared to 77.4 per cent for males. In Pakistan, three quarters of employed women work in the agricultural sector, the large majority of them in vulnerable employment conditions.

Inflationary pressures remained persistently high in most South Asian economies over the past year (figure IV.8). Consumer price inflation averaged 11.6 per cent in the region in 2012, slightly up from 11.2 per cent in 2011. The renewed rise in inflation can be attributed to several factors: droughts in parts of the region, higher world food prices, significant depreciation of local currencies, and increases in administered fuel and electricity prices. Deeply entrenched inflationary expectations and large fiscal deficits, particularly in India and Pakistan, further added to the price pressures. Year-on-year inflation rose to about 25 per cent in the Islamic Republic of Iran in late 2012, as the removal of government subsidies and the fall of the rial against the dollar drove up domestic prices.

 Inflation remains persistently high

Bangladesh and Pakistan, in contrast, experienced a moderate decline in inflation over the course of 2012, partly owing to more subdued growth of private sector credit. In the outlook, consumer price inflation is projected to decline slightly in most economies, averaging 10.6 per cent in 2013 and 9.9 per cent in 2014 for the region as a whole. More stable local currencies, lower global food prices and slower money supply growth are expected to reduce price pressures. However, persistently high inflation expectations, severe supply bottlenecks and the need to further raise administered energy prices will impede progress in reducing inflation.

Figure IV.8
Consumer price inflation in selected South Asian countries, January 2010-October 2012 (year-on-year percentage change)

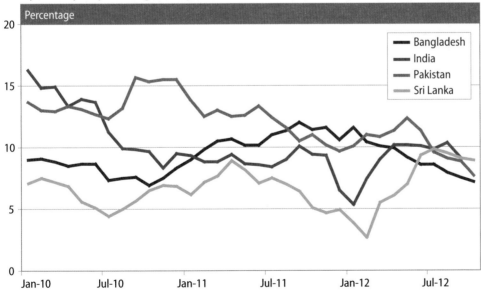

Source: UN/DESA, based on data from national sources.
Notes: For India, inflation in consumer price index numbers for industrial workers was used, provided by the Labour Bureau of the Government of India.

Persistent inflationary pressures and large fiscal deficits continue to limit the scope for monetary policy easing in response to slowing economic growth. The central banks of Bangladesh and Sri Lanka raised policy rates in early 2012, but left the monetary stance unchanged in the remainder of the year. Authorities of both countries are expected to maintain the current policy stance unless growth slows more sharply than expected. The Reserve Bank of India (RBI), which had increased its benchmark repo rate 13 times between March 2010 and October 2011, cut interest rates only slightly in 2012, even though investment demand slumped. To boost liquidity in the banking system, the RBI also reduced the cash reserve ratio for banks. While India's monetary authorities remain focused on containing inflation and anchoring inflation expectations, continued weakness in private capital spending is expected to prompt further monetary easing in the quarters ahead. Unlike the RBI, the State Bank of Pakistan (SBP) has fully shifted its focus to strengthening private investment, which has declined for four consecutive years, and supporting domestic demand. The SBP cut its main policy rate from 12 per cent to 10 per cent in 2012. If inflation continues to slow in the coming quarters, additional interest rate reductions are likely.

Slower growth and higher subsidy bills weigh on fiscal balances

Weakening growth of tax revenues, rising expenditures on energy, food and fertilizer subsidies, and higher security spending have all put additional pressures on fiscal balances in South Asia. In almost all countries, the deficit reduction targets for the past fiscal year were missed by a considerable margin. Despite increased efforts to lower spending on subsidies, this trend is likely to continue as Governments face major fiscal challenges, including strong expenditure demands that will address energy shortages, enhance welfare spending, and narrow tax bases. In India, the government deficit widened to 5.8 per cent of GDP in 2011/12, well above the target of 4.6 per cent. The shortfall can be primarily attributed to lower-than-expected corporate tax revenues, following the marked economic slowdown, and higher subsidy expenditure as food and fuel prices remained elevated. Actual government deficits also exceeded initial targets in other South Asian economies during the past fiscal year, accounting for 5.2 per cent of GDP in Bangladesh, 6.2 per cent in Sri Lanka and 6.3 per cent in Pakistan.

Trade deficits widened further as exports were hit by the global slowdown

In most South Asian economies, trade and current-account deficits widened significantly in 2012. Exports were hit hard by weakening demand in key markets, including the EU, the United States and China. The annual value of merchandise exports declined moderately in India, Pakistan and Sri Lanka, reflecting both lower volumes and lower prices of major export commodities like rubber and cotton. In the Islamic Republic of Iran, export earnings contracted by more than 25 per cent in 2012 following the tightening of sanctions. In most South Asian countries, import spending growth also declined sharply in 2012, although import bills continued to be pushed up by high oil prices and still robust consumer spending. An important factor behind the slowdown in import spending was the sharp depreciation of local currencies. The Indian rupee, for example, lost more than 25 per cent of its value against the dollar between June 2011 and June 2012. The weakness in the region's currencies can be attributed to large and rising current-account deficits as well as a sharp decline in portfolio inflows amid recurring concerns over the regional and global outlook. Workers' remittance flows to Bangladesh, Pakistan and Sri Lanka continued to grow at a strong pace in 2012, partially offsetting the large trade deficits. In the outlook period, South Asia's economies will continue to record large and partly widening current-account deficits.

Downside risks to the economic outlook for South Asia are related to the continued weakness of the global macroeconomic environment and to regional or domestic economic vulnerabilities. On the external side, a further economic downturn in the United States or Europe or a hard landing of China's economy would further weaken South Asia's exports, while also reducing inflows from workers' remittances. Widening current-account deficits, coupled with lower portfolio capital inflows, could add pressure on the balance of payments, possibly requiring contractionary policy adjustment. Political instability and deteriorating security conditions represent downside risks for several countries, notably the Islamic Republic of Iran, Nepal and Pakistan.

Western Asia: economic growth diverges between oil and non-oil economies

Economic performance in Western Asia strongly diverged in 2012, with most oil-exporting countries continuing to experience robust though decelerating growth, supported by record-high oil revenues and government spending. By contrast, economic activity weakened sharply in oil-importing countries, burdened by higher import bills, declining external demand and shrinking policy space. The divergence is expected to continue in the outlook for 2013, but there may be some convergence in 2014. On average, GDP growth in the region is estimated to decline from 6.7 per cent in 2011 to 3.3 per cent in 2012 (figure IV.9). It is forecast to stagnate in 2013 before picking up to 4.1 per cent in 2014.

Figure IV.9
GDP growth in Western Asia

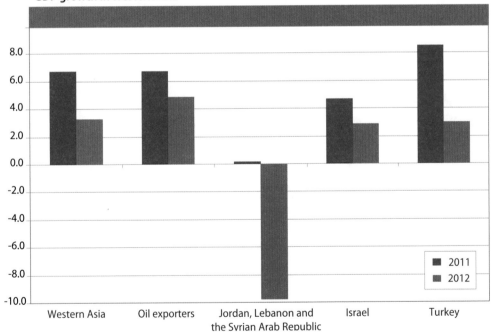

Source: UN/DESA.

Most oil-exporting countries benefitted from record-high oil prices and rising oil output in 2012, especially Iraq, Kuwait and Saudi Arabia. Strong growth in Saudi Arabia was further underpinned by the expansion of domestic demand and a dynamic real estate sector. Public and private investments bolstered growth in Qatar. Economic activity grew more modestly in Bahrain, Oman and the United Arab Emirates as the financial and real estate sectors gradually recovered. Political instability delayed any possible recovery in Yemen.

Negative spillover from the Syrian crisis affected neighbouring countries and the region at large

Social unrest and political instability, notably the civil war in the Syrian Arab Republic, weighed on risk perception in the entire region (box IV.3). Neighbouring Jordan and Lebanon were further affected by subdued cross-border economic activities, including trade, investment and tourism.

Box IV.3

The economic impact of the Syrian crisis

Lasting armed violence in the Syrian Arab Republic caused a humanitarian crisis and inflicted significant economic damage, including the destruction of commercial and residential properties, infrastructures and production facilities. In his address to the parliament on October 2, the Syrian Prime Minister estimated the cost of total damages at 2000 billion Syrian pounds,[a] which amounts to 55 per cent of the 2010 GDP after adjusting for inflation. Furthermore, at least one third of the 2010 capital stock may have been destroyed as of October 2012. Despite the Government's effort to increase employment in the public sector, unemployment increased significantly from an annual average rate of 8.6 per cent in 2010 to 14.9 per cent in 2011[b] and the situation worsened significantly in 2012 as a growing number of workers became unemployed, underemployed, were deterred from reporting to work, were displaced domestically or became political refugees abroad. Under these conditions, the Syrian economy will need several years to recover after the internal armed conflict comes to an end.

Economic sanctions imposed by the United States, the EU and the League of Arab States also negatively impacted the Syrian economy. The oil embargo caused an export revenue loss of about $4 billion, cutting government revenue by about 25 per cent in 2012. Financial sanctions further hampered trade by complicating trade financing and exerting pressures on the Syrian currency. In January, the central bank had to introduce a managed float of its exchange rate, allowing the Syrian pound to devaluate by more than 30 per cent before stabilizing around SYP70/$. Although imports of many essential goods were liberalized, trade of non-sanctioned goods, such as wheat and pharmaceuticals, declined significantly. Despite the imposition of a profit ceiling on wholesalers, prices kept rising rapidly, and in August 2012, the year-on-year consumer inflation rate reached 39.5 per cent. As a consequence of ongoing armed violence and sanctions, the number of tourists had dropped by 76 per cent year on year in the first quarter of 2012 and investments from Gulf countries in tourism infrastructure have been put off indefinitely.

The Syrian economy showed some signs of resilience, however, as the public and private sectors both made efforts to maintain basic infrastructure and business activities during disastrous economic, social and security conditions.

Spillover effects on neighbouring countries and intraregional trade

Political instability and precarious security conditions affected risk perception across the region, especially regarding Iraq, Jordan and Lebanon. Capital inflows and tourist arrivals, which were the main drivers of the recent economic expansion in Jordan and Lebanon, came to a halt. As demand for foreign currencies surged in the region, the Jordanian central bank had to raise interest rates and sell foreign reserves to defend the Jordanian dinar, and the Iraqi dinar depreciated against the United States dollar. Higher risk profiles and weak currencies kept funding costs elevated in those countries, even as they declined in other parts of the region.

The Syrian crisis further affected intraregional trade (table). Bilateral trade flows between the Syrian Arab Republic and neighbouring countries decreased substantially in the first half of 2012, with the exception of Lebanon through which a rising share of Syrian imports transit to Damascus and Southern regions. The transit of goods through Syrian territory almost came to a halt, diverting to alternate routes, and new trading partnerships and networks are being formed. Turkey may have benefitted most from the partial reshuffling of bilateral trade flows in the region. Iraqi exports to Lebanon and Turkey expanded as well, whereas Jordanian exports, by contrast, appear to have suffered from the precarious security conditions along its border with the Syrian Arab Republic. Bilateral trade flows with Turkey nonetheless expanded, albeit from very low initial levels.

a Syrian Arab News Agency (SANA), "Premier al-Halqi: Syria Paying for Its Stances", October 2, available from http://sana.sy/eng/21/2012/10/02/444919.htm- (accessed on 10 October 2012).

b Data from Syrian Arab Republic Central Bureau of Statistics, available from http://www.cbssyr.org/work/2011/compare/TAB2.htm (accessed on 10 October 2012).

Box IV.3 (cont'd)

Prolonged armed violence is affecting sensitive social fabrics. While the ongoing destruction of physical and human capital in the Syrian Arab Republic will complicate efforts to rebuild the country and create a new form of social cohesion, the Syrian crisis is also progressively dismantling and reshaping trade and knowledge networks in the region with potentially long-lasting effects.

Year-on-year change in goods trade flow, January–July, 2011 and 2012

Percentage	From Jordan	From Lebanon	From Syrian Arab Republic	From Turkey
To Iraq	-14.2	-3.2	N.A.	37.2
To Jordan		14.6	-51.6	30.2
To Lebanon	-19.0		-14.4	17.1
To Syrian Arab Republic	-17.6	28.5		-67.4
To Turkey	102.2	-35.3	-82.9	

Sources: Jordan Department of Statistics, available from http://www.dos.gov.jo/dos_home_e/main/index.htm (accessed on October 15, 2012); Lebanese Customs http://www.customs.gov.lb/customs/index.htm (accessed on October 15, 2012); Turkish Statistical Institute, available from http://www.turkstat.gov.tr/Start.do (accessed on October 15, 2012).

The deteriorating external environment increasingly affected economic activity in Israel, while weakening domestic demand contributed to a sharp decline in economic growth in Turkey.

Social unrest associated with the Arab Spring surged in part because of the weak absorption capacity of labour markets across the region, which generates underemployment and unemployment. Low official unemployment rates disguise the true extent of underutilization of labour because of low participation rates. Governments of the Gulf Cooperation Council (GCC) countries have responded to social unrest by raising wages and creating new jobs in the public sector, including by strengthening security forces. Meanwhile, migrant labour represents about 90 per cent of the private sector work force across GCC countries, as a consequence of uncompetitive compensation compared to the public sector and poorly coordinated education and industrial policies that result in a skills mismatch. In Saudi Arabia, for instance, the unemployment scheme created in the wake of the Arab Spring, attracted more than a million unemployed workers, many of them women not previously considered part of the labour force.

New unemployment scheme in Saudi Arabia reveals large hidden unemployment

In Jordan, the unemployment rate declined by 0.9 percentage points to average 12.0 per cent over the first three quarters of 2012, but underemployment and vulnerable employment is widespread. In Turkey, unemployment declined slightly to almost 9 per cent in 2012. In Israel, new unemployment estimates (now aligned with OECD definitions) showed an increase in the rate by more than one percentage point to almost 7 per cent in 2012, contrasting with earlier estimates and thereby undermining claims that the country would be coping with the global slowdown with relative ease.

Fiscal policy in Western Asia was durably affected by the Arab Spring. Temporary and permanent increases in public expenditures will drag on public finances in many countries in the years ahead. While medium-run fiscal balances remain strong in many Gulf countries, the break-even price of oil for GCC countries as a whole is estimated

Budget deficits increased in oil-importing countries

to have increased from \$49 per barrel in 2008 to \$79 in 2012, with Bahrain and Oman being most vulnerable to a potential drop in oil price.

Oil-importing countries possessing limited policy buffers reacted more cautiously to political unrest. Civil servant pay raises and energy subsidies widened the budget deficit to over 6 per cent of GDP in Jordan. Lebanon's fiscal stance remained neutral during the first half of 2012, but a proposed public sector salary increase may widen the budget deficit.

In Israel, several recommendations of the Trajtenberg Committee, created in 2011 in the wake of social unrest, have been accepted by the Government, but the projected rise of the budget deficit to 3.4 per cent of GDP in 2012 is more directly related to steady military spending, which amounted to more than 6 per cent of GDP. In Turkey, slowing growth is expected to have increased the budget deficit from an estimated 1.4 per cent of GDP in 2011 to more than 2.0 per cent in 2012. Fiscal balances in Turkey and across the region are forecast to deteriorate next year.

High food and energy prices spurred weak inflationary pressures

Inflation declined across the region during the first three quarters of 2012 in the context of high commodity prices but weakening external and domestic demand. In GCC countries, inflation remained at about 3 per cent or below, except in Saudi Arabia. The housing component of the consumer price index was negative in Bahrain, Qatar and the United Arab Emirates, caused by excess supply and limited domestic demand pressures. The pass-through effect of high food and energy prices may keep inflation above 10 per cent in Yemen. In Jordan and Lebanon, inflation is likely to remain above 4 per cent in 2012, a slight decline compared to 2011.

In Israel, the consumer price index grew by 2.1 per cent during the first three quarters of 2012 following high food and housing prices, about one percentage point lower than last year. In Turkey, demand-led inflationary pressures progressively weakened during the year, but higher food and energy prices as well as value-added tax increases pushed up inflation, which may decelerate to 7 per cent at the end of the year. Barring a revival of domestic and external demand pressures or a crisis that pushes up commodity prices, inflation will likely decline further across the region in 2013.

Borrowing costs declined in most countries

Policies related to the use of conventional monetary instruments remained unchanged in most countries of the region in 2012. Policy rates in GCC countries that have their currencies pegged to the dollar remained constant, almost mirroring the stance of the Fed. Growing money stock improved liquidity conditions, contributing to slightly lower funding costs, which had increased in the wake of the Arab Spring. Meanwhile, Jordan raised its policy rate by 50 basis points in February to defend the national currency, setting the overnight repurchase agreement rate at 4.75 per cent.

The depreciating Turkish lira stabilized against the dollar at the end of 2011, as the central bank tightened monetary policy by raising overnight lending rates and widening the interest rate corridor. In parallel, reserve requirement ratios were reduced in order to prevent an undesirable tightening in liquidity conditions. In 2012, as the current-account deficit progressively declined along with domestic demand, monetary authorities continued to reduce the effective funding rate from 11 per cent in January to less than 7 per cent in September. Inflation remained above target. In Israel, weakening demand-driven inflationary pressures led the central bank to loosen monetary policy three times during the first half of the year, setting the interest rate at 2.25 per cent. As most countries across the region tie their monetary policy to the stance of central banks in advanced economies, the monetary loosening required to respond to the a grim growth perspective may only occur in those countries with independent monetary policies in 2013.

The diverging economic performance in the region is also reflected in differing trends in external imbalances. While record oil revenues boosted external surpluses in oil-exporting countries, higher import bills burdened existing deficits in oil-importing countries. In the GCC countries, current-account surpluses range from about 8 per cent of GDP in the United Arab Emirates to more than 40 per cent in Kuwait. Oil production outages caused by pipeline attacks in Yemen contributed to the external deficit.

Jordan's and Lebanon's current-account deficits widened as a result of high commodity prices and related increases in import bills, weaker export demand and declining revenue from tourism. Foreign reserves dropped by 37 per cent in Jordan over the first half of the year and reserve accumulation stalled in Lebanon.

The trade deficit also widened in Israel, putting the current-account balance into deficit in 2012. Weakening external demand led to a drop in manufacturing exports, including for high-tech goods. Turkish manufactures have started to penetrate markets in Asia, making the country less dependent on exports to European markets. The current-account deficit is expected to remain high at about 7 per cent in 2010. While external imbalances across the region are structural, their magnitude in the years ahead largely depends on commodity price developments. The discovery of gas resources in the Mediterranean is expected to generate external surpluses for Israel from 2014.

In the outlook, Western Asia faces three major downside risks. First, a more pronounced jump in oil prices—owing, for example, to renewed domestic social unrest or rising tensions around the Strait of Hormuz—could raise the oil-price risk premium and exacerbate existing current-account and fiscal imbalances. Second, if the financial woes and deeper fiscal austerity in developed countries were to trigger a global downturn, a sustained drop in the oil price would negatively affect fiscal and, eventually, social stability in oil-exporting countries. Finally, inaction in relation to the dire employment situation and, more broadly, the failure to implement effective diversification strategies based on a more inclusive development paradigm represent major risks to long-run stability and prosperity in the region.

Record-high oil prices widened external imbalances in oil-exporting and importing countries

Uncertain outlook for oil prices weighs on risk perceptions in the region

Latin America and the Caribbean: a modest acceleration in growth is expected

Latin America and the Caribbean are expected to see a modest acceleration in growth to 3.9 per cent in 2013, up from 3.1 per cent in 2012. This continued solid growth trajectory is closely tied to the performance of the Brazilian economy, which is expected to expand by 4.0 per cent in 2013. Mexico and Central America are forecast to average a growth rate of 3.9 per cent, similar to that of 2012, but vulnerable to economic conditions in the United States. In line with the regional picture, the Caribbean countries will register an acceleration in growth to 3.7 per cent in 2013, 0.8 percentage points higher than in 2012 (figure IV.10).

During 2012, economic conditions deteriorated as the stagnation in the developed world and the slowdown in China affected exports from the region. As a result, GDP growth decelerated to 3.1 per cent in 2012, from 4.3 per cent in 2011 and 6.0 per cent in 2010. Economic growth in South American countries slowed to 2.7 per cent, with Brazil and Argentina contributing greatly to the overall picture. Resilient domestic demand continues to drive growth in most of Latin America. Net export demand expanded in Mexico and Central America, benefitting from the fragile recovery in the United States, while South American economies were mainly affected by the economic slowdown in China

Figure IV.10
GDP growth forecasts in Latin America and the Caribbean, 2013

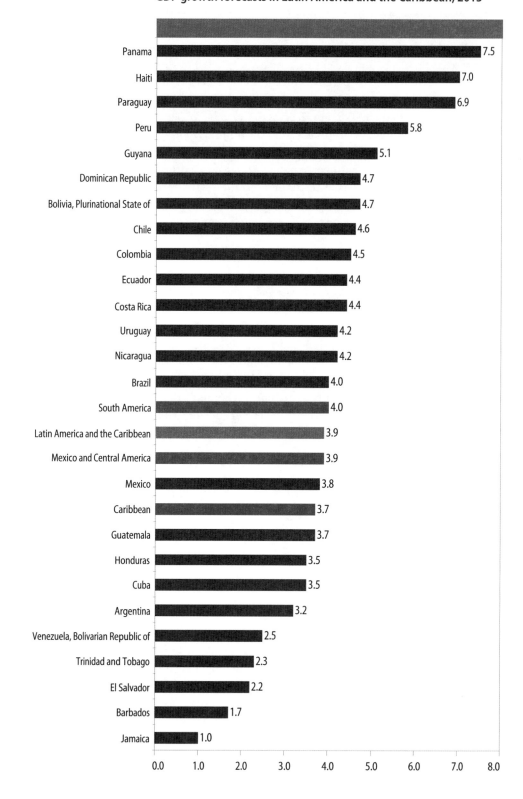

and the euro area recession. Indeed, the trade sector constitutes the main impact channel of the global downturn in the region (box IV.4). The dire economic situation in Europe is further transmitted to the region through lower workers' remittances, affecting Colombia and Ecuador in particular.

Despite the 2012 slowdown, labour market indicators continued to show a good performance, evidenced by continued increases in employment rates, higher real wages, increased female participation rates and lower unemployment. For the region as a whole, urban unemployment reached a historic low of 6.4 per cent in 2012. In the first half of the year, it was less than 6 per cent in Brazil, Ecuador, Mexico, Panama and Uruguay. Improved employment conditions strengthened private consumption, a key driver of GDP growth in recent years. During 2012, however, some signs of weakening emerged. Job creation slowed in Argentina, the Bolivarian Republic of Venezuela, Paraguay and Peru. Nonetheless, employment conditions are likely to remain steady without much further improvement during 2013.

Labour market indicators will remain strong

The outlook for inflation is fairly stable. The average annual inflation rate for the region was 6.0 per cent in 2012, down by 0.9 percentage points from 2011, and is expected to average 6.0 per cent in 2013. Increasing inflationary pressures might emerge if the shifts towards more expansionary monetary policies are pushed much further, or if there is a new surge in international food prices, especially for grains, which would affect inflation in Central America and the Caribbean in particular. However, there is no clear sign that core inflation is trending upward.

Most countries in the region still have monetary policy space to promote economic activity should global or domestic economic conditions deteriorate in 2013. However, given already robust private consumer demand, monetary expansion would need to be cautious. About half of the economies in the region began providing more monetary stimulus when the global downturn began to affect exports and economic growth. The most notable case is Brazil, which started to reduce interest rates in August 2011. The central bank has since reduced the reference rate by 525 basis points to a historic low of 7.25 per cent. Colombia, the Dominican Republic, Guatemala and Paraguay also reduced policy rates.

Monetary policy has shifted from targeting inflation to promoting economic activity

The exchange rates remain at higher levels compared to those before the global downturn, but there were diverging trends during 2012. Colombia, Chile and Peru have experienced an appreciation of their domestic currencies, while Brazil and Argentina saw theirs depreciate. The volatile behaviour of capital markets and exchange rates led many central banks, for example those of Argentina, Bahamas, Brazil, Colombia, Peru and Uruguay, to intervene actively in foreign-exchange markets. The tendency towards foreign-exchange purchases suggests that central banks were more concerned about avoiding local currency appreciation than depreciation. As a result, most countries increased their level of international reserves in the last year. Looking ahead, the QE measures in developed economies will likely underpin further appreciation pressures, which might lead to additional interventions. Some countries continued to implement other macroprudential policies, like financial regulation reforms, changes to the reserve requirements and liquidity injections. The Government of the Plurinational State of Bolivia, for example, implemented a temporary tax on dollar sales, amounting to 0.7 per cent of the transaction value.

Fiscal balances are expected to move towards further consolidation in 2013. The budget deficit averaged 2.0 per cent of GDP for the region as a whole in 2012. The primary budget balance also showed a small deficit of 0.1 per cent of GDP. Nevertheless, fiscal conditions vary widely across countries. Many have ample space to conduct countercyclical

Many countries are well positioned to implement countercyclical fiscal policies

fiscal policies. South American countries like Chile, Peru and the Plurinational State of Bolivia have relatively more fiscal space. In addition, Chile, Ecuador and Peru recently introduced tax reforms aimed at increasing the tax base. By contrast, chronic deficits in Central America have become a concern, but recent tax and other fiscal reforms in El Salvador, Guatemala, Honduras, Nicaragua and Panama are expected to improve fiscal balances in the coming years. Meanwhile, Caribbean public deficits also widened during the crisis owing to increased spending. In most Caribbean countries, public debt as a percentage of GDP remains very high.

The region's current-account deficit is widening

Given the slowdown in exports, current-account balances in the region are expected to deteriorate for the mineral exporters, in particular. For the region as a whole, trade surplus declined in value terms in 2012, as export growth slowed to 2.0 per cent while import growth accelerated to 7.5 per cent. The export growth slowdown is attributable mainly to the fall in exports from South America to the EU and China, with Argentina, Brazil and Chile being especially affected by the decline in exports to China (box IV.4). By contrast, exports from Central America and Mexico to the EU still increased. In addition, international prices for the region's main export commodities showed declines in 2012, so that the regional terms of trade also suffered a slight decline. Only the hydrocarbon-exporting countries and exporters of food products, like Argentina, Paraguay and Uruguay, posted an increase in their terms of trade.

Downside risks will affect South America more strongly

The major risks are tilted towards the downside of the baseline estimations. A more pronounced slowdown or renewed financial turmoil in the euro area would have a relatively modest effect in the region as a whole, but it would affect South America more strongly. South American countries in particular, however, have policy space left to respond with countercyclical measures. A worsening scenario in the United States would most strongly affect the Caribbean, Central America and Mexico through export, tourism and workers' remittances channels. Additionally, a hard landing in China would strongly affect the countries in South America that are heavily reliant on primary commodity exports. Finally, there is also an increasing concern in relation to the QE measures implemented in developed countries, particularly regarding the potential effects of capital flow and exchange-rate volatility. Considering the current slowdown in regional exports, further currency appreciation would provide a disincentive to economic diversification.

Box IV.4

The effects of the global downturn on Latin American exports

Over the past decade, a main driver of growth in Latin America and the Caribbean has been the higher demand for its export products, most notably the primary goods exported by South American countries. However, the current global economic slowdown reduced the region's growth rate of merchandise exports from 28 per cent in the first half of 2011 to a mere 4 per cent in the first half of 2012. This slowdown reflects less rapid growth in volumes and a fall in the prices of export goods. The most significant decline has been seen in shipments to the EU, with export values falling by 4 per cent during the period (table). While the average price of export goods decreased by 3.4 per cent, the prices for mineral and metal exports declined more significantly by 9.1 per cent.

The global downturn has brought about a deceleration in growth across the board for Latin American exports, but the severity of the impact varies considerably. South American countries have been most adversely affected, largely owing to their heavy dependence on primary commodities as principal export products. The mineral and metal exporters (Chile, Peru), and Brazil have seen the highest reduction in the value of their exports during the first half of 2012. Although this result

Box IV.4 (cont'd)

can partly be attributed to a deceleration in the growth of export volumes, it is predominantly owing to a significant drop in the prices of the raw materials exported by these countries. In the first half of 2012, prices of raw materials declined on average by 6 per cent from a year ago. A second factor behind the fall in the value of South American exports is the relative importance of the EU as a destination market. In fact, the most severe drop in exports for these countries in 2012 was registered in their trade with the euro area. By contrast, South America's energy exporters experienced a significant increase in the export value, averaging 9.9 per cent in the first half of 2012. This can be attributed to the sustained high price of oil and increased oil demand from European countries, following the tightening of EU sanctions against the Islamic Republic of Iran.

While Mexico and the Central American countries have also seen a significant slowdown in export growth in 2012, these countries still continued to register a moderate increase compared to the previous year. Costa Rica even saw a higher growth rate in the first half of 2012 compared to 2011, rising from 8 per cent to 12 per cent. The relatively stronger performance of this subregion reflects the greater share of manufactured goods in the export basket and the predominance of the United States as trading partner. Over the past year, growth of import demand in the United States, while still sluggish, outpaced that of other developed regions.

In sum, the global downturn has affected the economies of Latin America and the Caribbean primarily through the export channel, with significant reductions in the prices of many major export products. This slowdown in export growth not only affects GDP growth directly but also indirectly through cutbacks or delays in investment. Indeed, many investment decisions in natural resource sectors in Latin America are mainly driven by the fluctuations of international commodity prices. This situation highlights the prospective additional constraints that the current quantitative easing measures in the developed world—through their potential effect on the region's currencies—might put on regional growth.

Latin America: year-on-year export changes, first half of 2012

Percentages

Region/Countries	Value	Volume	Price	Value by destination			
				USA	EU	Asia	Latin America
Latin America	4.1	7.5	-3.4	4.3	-4.0	7.5	3.1
Central America	4.2	7.4	-3.2	4.8	2.5	10.1	5.5
Exporters of hydrocarbons[a]	9.9	10.9	-1.0	-2.9	4.7	18.2	12.6
Exporters of minerals & metals[b]	-1.0	8.1	-9.1	-3.1	-16.0	4.4	2.2
Exporters of food[c]	-0.6	2.6	-3.2	8.7	-17.0	-1.4	-0.6
Brazil	-0.9	6.7	-7.6	17.4	-6.2	5.3	-7.9
Mexico	7.6	6.4	1.2	5.5	19.2	18.0	18.6

Source: UN/ECLAC.

a Plurinational State of Bolivia, Ecuador, Bolivarian Republic of Venezuela and Colombia.
b Chile and Peru.
c Argentina, Paraguay, Uruguay.

Statistical annex

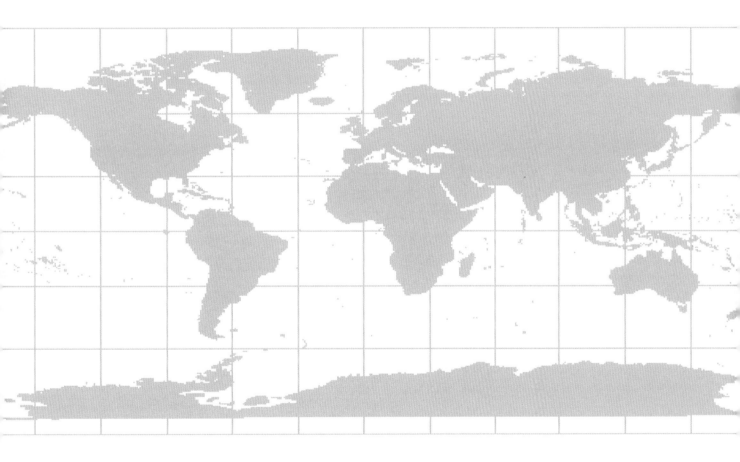

Country classification

Data sources, country classifications and aggregation methodology

The statistical annex contains a set of data that the *World Economic Situation and Prospects (WESP)* employs to delineate trends in various dimensions of the world economy.

Data sources

The annex was prepared by the Development Policy and Analysis Division (DPAD) of the Department of Economic and Social Affairs of the United Nations Secretariat (UN/DESA). It is based on information obtained from the Statistics Division and the Population Division of UN/DESA, as well as from the five United Nations regional commissions, the United Nations Conference on Trade and Development (UNCTAD), the United Nations World Tourism Organization (UNWTO), the International Monetary Fund (IMF), the World Bank, the Organization for Economic Cooperation and Development (OECD), and national and private sources. Estimates for the most recent years were made by DPAD in consultation with the regional commissions, UNCTAD, UNWTO and participants in Project LINK, an international collaborative research group for econometric modelling coordinated jointly by DPAD and the University of Toronto. Forecasts for 2013 and 2014 are primarily based on the World Economic Forecasting Model of DPAD, with support from Project LINK.

Data presented in *WESP* may differ from those published by other organizations for a series of reasons, including differences in timing, sample composition and aggregation methods. Historical data may differ from those in previous editions of *WESP* because of updating and changes in the availability of data for individual countries.

Country classifications

For analytical purposes, *WESP* classifies all countries of the world into one of three broad categories: developed economies, economies in transition and developing economies. The composition of these groupings, specified in tables A, B and C, is intended to reflect basic economic country conditions. Several countries (in particular the economies in transition) have characteristics that could place them in more than one category; however, for purposes of analysis, the groupings have been made mutually exclusive. Within each broad category, some subgroups are defined based either on geographical location or on ad hoc criteria, such as the subgroup of "major developed economies", which is based on the membership of the Group of Seven. Geographical regions for developing economies are as follows: Africa, East Asia, South Asia, Western Asia, and Latin America and the Caribbean.[a]

In parts of the analysis, a distinction is made between fuel exporters and fuel importers from among the economies in transition and the developing countries. An economy is classified as a fuel exporter if the share of fuel exports in its total merchandise

---

a   Names and composition of geographical areas follow those specified in the statistical paper entitled "Standard country or area codes for statistical use" (ST/ESA/STAT/SER.M/49/Rev. 4).

exports is greater than 20 per cent and the level of fuel exports is at least 20 per cent higher than that of the country's fuel imports. This criterion is drawn from the share of fuel exports in the total value of world merchandise trade. Fuels include coal, oil and natural gas (table D).

For other parts of the analysis, countries have been classified by their level of development as measured by per capita gross national income (GNI). Accordingly, countries have been grouped as high-income, upper middle income, lower middle income and low-income (table E). To maintain compatibility with similar classifications used elsewhere, the threshold levels of GNI per capita are those established by the World Bank. Countries with less than $1,025 GNI per capita are classified as low-income countries, those with between $1,026 and $4,035 as lower middle income countries, those with between $4,036 and $12,475 as upper middle income countries, and those with incomes of more than $12,476 as high-income countries. GNI per capita in dollar terms is estimated using the World Bank Atlas method,[b] and the classification in table E is based on data for 2011.

The list of the least developed countries (LDCs) is decided upon by the United Nations Economic and Social Council and, ultimately, by the General Assembly, on the basis of recommendations made by the Committee for Development Policy. The basic criteria for inclusion require that certain thresholds be met with regard to per capita GNI, a human assets index and an economic vulnerability index.[c] As at 30 November 2012, there were 48 LDCs (table F).

WESP also makes reference to the group of heavily indebted poor countries (HIPCs), which are considered by the World Bank and IMF as part of their debt-relief initiative (the Enhanced HIPC Initiative).[d] In September 2012, there were 39 HIPCs (see table G).

Aggregation methodology

Aggregate data are either sums or weighted averages of individual country data. Unless otherwise indicated, multi-year averages of growth rates are expressed as compound annual percentage rates of change. The convention followed is to omit the base year in a multi-year growth rate. For example, the 10-year average growth rate for the decade of the 2000s would be identified as the average annual growth rate for the period from 2001 to 2010.

WESP utilizes exchange-rate conversions of national data in order to aggregate output of individual countries into regional and global totals. The growth of output in each group of countries is calculated from the sum of gross domestic product (GDP) of individual countries measured at 2005 prices and exchange rates. Data for GDP in 2005 in national currencies were converted into dollars (with selected adjustments) and extended forwards and backwards in time using changes in real GDP for each country. This method supplies a reasonable set of aggregate growth rates for a period of about 15 years, centred on 2005.

---

b	See http://data.worldbank.org/about/country-classifications.
c	*Handbook on the Least Developed Country Category: Inclusion, Graduation and Special Support Measures* (United Nations publication, Sales No. E.07.II.A.9). Available from http://www.un.org/esa/analysis/devplan/cdppublications/2008cdphandbook.pdf.
d	IMF, Debt Relief Under the Heavily Indebted Poor Countries (HIPC) Initiative. Available from http://www.imf.org/external/np/exr/facts/pdf/hipc.pdf.

The exchange-rate based method differs from the one mainly applied by the IMF and the World Bank for their estimates of world and regional economic growth, which is based on purchasing power parity (PPP) weights. Over the past two decades, the growth of world gross product (WGP) on the basis of the exchange-rate based approach has been below that based on PPP weights. This is because developing countries, in the aggregate, have seen significantly higher economic growth than the rest of the world in the 1990s and 2000s and the share in WGP of these countries is larger under PPP measurements than under market exchange rates.

Table A
Developed economies

Europe		Other countries	Major developed economies (G7)
European Union	*Other Europe*		
EU-15	Iceland	Australia	Canada
Austria	Norway	Canada	Japan
Belgium	Switzerland	Japan	France
Denmark		New Zealand	Germany
Finland		United States	Italy
France			United Kingdom
Germany			United States
Greece			
Ireland			
Italy			
Luxembourg			
Netherlands			
Portugal			
Spain			
Sweden			
United Kingdom			
New EU member States			
Bulgaria			
Cyprus			
Czech Republic			
Estonia			
Hungary			
Latvia			
Lithuania			
Malta			
Poland			
Romania			
Slovakia			
Slovenia			

Table B
Economies in transition

South-Eastern Europe	Commonwealth of Independent States and Georgia[a]
Albania	Armenia
Bosnia and Herzegovina	Azerbaijan
Croatia	Belarus
Montenegro	Georgia[a]
Serbia	Kazakhstan
The former Yugoslav Republic of Macedonia	Kyrgyzstan
	Republic of Moldova
	Russian Federation
	Tajikistan
	Turkmenistan
	Ukraine
	Uzbekistan

[a] Georgia officially left the Commonwealth of Independent States on 18 August 2009. However, its performance is discussed in the context of this group of countries for reasons of geographic proximity and similarities in economic structure.

Table C
Developing economies by region[a]

Africa	Asia	Latin America and the Caribbean
North Africa	**East Asia**	**Caribbean**
Algeria	Brunei Darussalam	Barbados
Egypt	China	Cuba
Libya[b]	Hong Kong SAR[c]	Dominican Republic
Morocco	Indonesia	Guyana
Tunisia	Malaysia	Haiti
Sub-Saharan Africa	Myanmar	Jamaica
Central Africa	Papua New Guinea	Trinidad and Tobago
Cameroon	Philippines	**Mexico and Central America**
Central African Republic	Republic of Korea	Costa Rica
Chad	Singapore	El Salvador
Congo	Taiwan Province of China	Guatemala
Equatorial Guinea	Thailand	Honduras
Gabon	Viet Nam	Mexico
Sao Tome and Prinicipe	**South Asia**	Nicaragua
East Africa	Bangladesh	Panama
Burundi	India	**South America**
Comoros	Iran (Islamic Republic of)	Argentina
Democratic Republic of the Congo	Nepal	Bolivia (Plurinational State of)
Djibouti	Pakistan	Brazil
Eritrea	Sri Lanka	Chile
Ethiopia	**Western Asia**	Colombia
Kenya	Bahrain	Ecuador
Madagascar	Iraq	Paraguay
Rwanda	Israel	Peru
Somalia	Jordan	Uruguay
Sudan	Kuwait	Venezuela (Bolivarian Republic of)
Uganda	Lebanon	
United Republic of Tanzania	Oman	
Southern Africa	Qatar	
Angola	Saudi Arabia	
Botswana	Syrian Arab Repuplic	
Lesotho	Turkey	
Malawi	United Arab Emirates	
Mauritius	Yemen	
Mozambique		
Namibia		
South Africa		
Zambia		
Zimbabwe		
West Africa		
Benin		
Burkina Faso		
Cape Verde		
Côte d'Ivoire		
Gambia		
Ghana		
Guinea		
Guinea-Bissau		
Liberia		
Mali		
Mauritania		
Niger		
Nigeria		
Senegal		
Sierra Leone		
Togo		

a Economies systematically monitored by the Global Economic Monitoring Unit of DPAD.
b The name of the Libyan Arab Jamahiriya was officially changed to Libya on 16 September 2011.
c Special Administrative Region of China.

Table D
Fuel-exporting countries

Economies in transition	Developing countries				
	Latin America and the Caribbean	*Africa*	*East Asia*	*South Asia*	*Western Asia*
Azerbaijan	Bolivia	Algeria	Brunei Darussalam	Iran (Islamic	Bahrain
Kazakhstan	(Plurinational State of)	Angola	Indonesia	Republic of)	Iraq
Russian Federation	Colombia	Cameroon	Viet Nam		Kuwait
Turkmenistan	Ecuador	Chad			Oman
Uzbekistan	Trinidad and Tobago	Congo			Qatar
	Venezuela	Côte d'Ivoire			Saudi Arabia
	(Bolivarian Republic of)	Egypt			United Arab
		Equatorial Guinea			Emirates
		Gabon			Yemen
		Libya			
		Nigeria			
		Sudan			

Table E
Economies by per capita GNI in 2011[a]

High-income	Upper middle income	Lower middle income	Low-income
Australia	Algeria	Albania[d]	Bangladesh
Austria	Angola[c]	Armenia	Benin
Bahrain	Argentina	Bolivia (Plurinational	Burkina Faso
Barbados	Azerbaijan	State of)	Burundi
Belgium	Belarus	Cameroon	Central African Republic
Brunei Darussalam	Bosnia and Herzegovina	Cape Verde	Chad
Canada	Botswana	Congo	Comoros
Croatia	Brazil	Côte d'Ivoire	Democratic Republic of
Cyprus	Bulgaria	Djibouti	the Congo
Czech Republic	Chile	Egypt	Eritrea
Denmark	China	El Salvador	Ethiopia
Equatorial Guinea	Colombia	Georgia	Gambia
Estonia	Costa Rica	Ghana	Guinea
Finland	Cuba	Guatemala	Guinea-Bissau
France	Dominican Republic	Guyana	Haiti
Germany	Ecuador	Honduras	Kenya
Greece	Gabon	India	Kyrgyzstan
Hong Kong SAR[b]	Iran (Islamic Republic of)	Indonesia	Liberia
Hungary	Jamaica	Iraq	Madagascar
Iceland	Jordan	Lesotho	Malawi
Ireland	Kazakhstan	Morocco	Mali
Israel	Latvia	Nicaragua	Mauritania[d]
Italy	Lebanon	Niger	Mozambique
Japan	Libya	Nigeria	Myanmar
Kuwait	Lithuania	Pakistan	Nepal
Montenegro	Malaysia	Paraguay	Niger
Luxembourg	Mauritius	Philippines	Rwanda
Malta	Mexico	Republic of Moldova	Sierra Leone
Netherlands	Namibia	Sao Tome and Prinicipe	Somalia
New Zealand	Panama	Senegal	Tajikistan
Norway	Papua New Guinea	Sri Lanka	Togo
Oman	Peru	Sudan	Uganda
Poland	Romania	Syrian Arab Repuplic	United Republic of
Portugal	Russian Federation	Ukraine	Tanzania
Qatar	Serbia	Uzbekistan	Zimbabwe
Republic of Korea	South Africa	Viet Nam	
Saudi Arabia	Thailand	Yemen	
Singapore	The former Yugoslav	Zambia	
Slovakia	Republic of Macedonia		
Slovenia	Tunisia		
Spain	Turkey		
Sweden	Turkmenistan[c]		
Switzerland	Uruguay		
Taiwan Province of	Venezuela		
China	(Bolivarian Republic of)		
Trinidad and Tobago			
United Arab Emirates			
United Kingdom			
United States			

a Economies systematically monitored for the World Economic Situation and Prospects report and included in the United Nations' global economic forecast.

b Special Administrative Region of China.

c Indicates the country has been shifted upward by one category from previous year's classification.

d Indicates the country has been shifted downward by one category from previous year's classification.

Table F
Least developed countries

As of November 2011				
Africa	*East Asia*	*South Asia*	*Western Asia*	*Latin America and the Caribbean*
Angola	Cambodia[a]	Afghanistan[a]	Yemen	Haiti
Benin	Kiribati[a]	Bangladesh		
Burkina Faso	Lao People's	Bhutan[a]		
Burundi	Democratic Republic[a]	Nepal		
Central African Republic	Myanmar			
Chad	Samoa[a, b]			
Comoros	Solomon Islands[a]			
Democratic Republic	Timor Leste[a]			
of the Congo	Tuvalu[a]			
Djibouti	Vanuatu[a]			
Equatorial Guinea				
Eritrea				
Ethiopia				
Gambia				
Guinea				
Guinea-Bissau				
Lesotho				
Liberia				
Madagascar				
Malawi				
Mali				
Mauritania				
Mozambique				
Niger				
Rwanda				
Sao Tome and Principe				
Senegal				
Sierra Leone				
Somalia				
Sudan				
Togo				
Uganda				
United Republic of Tanzania				
Zambia				

Note: At its sixty-seventh session, the United Nations General Assembly will formally include the Republic of South Sudan, which became a State Member of the United Nations on 14 July 2011, in the least developed country category.

a   Not included in the *WESP* discussion because of insufficient data.

b   Samoa will graduate from the list of the least developed countries in January 2014.

Table G
Heavily indebted poor countries

As of September 2012		
Post-completion point HIPCs[a]	*Interim HIPCs*[b]	*Pre-decision point HIPCs*[c]
Afghanistan	Chad	Eritrea
Benin	Comoros	Somalia
Bolivia		Sudan
Burkina Faso		
Burundi		
Cameroon		
Central African Republic		
Congo		
Côte d'Ivoire		
Democratic Republic of the Congo		
Ethiopia		
Gambia		
Ghana		
Guinea		
Guinea-Bissau		
Guyana		
Haiti		
Honduras		
Liberia		
Madagascar		
Malawi		
Mali		
Mauritania		
Mozambique		
Nicaragua		
Niger		
Rwanda		
Sao Tome and Principe		
Senegal		
Sierra Leone		
Togo		
Uganda		
United Republic of Tanzania		
Zambia		

Note: South Sudan is not eligible or potentially eligible for debt relief under the HIPC Initiative given that, as a newly created country, it cannot meet the HIPC indebtedness criterion which is bound by the end-2004 and end-2010 cut-off dates. See, IMF, "Eligibility to use the Fund's facilities for concessional financing: Republic of South Sudan", 1 August 2012, available from http://www.imf.org/external/np/pp/eng/2012/080112.pdf.

a   Countries that have qualified for irrevocable debt relief under the HIPC Initiative.

b   Countries that have qualified for assistance under the HIPC Initiative (that is to say, have reached decision point), but have not yet reached completion point.

c   Countries that are potentially eligible and may wish to avail themselves of the HIPC Initiative or the Multilateral Debt Relief Initiative (MDRI).

Table H
Small island developing States

American Samoa	Mauritius
Anguilla	Micronesia (Federated States of)
Antigua and Barbuda	Montserrat
Aruba	Nauru
Bahamas	Netherlands Antilles
Barbados	New Caledonia
Belize	Niue
British Virgin Islands	Palau
Cape Verde	Papua New Guinea
Commonwealth of Northern Marianas	Puerto Rico
Comoros	Samoa
Cook Islands	Sao Tome and Principe
Cuba	Seychelles
Dominica	Singapore
Dominican Republic	Solomon Islands
Fiji	St. Kitts and Nevis
French Polynesia	St. Lucia
Grenada	St. Vincent and the Grenadines
Guam	Suriname
Guinea-Bissau	Timor-Leste
Guyana	Tonga
Haiti	Trinidad and Tobago
Jamaica	Tuvalu
Kiribati	U.S. Virgin Islands
Maldives	Vanuatu
Marshall Islands	

Table I
Landlocked developing countries

Afghanistan	Republic of Moldova
Armenia	Mongolia
Azerbaijan	Nepal
Bhutan	Niger
Bolivia (Plurinational State of)	Paraguay
Botswana	Rwanda
Burkina Faso	Swaziland
Burundi	Tajikistan
Central African Republic	The former Yugoslav Republic of Macedonia
Chad	Turkmenistan
Ethiopia	Uganda
Kazakhstan	Uzbekistan
Kyrgystan	Zambia
Lao People's Democratic Republic	Zimbabwe
Lesotho	
Malawi	
Mali	

Annex tables

Annex

List of tables

Table A.1
Developed economies: rates of growth of real GDP, 2004–2014

Annual percentage change												
	2004-2011[a]	2004	2005	2006	2007	2008	2009	2010	2011	2012[b]	2013[c]	2014[c]
Developed economies	**1.1**	**2.9**	**2.4**	**2.8**	**2.6**	**0.0**	**-3.8**	**2.6**	**1.4**	**1.1**	**1.1**	**2.0**
United States	1.2	3.5	3.1	2.7	1.9	-0.3	-3.1	2.4	1.8	2.1	1.7	2.7
Canada	1.7	3.2	3.1	2.7	2.1	1.1	-2.8	3.2	2.6	1.8	1.5	2.8
Japan	0.3	2.4	1.3	1.7	2.2	-1.0	-5.5	4.5	-0.7	1.5	0.6	0.8
Australia	2.7	3.8	3.3	2.6	4.9	2.2	1.5	2.4	2.3	3.0	2.6	3.3
New Zealand	1.2	4.3	3.1	2.3	2.9	-0.2	-2.3	1.7	1.3	2.1	2.1	2.7
European Union	**1.2**	**2.6**	**2.1**	**3.3**	**3.2**	**0.3**	**-4.3**	**2.1**	**1.5**	**-0.3**	**0.6**	**1.7**
EU-15	1.0	2.4	1.9	3.1	3.0	0.1	-4.4	2.1	1.4	-0.4	0.5	1.6
Austria	1.7	2.6	2.4	3.7	3.7	1.4	-3.8	2.1	2.7	0.8	1.3	2.0
Belgium	1.4	3.3	1.8	2.7	2.9	1.0	-2.8	2.4	1.8	-0.3	0.5	1.5
Denmark	0.4	2.3	2.4	3.4	1.6	-0.8	-5.8	1.3	0.8	1.1	1.2	1.3
Finland	1.4	4.1	2.9	4.4	5.3	0.3	-8.5	3.3	2.7	1.5	1.2	1.6
France	0.9	2.5	1.8	2.5	2.3	-0.1	-3.1	1.7	1.7	0.1	0.3	1.1
Germany	1.5	1.2	0.7	3.7	3.3	1.1	-5.1	4.2	3.0	0.8	1.0	1.8
Greece	-0.5	4.4	2.3	5.5	3.0	-0.2	-3.3	-3.5	-6.9	-6.1	-1.8	0.6
Ireland	1.3	4.4	5.9	5.4	5.4	-2.1	-5.5	-0.8	1.4	0.5	1.7	2.4
Italy	0.0	1.7	0.9	2.2	1.7	-1.2	-5.5	1.8	0.4	-2.4	-0.3	1.4
Luxembourg	2.3	4.4	5.3	4.9	6.6	-0.7	-4.1	2.9	1.7	-0.1	0.9	2.0
Netherlands	1.4	2.2	2.0	3.4	3.9	1.8	-3.7	1.6	1.0	-0.5	0.7	1.4
Portugal	0.2	1.6	0.8	1.4	2.4	0.0	-2.9	1.4	-1.7	-3.2	-2.2	0.2
Spain	1.2	3.3	3.6	4.1	3.5	0.9	-3.7	-0.3	0.4	-1.6	-1.4	0.8
Sweden	2.2	4.2	3.2	4.3	3.3	-0.6	-5.0	6.6	3.9	1.7	1.8	2.8
United Kingdom	0.9	2.9	2.8	2.6	3.6	-1.0	-4.0	1.8	0.9	-0.3	1.2	2.3
New EU member States	3.3	5.6	4.8	6.5	6.0	4.1	-3.6	2.3	3.1	1.2	2.0	2.9
Bulgaria	3.1	6.7	6.4	6.5	6.4	6.2	-5.5	0.4	1.7	1.0	2.3	3.5
Cyprus	2.3	4.2	3.9	4.1	5.1	3.6	-1.9	1.1	0.5	-1.2	0.5	1.3
Czech Republic	3.1	4.7	6.8	7.0	5.7	3.1	-4.5	2.5	1.7	-0.9	1.1	2.0
Estonia	2.5	6.3	8.9	10.1	7.5	-4.2	-14.1	3.3	8.3	3.0	3.0	3.5
Hungary	0.7	4.8	4.0	3.9	0.1	0.9	-6.8	1.3	1.6	-1.0	0.6	2.2
Latvia	1.6	8.9	10.1	11.2	9.6	-3.3	-17.7	-0.9	5.5	4.0	4.0	4.0
Lithuania	2.7	7.4	7.8	7.8	9.8	2.9	-14.8	1.5	5.9	3.0	3.0	3.0
Malta	2.4	-0.5	3.7	2.9	4.3	4.1	-2.7	2.3	2.1	-0.7	1.1	1.8
Poland	4.5	5.3	3.6	6.2	6.8	5.1	1.6	3.9	4.3	2.6	2.6	3.5
Romania	2.7	8.5	4.2	7.9	6.3	7.3	-6.6	-1.6	2.5	1.0	2.3	3.0
Slovakia	4.7	5.1	6.7	8.3	10.5	5.8	-4.9	4.4	3.2	2.4	2.0	2.6
Slovenia	1.9	4.4	4.0	5.8	7.0	3.4	-7.8	1.2	0.6	-2.0	0.5	2.2
Other Europe	**1.7**	**3.2**	**2.8**	**3.2**	**3.4**	**1.2**	**-1.9**	**1.9**	**1.7**	**1.7**	**1.5**	**1.9**
Iceland	1.5	7.8	7.2	4.7	6.0	1.2	-6.6	-4.0	2.6	2.6	2.7	2.6
Norway	1.2	4.0	2.6	2.5	2.7	0.0	-1.7	0.7	1.4	3.5	2.2	2.4
Switzerland	2.2	2.4	2.7	3.8	3.8	2.2	-1.9	3.0	1.9	0.3	0.8	1.4
Memorandum items:												
North America	1.2	3.4	3.1	2.7	1.9	-0.2	-3.0	2.5	1.9	2.1	1.7	2.7
Western Europe	1.2	2.6	2.1	3.3	3.2	0.4	-4.2	2.1	1.5	-0.2	0.6	1.7
Asia and Oceania	0.7	2.6	1.6	1.8	2.6	-0.5	-4.4	4.1	-0.2	1.7	1.0	1.3
Major developed economies	1.0	2.8	2.3	2.6	2.3	-0.3	-3.9	2.8	1.4	1.2	1.2	2.1
Euro area	1.0	2.2	1.7	3.3	3.0	0.4	-4.4	2.1	1.5	-0.5	0.3	1.4

Source: UN/DESA, based on data of the United Nations Statistics Division and individual national sources.

Note: Country groups are calculated as a weighted average of individual country growth rates of gross domestic product (GDP), where weights are based on GDP in 2005 prices and exchange rates.

a Average percentage change.
b Partly estimated.
c Baseline scenario forecasts, based in part on Project LINK and the UN/DESA World Economic Forecasting Model.

Table A.2
Economies in transition: rates of growth of real GDP, 2004–2014

Annual percentage change												
	2004-2011[a]	2004	2005	2006	2007	2008	2009	2010	2011	2012[b]	2013[c]	2014[c]
Economies in transition	**4.3**	**7.7**	**6.5**	**8.3**	**8.6**	**5.2**	**-6.6**	**4.4**	**4.5**	**3.5**	**3.6**	**4.2**
South-Eastern Europe	2.3	5.8	5.1	4.8	5.5	3.7	-4.3	0.4	1.1	-0.6	1.2	2.6
Albania	4.8	5.7	5.8	5.4	5.9	7.5	3.3	3.9	2.0	1.5	2.5	3.0
Bosnia and Herzegovina	3.5	6.3	8.0	6.0	6.1	5.6	-2.9	0.7	1.7	0.2	1.0	2.1
Croatia	1.1	4.1	4.3	4.9	5.1	2.1	-6.9	-1.4	0.0	-1.3	0.8	2.5
Montenegro	4.2	4.4	4.2	8.6	10.7	6.9	-5.7	2.5	3.2	0.4	1.5	3.0
Serbia	2.4	9.3	5.4	3.6	5.4	3.8	-3.5	1.0	1.6	-1.0	1.3	2.8
The former Yugoslav Republic of Macedonia	3.6	4.6	4.4	5.0	6.1	5.0	-0.9	2.9	3.0	1.0	2.3	2.5
Commonwealth of Independent States and Georgia[d]	4.5	7.9	6.7	8.7	8.9	5.3	-6.8	4.8	4.8	3.8	3.8	4.4
Net fuel exporters	4.6	7.3	7.0	8.8	8.9	5.4	-6.3	4.7	4.7	4.0	3.8	4.4
Azerbaijan	15.3	10.2	26.4	34.5	25.1	10.8	9.3	5.0	0.1	1.2	2.5	3.8
Kazakhstan	6.9	9.6	9.7	10.6	8.9	3.3	1.2	7.3	7.5	5.5	5.0	5.5
Russian Federation	4.0	7.2	6.4	8.2	8.5	5.2	-7.8	4.3	4.3	3.7	3.6	4.2
Turkmenistan	11.5	5.0	13.0	11.4	11.8	14.7	6.1	9.2	14.7	9.0	8.0	7.0
Uzbekistan	8.2	7.7	7.0	7.3	9.5	9.0	8.1	8.5	8.3	7.0	6.9	6.1
Net fuel importers	3.7	11.4	5.0	8.1	8.4	4.6	-9.8	5.2	5.4	2.8	3.3	4.3
Armenia	5.4	10.5	13.9	13.2	13.7	6.9	-14.1	2.2	4.7	3.8	4.0	4.0
Belarus	7.3	11.4	9.4	10.0	8.6	10.2	0.2	7.7	5.3	3.9	3.1	5.0
Georgia[d]	6.1	5.9	9.6	9.4	12.3	2.3	-3.8	6.3	7.2	4.8	5.0	4.0
Kyrgyzstan	3.9	7.0	-0.2	3.1	8.5	8.4	2.9	-0.5	5.7	0.2	3.5	4.0
Republic of Moldova	4.3	7.4	7.5	4.8	3.0	7.8	-6.0	7.1	6.4	0.6	2.0	3.0
Tajikistan	6.7	10.3	6.7	6.6	7.8	7.6	4.0	6.5	7.4	7.0	5.7	5.0
Ukraine	1.8	12.1	2.7	7.3	7.9	2.3	-14.8	4.2	5.2	2.0	3.2	4.0

Source: UN/DESA, based on data of the United Nations Statistics Division and individual national sources.

Note: Country groups are calculated as a weighted average of individual country growth rates of gross domestic product (GDP), where weights are based on GDP in 2005 prices and exchange rates.

a Average percentage change.
b Partly estimated.
c Baseline scenario forecasts, based in part on Project LINK and the UN/DESA World Economic Forecasting Model.
d Georgia officially left the Commonwealth of Independent States on 18 August 2009. However, its performance is discussed in the context of this group of countries for reasons of geographic proximity and similarities in economic structure.

Table A.3
Developing economies: rates of growth of real GDP, 2004-2014

Annual percentage change												
	2004-2011[a]	2004	2005	2006	2007	2008	2009	2010	2011	2012[b]	2013[c]	2014[c]
Developing countries[d]	**6.2**	**7.2**	**6.8**	**7.6**	**7.9**	**5.1**	**2.7**	**7.7**	**5.7**	**4.7**	**5.1**	**5.6**
Africa	4.5	5.9	5.8	5.9	6.2	5.2	2.7	4.7	1.1	5.0	4.8	5.1
North Africa	2.9	4.8	5.1	5.4	4.7	4.6	3.2	4.1	-6.0	7.5	4.4	4.9
Sub-Saharan Africa	5.2	6.4	6.1	6.2	6.9	5.5	2.5	5.0	4.5	3.9	5.0	5.2
Net fuel exporters	4.6	6.7	6.6	5.9	7.0	5.9	4.2	5.1	-2.1	6.4	5.2	5.4
Net fuel importers	4.4	5.1	5.0	5.9	5.4	4.6	1.4	4.3	4.2	3.7	4.4	4.8
East and South Asia	7.7	7.8	8.1	9.0	9.9	5.8	5.5	9.0	6.8	5.5	6.0	6.3
East Asia	7.9	7.9	8.0	9.2	10.2	6.4	5.2	9.2	7.1	5.8	6.2	6.5
South Asia	7.1	7.5	8.2	8.3	8.9	3.3	7.0	8.3	5.8	4.4	5.0	5.7
Net fuel exporters	5.4	5.2	5.7	6.0	7.2	3.9	4.4	6.1	4.7	3.2	3.7	4.7
Net fuel importers	8.0	8.1	8.3	9.3	10.2	6.0	5.6	9.3	7.0	5.7	6.2	6.5
Western Asia	4.8	8.4	6.6	6.9	4.7	3.8	-1.5	6.7	6.7	3.3	3.3	4.1
Net fuel exporters	5.0	8.5	6.0	7.3	4.4	5.6	-0.6	5.7	6.6	4.9	3.9	3.5
Net fuel importers	4.6	8.3	7.3	6.4	5.1	1.9	-2.5	7.8	6.9	1.6	2.7	4.7
Latin America and the Caribbean	4.0	5.9	4.6	5.7	5.6	4.0	-1.9	6.0	4.3	3.1	3.9	4.4
South America	4.8	7.1	5.1	5.6	6.7	5.4	-0.2	6.5	4.5	2.7	4.0	4.4
Mexico and Central America	2.5	4.1	3.4	5.3	3.6	1.5	-5.3	5.4	4.0	4.0	3.9	4.6
Caribbean	5.0	3.7	8.1	10.3	6.4	3.5	0.9	3.5	2.7	2.9	3.7	3.8
Net fuel exporters	4.6	10.6	7.1	8.0	7.0	4.6	-0.7	1.6	5.0	4.5	3.6	3.9
Net fuel importers	3.9	5.2	4.2	5.3	5.4	3.9	-2.1	6.7	4.2	2.9	4.0	4.5
Memorandum items												
Least developed countries	6.7	7.7	7.9	7.9	9.0	7.8	5.1	5.8	3.7	3.7	5.7	5.5
Sub-Saharan Africa (excluding Nigeria and South Africa)	6.0	6.6	6.7	6.7	8.1	6.7	4.0	5.5	4.4	3.9	5.5	5.3
Africa sub-regions as classified by the Economic Commission for Africa[e]												
Central Africa	4.5	9.3	5.3	2.5	5.9	5.0	3.0	4.8	5.0	5.0	4.7	4.4
Eastern Africa	6.6	7.0	7.6	7.0	7.6	6.7	4.4	7.0	6.3	5.6	6.1	6.2
North Africa	3.3	4.9	5.2	5.8	5.2	4.9	3.7	4.1	-5.6	5.4	4.2	4.6
Southern Africa	4.5	5.3	6.1	6.7	7.3	4.9	-0.3	3.5	3.7	3.5	4.1	4.4
West Africa	5.9	7.6	5.8	5.1	5.6	5.9	5.6	6.8	6.5	6.3	6.6	6.8
East Asia (excluding China)	4.5	5.9	5.0	5.7	6.0	2.8	0.2	7.7	4.2	3.1	3.7	4.2
South Asia (excluding India)	4.9	5.9	6.0	6.2	7.1	2.1	4.1	5.4	3.4	1.5	2.3	3.5
Western Asia (excluding Israel and Turkey)	4.9	8.4	5.9	7.0	4.6	5.6	0.0	5.6	6.0	3.6	3.4	3.7
Arab States[f]	4.3	7.2	5.6	6.6	4.8	5.4	1.2	5.1	2.2	4.1	3.6	3.9
Landlocked developing economies	7.1	7.6	8.3	9.1	8.7	6.6	3.4	7.4	6.5	4.9	5.3	5.3
Small island developing economies	5.4	6.0	7.2	8.6	7.4	3.0	0.1	8.4	3.7	2.1	2.9	3.5
Major developing economies												
Argentina	7.4	9.0	9.2	8.5	8.7	6.8	0.8	9.2	8.9	2.5	3.2	4.2
Brazil	4.0	5.7	3.2	4.0	6.1	5.2	-0.3	7.5	2.7	1.3	4.0	4.4

Table A.3 (cont'd)

	2004-2011ᵃ	2004	2005	2006	2007	2008	2009	2010	2011	2012ᵇ	2013ᶜ	2014ᶜ
Chile	4.5	7.0	6.2	5.7	5.2	3.3	-1.0	6.1	6.0	5.1	4.6	4.9
China	10.9	10.1	11.3	12.7	14.2	9.6	9.2	10.3	9.2	7.7	7.9	8.0
Colombia	4.8	5.3	4.7	6.7	6.9	3.5	1.7	4.0	5.9	4.4	4.5	4.8
Egypt	5.3	4.1	4.5	6.8	7.1	7.2	4.6	5.2	1.8	1.1	3.2	4.7
Hong Kong SARᵍ	4.5	8.5	7.1	7.0	6.4	2.3	-2.6	7.0	5.0	1.4	2.5	3.1
India	8.1	8.3	9.3	9.3	9.8	3.9	8.2	9.6	6.9	5.5	6.1	6.5
Indonesia	5.8	5.0	5.7	5.5	6.3	6.0	4.6	6.2	6.5	6.2	6.2	6.3
Iran, Islamic Republic of	4.5	5.1	5.3	6.1	8.3	0.6	4.0	5.9	2.0	-1.9	-0.9	1.5
Israel	4.5	4.9	4.9	5.8	5.9	4.1	1.1	5.0	4.6	2.9	2.8	6.0
Korea, Republic of	3.8	4.6	4.0	5.2	5.1	2.3	0.3	6.3	3.6	2.1	3.0	3.5
Malaysia	4.6	6.8	5.3	5.6	6.3	4.8	-1.5	7.2	5.1	5.0	4.4	4.9
Mexico	2.3	4.1	3.2	5.2	3.3	1.2	-6.0	5.5	3.9	3.9	3.8	4.6
Nigeria	6.8	10.5	6.5	6.0	6.5	6.3	6.9	7.8	7.4	6.4	6.8	7.2
Pakistan	4.4	7.4	7.7	6.2	5.7	1.6	3.6	3.5	3.0	3.8	4.2	4.4
Peru	7.1	5.0	6.8	7.7	8.9	9.8	0.8	8.8	6.9	6.0	5.8	5.6
Philippines	4.7	6.7	4.8	5.2	6.6	4.2	1.1	7.6	3.7	6.2	5.4	5.5
Saudi Arabia	3.8	5.3	5.6	3.2	2.0	4.2	0.1	4.6	6.8	5.5	3.7	3.0
Singapore	6.4	9.2	7.4	8.8	8.9	1.7	-1.0	14.8	4.9	1.4	2.5	3.3
South Africa	3.5	4.6	5.3	5.6	5.5	3.6	-1.5	2.9	3.1	2.5	3.1	3.8
Taiwan Province of China	4.2	6.2	4.7	5.4	6.0	0.7	-1.8	10.7	4.0	1.1	2.4	2.9
Thailand	3.2	6.3	4.2	4.9	5.4	1.6	-1.1	7.5	0.1	5.3	4.6	5.0
Turkey	4.7	9.4	8.4	6.9	4.7	0.7	-4.8	9.2	8.5	3.0	3.4	4.2
Venezuela, Bolivarian Republic of	4.7	18.3	10.3	9.9	8.8	5.3	-3.2	-1.5	4.0	5.1	2.5	2.9

Source: UN/DESA, based on data of the United Nations Statistics Division and individual national sources.

Note: Country groups are calculated as a weighted average of individual country growth rates of gross domestic product (GDP), where weights are based on GDP in 2005 prices and exchange rates.

a   Average percentage change.
b   Partly estimated.
c   Baseline scenario forecasts, based in part on Project LINK and the UN/DESA World Economic Forecasting Model.
d   Covering countries that account for 98 per cent of the population of all developing countries.
e   The United Nations Economic Commission for Africa maintains a classification of countries which is not fully compatible with the current WESP classification.
f   Currently includes data for Algeria, Bahrain, Comoros, Djibouti, Egypt, Iraq, Jordan, Kuwait, Lebanon, Libya, Mauritania, Morocco, Oman, Qatar, Saudi Arabia, Somalia, Sudan, Syrian Arab Republic, Tunisia, United Arab Emirates and Yemen.
g   Special Administrative Region of China.

Table A.4
Developed economies: consumer price inflation, 2004–2014

Annual percentage change[a]	2004	2005	2006	2007	2008	2009	2010	2011	2012[b]	2013[c]	2014[c]
Developed economies	**2.0**	**2.4**	**2.3**	**2.1**	**3.5**	**-0.1**	**1.8**	**2.6**	**1.9**	**1.5**	**1.8**
United States	2.7	3.7	3.2	2.6	4.3	-0.8	2.5	3.1	2.0	1.3	1.8
Canada	1.9	2.2	2.0	2.1	2.4	0.3	1.8	2.9	1.7	1.9	1.9
Japan	0.0	-0.3	0.2	0.1	1.4	-1.3	-0.7	-0.3	0.3	0.4	1.8
Australia	2.3	2.7	3.5	2.3	4.4	1.8	2.8	3.4	1.7	2.5	2.0
New Zealand	2.3	3.0	3.4	2.4	4.0	2.1	2.3	4.0	1.2	1.8	2.1
European Union	**2.1**	**2.2**	**2.2**	**2.2**	**3.5**	**0.8**	**2.0**	**3.0**	**2.4**	**2.0**	**1.9**
EU-15	1.9	2.1	2.2	2.1	3.3	0.7	1.9	3.0	2.3	1.9	1.8
Austria	2.0	2.1	1.7	2.2	3.2	0.4	1.7	3.6	2.3	2.0	2.0
Belgium	1.9	2.5	2.3	1.8	4.5	0.0	2.3	3.5	0.6	2.9	0.9
Denmark	0.9	1.7	1.9	1.7	3.6	1.1	2.2	2.6	2.3	1.5	1.3
Finland	0.1	0.8	1.3	1.6	3.9	1.6	1.7	3.3	2.9	2.2	1.6
France	2.3	1.9	1.9	1.6	3.2	0.1	1.7	2.3	2.3	2.2	2.1
Germany	1.8	1.9	1.8	2.3	2.8	0.2	1.2	2.5	1.9	1.8	1.6
Greece	3.0	3.5	3.3	3.0	4.2	1.4	4.7	3.1	1.1	0.4	1.0
Ireland	2.3	2.2	2.7	2.9	3.1	-1.7	-1.6	1.2	2.0	1.3	1.5
Italy	2.3	2.2	2.2	2.0	3.5	0.8	1.6	2.9	2.9	1.8	2.1
Luxembourg	2.2	2.5	2.7	2.3	3.4	0.4	2.3	3.7	2.6	2.7	2.0
Netherlands	1.4	1.5	1.7	1.6	2.2	1.0	0.9	2.5	2.3	2.0	2.0
Portugal	2.5	2.1	3.0	2.4	2.7	-0.9	1.4	3.6	2.8	1.9	1.5
Spain	3.1	3.4	3.6	2.8	4.1	-0.2	2.1	3.1	2.4	2.4	2.2
Sweden	1.0	0.8	1.5	1.7	3.4	1.9	1.9	1.4	1:1	0.8	1.3
United Kingdom	1.3	2.1	2.3	2.3	3.6	2.2	3.3	4.5	2.7	2.0	1.7
New EU member States	5.1	3.4	3.1	4.1	6.0	3.1	2.9	3.8	3.7	3.2	2.8
Bulgaria	6.4	6.0	7.3	7.6	12.3	2.5	3.0	3.4	2.9	3.0	3.5
Cyprus	2.5	2.7	2.6	2.4	4.7	0.4	2.5	3.5	3.6	2.6	3.0
Czech Republic	2.6	1.6	2.1	3.0	6.2	0.6	1.3	2.2	3.0	2.7	2.5
Estonia	3.0	4.1	4.4	6.6	10.4	0.2	3.0	5.0	4.0	3.8	3.0
Hungary	6.8	3.5	4.0	7.9	6.0	4.0	4.8	4.0	5.7	4.5	3.5
Latvia	6.2	6.9	6.5	10.1	15.4	3.3	-1.0	4.2	2.5	2.7	2.5
Lithuania	1.1	2.7	3.8	5.7	11.1	4.2	1.2	4.1	3.4	3.0	3.0
Malta	2.9	3.3	2.6	1.7	3.8	2.8	0.5	2.8	2.9	3.9	1.0
Poland	3.6	2.2	1.3	2.6	4.2	4.0	2.7	3.9	3.6	3.0	2.8
Romania	12.0	8.9	6.6	4.8	7.9	5.6	6.2	5.8	3.5	4.0	3.0
Slovakia	7.5	2.8	4.3	1.9	3.9	0.9	0.7	4.1	3.7	2.4	2.5
Slovenia	3.6	2.5	2.5	3.8	5.5	0.9	2.1	2.1	2.5	2.1	1.9
Other Europe	**0.8**	**1.4**	**1.8**	**0.9**	**3.0**	**0.9**	**1.5**	**0.7**	**0.1**	**0.7**	**1.3**
Iceland	3.3	4.1	6.7	5.1	12.7	12.0	5.4	4.0	5.3	3.5	3.8
Norway	0.6	1.5	2.5	0.7	3.4	2.3	2.4	1.3	0.9	1.6	2.1
Switzerland	0.8	1.2	1.0	0.8	2.3	-0.7	0.6	0.1	-0.7	-0.1	0.5
Memorandum items:											
North America	2.6	3.6	3.1	2.6	4.1	-0.7	2.4	3.1	2.0	1.3	1.8
Western Europe	2.1	2.1	2.2	2.2	3.5	0.8	1.9	2.9	2.3	2.0	1.8
Asia and Oceania	0.4	0.2	0.7	0.5	1.9	-0.8	-0.1	0.3	0.5	0.7	1.8
Major developed economies	1.9	2.4	2.3	2.0	3.4	-0.3	1.7	2.5	1.8	1.4	1.8
Euro area	2.2	2.2	2.2	2.1	3.3	0.3	1.6	2.7	2.2	2.0	1.9

Source: UN/DESA, based on OECD, *Main Economic Indicators*; Eurostat; and individual national sources.

a   Data for country groups are weighted averages, where weights for each year are based on 2005 GDP in United States dollars.
b   Partly estimated.
c   Baseline scenario forecasts, based in part on Project LINK and the UN/DESA World Economic Forecasting Model.

Table A.5
Economies in transition: consumer price inflation, 2004–2014

Annual percentage change[a]	2004	2005	2006	2007	2008	2009	2010	2011	2012[b]	2013[c]	2014[c]
Economies in transition	**9.9**	**11.7**	**9.2**	**9.0**	**14.6**	**10.7**	**6.8**	**9.5**	**6.6**	**7.4**	**5.8**
South-Eastern Europe	4.0	6.4	5.7	3.6	7.8	3.4	2.8	5.0	3.9	3.4	3.3
Albania	2.3	2.4	2.4	2.9	3.3	2.3	3.6	3.6	2.3	2.5	2.7
Bosnia and Herzegovina	-0.5	3.7	6.1	1.5	7.4	-0.3	2.2	3.7	2.5	2.5	3.0
Croatia	2.1	3.3	3.2	2.9	6.0	2.4	1.1	2.3	3.2	2.6	2.7
Montenegro	2.1	2.7	3.0	4.3	9.0	3.9	0.5	3.0	3.0	3.0	2.7
Serbia	11.0	16.1	11.7	6.4	12.4	8.2	6.2	11.2	6.5	5.8	5.0
The former Yugoslav Republic of Macedonia	-0.4	0.5	3.2	2.3	8.3	-0.8	1.5	3.9	3.2	3.0	2.6
Commonwealth of Independent States and Georgia[d]	10.5	12.2	9.5	9.5	15.2	11.4	7.2	9.9	6.9	7.7	6.1
Net fuel exporters	10.4	12.2	9.7	9.3	14.3	11.1	7.0	8.6	5.3	7.1	5.8
Azerbaijan	6.7	9.5	8.2	16.6	20.7	1.4	5.8	8.0	2.3	2.6	4.1
Kazakhstan	6.9	7.5	8.6	10.8	17.1	7.3	7.2	8.4	5.1	6.5	5.0
Russian Federation	10.9	12.7	9.7	9.0	14.0	11.7	7.0	8.5	5.1	7.0	5.7
Turkmenistan	5.9	10.7	8.2	6.3	14.5	-2.6	4.6	11.1	10.3	12.1	10.0
Uzbekistan	6.6	10.0	14.2	12.3	12.7	14.1	9.5	12.8	14.0	13.0	11.0
Net fuel importers	10.8	11.8	8.4	11.2	21.2	13.4	8.8	18.2	17.2	12.0	7.9
Armenia	7.0	0.6	2.9	4.4	8.9	3.4	8.2	7.7	4.2	4.3	4.3
Belarus	18.3	10.4	7.0	8.2	14.8	12.9	7.7	52.5	68.1	28.0	15.5
Georgia[d]	5.7	8.2	9.2	9.2	10.1	1.8	7.1	8.5	0.5	4.3	3.0
Kyrgyzstan	4.1	4.4	5.6	10.1	24.5	6.9	8.1	16.6	3.1	5.0	5.0
Republic of Moldova	12.5	12.0	12.8	12.3	12.8	-0.1	7.4	7.5	4.4	4.4	5.0
Tajikistan	7.1	7.2	10.0	13.4	20.9	6.4	6.5	12.5	12.4	8.0	9.0
Ukraine	9.0	13.5	9.1	12.8	25.2	15.9	9.4	8.0	2.3	8.0	6.0

Source: UN/DESA, based on data of the Economic Commission for Europe.

a Data for country groups are weighted averages, where weights for each year are based on 2005 GDP in United States dollars.
b Partly estimated.
c Baseline scenario forecasts, based in part on Project LINK and the UN/DESA World Economic Forecasting Model.
d Georgia officially left the Commonwealth of Independent States on 18 August 2009. However, its performance is discussed in the context of this group of countries for reasons of geographic proximity and similarities in economic structure.

Table A.6
Developing economies: consumer price inflation, 2004-2014

Annual percentage change[a]											
	2004	*2005*	*2006*	*2007*	*2008*	*2009*	*2010*	*2011*	*2012*[b]	*2013*[c]	*2014*[c]
Developing countries by region	**5.2**	**4.9**	**5.3**	**19.4**	**8.2**	**4.3**	**5.5**	**6.4**	**5.4**	**5.2**	**5.0**
Africa	7.8	8.2	12.4	157.6	10.9	7.8	6.4	8.0	8.1	6.6	5.9
North Africa	4.7	2.6	4.1	5.3	9.2	5.9	5.3	7.2	6.4	5.1	4.7
Sub-Saharan Africa	9.3	11.0	16.6	234.0	11.7	8.7	6.9	8.4	9.0	7.3	6.6
Net fuel exporters	9.8	8.2	5.9	6.0	10.9	8.6	8.7	9.6	10.1	8.1	6.9
Net fuel importers	5.9	8.1	18.4	298.4	10.9	7.0	4.3	6.5	6.3	5.2	5.1
East and South Asia	4.1	3.6	3.7	4.9	7.4	2.9	5.0	6.2	4.8	4.7	4.8
East Asia	3.5	2.9	2.7	3.9	6.0	0.6	3.2	4.9	2.9	3.1	3.4
South Asia	6.2	6.4	7.1	8.6	12.5	11.2	11.5	11.2	11.6	10.6	9.9
Net fuel exporters	9.3	11.2	11.9	10.5	17.0	8.0	7.2	12.3	11.7	10.6	9.9
Net fuel importers	3.5	2.8	2.8	4.3	6.4	2.3	4.8	5.6	4.1	4.1	4.3
Western Asia	4.7	5.4	7.1	7.2	10.3	4.1	5.8	4.8	5.1	4.5	4.4
Net fuel exporters	3.1	4.3	6.3	7.6	10.9	3.0	4.3	4.0	3.7	3.6	3.8
Net fuel importers	6.3	6.4	7.9	6.7	9.6	5.3	7.2	5.7	6.5	5.4	4.9
Latin America and the Caribbean	7.0	6.1	5.1	5.3	7.7	6.0	6.0	6.9	6.0	6.0	5.5
South America	7.0	7.1	5.7	5.7	8.8	6.7	7.1	8.8	7.2	7.3	6.7
Mexico and Central America	4.9	4.4	3.9	4.3	5.7	5.1	4.2	3.6	4.1	3.8	3.6
Caribbean	25.8	6.1	7.4	8.6	10.3	3.0	5.6	7.6	4.7	5.4	5.2
Net fuel exporters	12.0	9.4	8.2	10.8	17.7	14.5	13.9	13.1	12.0	12.2	11.3
Net fuel importers	6.2	5.6	4.6	4.5	6.2	4.7	4.8	6.0	5.1	5.1	4.7
Memorandum items											
Least developed countries	10.6	10.4	9.0	9.5	13.8	8.5	8.3	11.7	12.3	9.9	8.1
Sub-Saharan Africa (excluding Nigeria and South Africa)	15.2	15.7	30.3	499.4	13.1	8.8	6.8	10.2	10.9	8.5	7.0
Africa sub-regions as classified by the Economic Commission for Africa[d]											
Central Africa	0.4	3.9	4.3	1.1	6.5	4.3	2.9	2.0	3.8	3.4	3.4
East Africa	7.4	10.8	10.9	10.7	21.7	12.6	7.2	19.5	14.4	10.0	8.6
North Africa	5.1	3.2	4.4	5.6	9.7	6.4	6.2	8.1	8.6	6.7	5.5
Southern Africa	10.1	10.6	25.9	473.1	10.2	7.7	5.4	5.7	5.9	4.9	5.1
West Africa	10.9	14.1	7.3	5.5	11.2	9.4	9.1	8.5	9.8	8.7	8.0
East Asia (excluding China)	3.1	3.9	3.9	3.1	6.1	1.9	3.0	4.2	3.0	3.1	3.2
South Asia (excluding India)	11.1	11.1	9.9	13.1	21.3	11.7	10.6	15.8	16.2	14.1	12.9
Western Asia (excluding Israel and Turkey)	3.1	4.3	6.4	7.3	11.2	2.9	4.5	4.0	4.7	3.9	3.9
Arab States[e]	4.0	3.9	6.0	6.8	10.7	4.1	5.1	5.4	6.1	4.9	4.4
Landlocked developing economies	13.4	16.7	39.6	710.1	15.5	6.4	5.9	9.2	7.9	7.5	6.5
Small island developing economies	10.4	2.9	3.7	4.6	7.7	1.8	3.8	5.8	4.7	4.6	3.9

Table A.6 (cont'd)

	2004	2005	2006	2007	2008	2009	2010	2011	2012[b]	2013[c]	2014[c]
Major developing economies											
Argentina	4.4	9.6	10.9	8.8	8.6	6.3	10.8	15.7	11.3	10.2	9.8
Brazil	6.6	6.8	4.2	3.6	5.6	4.9	5.0	6.5	5.3	5.8	5.0
Chile	1.1	3.1	3.4	4.4	8.7	0.3	1.4	4.4	3.0	2.5	3.0
China	3.9	1.9	1.6	4.8	6.0	-0.6	3.5	5.5	2.8	3.1	3.7
Colombia	5.9	5.0	4.3	5.5	7.0	4.2	2.3	3.4	3.2	3.1	3.1
Egypt	11.3	4.9	7.6	9.3	18.3	11.8	11.3	11.5	8.3	9.1	8.0
Hong Kong SAR[f]	-0.4	0.9	2.1	2.0	4.2	0.6	2.4	5.3	3.9	3.2	3.0
India	3.8	4.2	5.8	6.4	8.3	10.9	12.0	8.9	9.4	8.9	8.4
Indonesia	6.0	10.5	13.1	6.5	10.2	4.4	5.1	5.4	4.3	4.8	4.9
Iran, Islamic Republic of	14.8	13.4	11.9	17.2	25.5	13.5	10.1	20.6	23.0	20.0	18.0
Israel	-0.4	1.3	2.1	0.5	4.6	3.3	2.7	3.4	2.4	2.1	3.0
Korea, Republic of	3.6	2.8	2.2	2.5	4.7	2.8	2.9	4.0	2.3	2.6	2.9
Malaysia	1.5	3.0	3.6	2.0	5.4	0.6	1.7	3.2	1.7	2.3	2.5
Mexico	4.7	4.0	3.6	4.0	5.1	5.3	4.2	3.4	4.0	3.7	3.5
Nigeria	15.0	17.9	8.2	5.4	11.5	11.5	13.5	10.8	12.5	11.0	9.8
Pakistan	7.4	9.1	7.9	7.6	20.3	13.6	13.9	11.9	9.7	8.5	8.2
Peru	3.7	1.6	2.0	1.8	5.8	2.9	1.5	3.4	3.6	3.1	2.5
Philippines	4.8	6.5	5.5	2.9	8.3	4.1	3.9	4.6	3.3	3.7	3.9
Saudi Arabia	0.3	0.7	2.2	4.2	9.9	5.1	5.4	5.0	4.9	4.4	4.0
Singapore	1.7	0.4	1.0	2.1	6.5	0.6	2.9	5.3	5.2	4.4	3.2
South Africa	-0.7	2.0	3.2	6.2	10.1	7.2	4.1	5.0	5.2	4.2	4.6
Taiwan Province of China	1.6	2.3	0.6	1.8	3.5	-0.9	1.0	1.4	2.1	1.9	1.8
Thailand	2.8	4.5	4.6	2.3	5.4	-0.9	3.3	3.8	3.1	3.5	3.2
Turkey	8.6	8.2	9.6	8.8	10.4	6.3	8.6	6.5	6.4	6.2	5.5
Venezuela, Bolivarian Republic of	21.7	16.0	13.7	18.7	31.4	28.6	29.1	26.0	23.1	24.2	22.5

Source: UN/DESA, based on IMF, International Financial Statistics.

a   Data for country groups are weighted averages, where weights are based on GDP in 2005 prices and exchange rates.

b   Partly estimated.

c   Baseline scenario forecasts, based in part on Project LINK and the UN/DESA World Economic Forecasting Model.

d   The United Nations Economic Commission for Africa maintains a classification of countries which is not fully compatible with the current WESP classification.

e   Currently includes data for Algeria, Bahrain, Comoros, Djibouti, Egypt, Iraq, Jordan, Kuwait, Lebanon, Libya, Mauritania, Morocco, Oman, Qatar, Saudi Arabia, Somalia, Sudan, Syrian Arab Republic, Tunisia, United Arab Emirates and Yemen.

f   Special Administrative Region of China.

Table A.7
Developed economies: unemployment rates,[a, b] 2004–2014

Percentage of labour force											
	2004	*2005*	*2006*	*2007*	*2008*	*2009*	*2010*	*2011*	*2012[c]*	*2013[d]*	*2014[d]*
Developed economies	**7.2**	**6.9**	**6.3**	**5.8**	**6.1**	**8.4**	**8.8**	**8.5**	**8.6**	**8.7**	**8.5**
United States	5.5	5.1	4.6	4.6	5.8	9.3	9.6	9.0	8.1	7.7	7.3
Canada	7.2	6.8	6.3	6.0	6.1	8.3	8.0	7.5	7.4	7.4	7.1
Japan	4.7	4.4	4.1	3.8	4.0	5.1	5.1	4.6	4.7	5.1	5.0
Australia	5.4	5.0	4.8	4.4	4.2	5.6	5.2	5.1	5.4	5.5	5.7
New Zealand	4.1	3.8	3.9	3.7	4.2	6.1	6.5	6.5	6.5	6.2	5.8
European Union	**9.2**	**9.0**	**8.3**	**7.2**	**7.0**	**9.0**	**9.6**	**9.6**	**10.4**	**10.9**	**10.6**
EU-15	8.3	8.3	7.8	7.1	7.2	9.1	9.6	9.6	10.6	11.1	10.9
Austria	5.0	5.2	4.8	4.4	3.8	4.8	4.4	4.1	4.4	4.6	4.6
Belgium	8.4	8.4	8.3	7.5	7.0	7.9	8.3	7.2	7.4	7.6	7.2
Denmark	5.5	4.8	3.9	3.8	3.4	6.1	7.4	7.6	7.9	8.1	7.8
Finland	8.8	8.4	7.7	6.9	6.4	8.2	8.4	7.8	7.7	7.6	7.5
France	9.3	9.3	9.3	8.4	7.8	9.5	9.7	9.6	10.4	10.9	10.7
Germany	10.5	11.3	10.3	8.7	7.5	7.8	7.1	6.0	5.5	5.6	5.8
Greece	10.5	9.9	8.9	8.3	7.7	9.5	12.6	17.7	24.0	26.2	27.7
Ireland	4.5	4.4	4.5	4.6	6.3	11.9	13.7	14.4	14.9	14.5	13.8
Italy	8.0	7.7	6.8	6.1	6.7	7.8	8.4	8.4	10.6	11.5	11.3
Luxembourg	5.0	4.6	4.6	4.2	4.9	5.1	4.6	4.8	5.4	6.4	6.4
Netherlands	5.1	5.3	4.3	3.6	3.1	3.7	4.5	4.5	5.2	5.7	5.8
Portugal	6.8	7.7	7.8	8.1	7.7	9.6	11.0	12.9	15.6	18.2	15.9
Spain	10.9	9.2	8.5	8.3	11.3	18.0	20.1	21.6	24.8	26.2	25.2
Sweden	7.4	7.6	7.0	6.1	6.2	8.3	8.4	7.5	7.6	7.9	7.7
United Kingdom	4.7	4.8	5.4	5.3	5.7	7.6	7.8	8.0	8.1	8.4	8.3
New EU member States	12.8	11.9	10.0	7.7	6.5	8.4	9.8	9.6	9.9	10.2	9.6
Bulgaria	12.0	10.1	9.0	6.9	5.6	6.8	10.2	11.0	11.7	11.2	10.3
Cyprus	4.7	5.5	4.7	4.1	3.8	5.5	6.4	7.9	12.1	12.9	13.2
Czech Republic	8.3	7.9	7.1	5.3	4.4	6.7	7.1	6.9	7.5	8.3	7.7
Estonia	10.0	7.9	5.9	4.6	5.4	13.8	16.8	12.3	11.4	10.9	9.5
Hungary	6.1	7.2	7.5	7.4	7.8	10.0	11.1	10.8	11.2	10.4	9.9
Latvia	9.9	8.9	6.8	6.0	7.5	17.1	18.6	15.4	16.0	15.3	14.7
Lithuania	11.3	8.3	5.6	4.3	5.8	13.7	17.8	15.3	15.5	14.9	14.5
Malta	7.2	7.3	6.9	6.5	6.0	6.9	6.9	6.5	6.3	6.3	6.2
Poland	19.0	17.8	13.9	9.6	7.1	8.2	9.6	9.8	10.0	11.0	10.1
Romania	7.7	7.2	7.3	6.4	5.8	6.9	7.3	7.3	7.1	6.9	6.7
Slovakia	18.4	16.4	13.5	11.2	9.6	12.1	14.5	12.6	13.9	13.8	13.7
Slovenia	6.3	6.5	6.0	4.9	4.4	5.9	7.3	7.3	8.1	8.8	8.5

Table A.7 (cont'd)	2004	2005	2006	2007	2008	2009	2010	2011	2012[c]	2013[d]	2014[d]
Other Europe	**4.3**	**4.3**	**3.7**	**3.2**	**3.1**	**3.9**	**4.2**	**3.8**	**3.1**	**3.6**	**3.6**
Iceland[e]	3.1	2.6	2.9	2.3	3.0	7.2	7.6	7.1	6.6	6.2	5.9
Norway	4.3	4.5	3.4	2.5	2.6	3.2	3.6	3.2	3.0	3.2	3.1
Switzerland	4.3	4.3	3.9	3.6	3.3	4.3	4.4	3.9	3.0	3.7	3.7
Memorandum items											
Major developed economies	6.4	6.2	5.8	5.5	5.9	8.1	8.2	7.7	7.5	7.5	7.3
Euro area	9.2	9.2	8.5	7.6	7.6	9.6	10.1	10.1	11.3	11.8	11.6

Source: UN/DESA, based on data of the OECD and Eurostat.

a   Unemployment data are standardized by the OECD and Eurostat for comparability among countries and over time, in conformity with the definitions of the International Labour Organization (see OECD, *Standardized Unemployment Rates: Sources and Methods* (Paris, 1985)).

b   Data for country groups are weighted averages, where labour force is used for weights.

c   Partly estimated.

d   Baseline scenario forecasts, based in part on Project LINK and the UN/DESA World Economic Forecasting Model.

e   Not standardized.

Table A.8
Economies in transition and developing economies: unemployment rates,[a] 2003-2012

Percentage of labour force	2003	2004	2005	2006	2007	2008	2009	2010	2011	2012[b]
South-Eastern Europe										
Albania[c]	15.0	14.4	14.1	13.8	13.2	12.5	13.6	13.5	13.3	13.1
Bosnia and Herzegovina	..	..	..	31.1	29.0	23.4	24.1	27.2	27.6	28.0
Croatia	13.9	13.7	12.6	11.1	9.6	8.4	9.1	12.3	14.2	14.8
Montenegro	33.4	31.1	30.3	29.6	19.4	16.8	19.1	19.7	19.7	20.0
Serbia	14.6	18.5	20.8	20.9	18.1	13.6	16.1	19.2	23.0	25.5
The former Yugoslav Republic of Macedonia	36.7	37.2	37.3	36.0	34.9	33.8	32.2	32.0	31.4	31.2
Commonwealth of Independent States and Georgia[d]										
Armenia[c]	10.2	9.4	7.6	7.2	6.4	6.3	6.8	7.1	6.0	5.8
Azerbaijan	10.7	8.4	7.6	6.8	6.5	6.0	5.9	5.6	5.4	5.4
Belarus[c]	3.1	1.9	1.5	1.1	1.0	0.8	0.9	0.7	0.6	0.5
Georgia[d]	11.5	12.6	13.8	13.6	13.3	16.5	16.9	16.3	15.1	14.3
Kazakhstan	8.8	8.4	8.1	7.8	7.3	6.6	6.6	5.8	5.4	5.2
Kyrgyzstan[c]	2.9	2.9	3.3	3.5	3.3	2.8	2.8	2.5	2.6	2.5
Republic of Moldova[c]	7.9	8.1	7.3	7.4	5.1	4.0	6.4	7.4	6.7	7.0
Russian Federation	8.2	7.8	7.2	7.2	6.1	6.4	8.4	7.5	6.6	6.1
Tajikistan[c]	2.3	2.0	2.1	2.3	2.5	2.1	2.1	2.2	2.1	2.1
Turkmenistan[c]	2.5	..	3.7	..	3.6	2.5	2.2	2.0	2.3	2.1
Ukraine	9.1	8.6	7.2	7.4	6.6	6.4	8.8	8.1	8.0	8.3
Uzbekistan[c]	0.3	0.4	0.3	0.3	0.2	0.2	0.2	0.2	0.2	0.2
Africa										
Algeria	23.7	17.7	15.3	12.3	13.8	11.3	10.2	10.0	10.0	..
Botswana	23.8	..	..	17.6	20.2	..	..	17.8	..	..
Egypt	11.9	10.3	11.2	10.7	8.9	8.7	9.4	9.0	12.2	12.6
Mauritius	7.7	8.4	9.6	9.1	8.5	7.2	7.3	7.8	7.9	8.0
Morocco	11.9	10.8	11.0	9.7	9.8	9.6	9.1	9.1	8.9	..
South Africa	29.8	27.0	26.6	25.5	23.3	22.9	24.0	24.9	24.2	24.5
Tunisia[e]	..	..	12.9	12.5	12.4	12.4	13.3	13.0	16.0	18.1
Developing America										
Argentina[f, g]	17.3	13.6	11.6	10.2	8.5	7.9	8.7	7.7	7.2	7.3
Barbados	11.0	9.8	9.1	8.7	7.4	8.1	10.0	10.8	11.2	12.1
Bolivia[f]	9.2	6.2	8.1	8.0	7.7	6.7	7.9	6.1	5.8	..
Brazil[h, i]	12.3	11.5	9.8	10.0	9.3	7.9	8.1	6.7	6.0	5.7
Chile	9.5	10.0	9.2	7.7	7.1	7.8	10.8	8.2	7.1	6.5
Colombia[j]	16.4	15.1	13.6	12.5	11.1	11.3	12.6	11.9	10.9	10.9
Costa Rica	6.7	6.7	6.9	6.0	4.8	4.8	8.5	7.1	7.7	..
Dominican Republic	16.7	18.4	17.9	16.2	15.6	14.1	14.9	14.3	14.6	14.5
Ecuador[k]	11.6	9.7	8.5	8.1	7.4	6.9	8.5	7.6	6.0	4.8
El Salvador	6.9	6.8	7.8	6.6	6.3	5.9	7.3	7.0	..	..
Guatemala	3.4	3.1	..	..	..	..	..	3.5	4.1	..
Honduras	7.6	8.0	6.5	4.9	4.0	4.1	4.9	6.4	6.8	..
Jamaica	11.4	11.7	11.3	10.3	9.8	10.6	11.4	12.4	12.6	13.7

Table A.8 (cont'd)

	2003	2004	2005	2006	2007	2008	2009	2010	2011	2012[b]
Mexico	4.6	5.3	4.7	4.6	4.8	4.9	6.7	6.4	6.0	5.8
Nicaragua	10.2	9.3	7.0	7.0	6.9	8.0	10.5	9.7	..	..
Panama	15.9	14.1	12.1	10.4	7.8	6.5	7.9	7.7	5.4	5.4
Paraguay[f]	11.2	10.0	7.6	8.9	7.2	7.4	8.2	6.8	7.0	7.2
Peru[f, l]	9.4	9.4	9.6	8.5	8.4	8.4	8.4	7.9	7.7	7.5
Trinidad and Tobago	10.5	8.4	8.0	6.2	5.6	4.6	5.3	5.9	5.8	..
Uruguay[f]	16.9	13.1	12.2	11.4	9.6	7.9	7.6	7.1	6.3	5.8
Venezuela, Bolivarian Republic of	18.0	15.3	12.4	09.9	8.4	7.3	7.9	8.7	8.3	8.6
Developing Asia										
China	4.3	4.2	4.2	4.1	4.0	4.2	4.3	4.2	4.1	4.1
Hong Kong SAR[m]	7.9	6.8	5.6	4.8	4.0	3.5	5.3	4.3	3.4	3.3
India	..	5.0	..	..	..	..	9.4	..	..	..
Indonesia	9.7	9.9	11.2	10.3	9.1	8.4	7.9	7.1	6.8	6.2
Iran, Islamic Republic of	..	10.3	11.5	..	10.5	10.3	11.5	13.5	12.3	..
Israel	10.7	10.4	9.0	8.4	7.3	6.1	7.6	6.6	5.6	6.8
Jordan	14.8	12.5	14.8	14.0	13.1	12.7	12.9	12.5	12.3	12.1
Korea, Republic of	3.6	3.7	3.7	3.5	3.2	3.2	3.6	3.7	3.4	3.3
Malaysia	3.6	3.5	3.5	3.3	3.2	3.3	3.7	3.2	3.1	3.0
Pakistan	8.3	7.7	7.7	6.2	5.3	5.2	5.5	5.8	6.0	..
Palestinian Occupied Territory	25.5	26.8	23.5	23.7	21.7	26.6	24.5	23.7	20.9	22.8
Philippines[n, o]	10.2	10.9	7.8	7.9	7.3	7.4	7.5	7.3	7.2	7.0
Saudi Arabia	5.6	5.8	6.1	6.3	6.1	6.3	6.3	6.2	5.9	..
Singapore	4.0	3.4	3.1	2.7	2.1	2.1	3.0	2.2	2.0	2.0
Sri Lanka[p]	8.1	8.1	7.2	6.5	6.0	5.2	5.7	4.9	4.0	3.9
Taiwan Province of China	5.0	4.4	4.1	3.9	3.9	4.1	5.8	5.2	4.4	4.3
Thailand	2.2	2.1	1.8	1.5	1.4	1.4	1.5	1.0	0.8	0.7
Turkey	9.3	9.0	9.2	8.8	8.9	9.7	12.6	10.7	9.8	9.1
Viet Nam[f]	5.8	5.6	5.3	4.8	4.6	4.7	4.6	4.3	3.6	..

Sources: UN/DESA, based on data of the Economic Commission for Europe (ECE); ILO LABORSTAT database and KILM 7th edition; Economic Commission for Latin America and the Caribbean (ECLAC); and national sources.

a   As a percentage of labour force. Reflects national definitions and coverage. Not comparable across economies.
b   Partly estimated.
c   End-of-period registered unemployment data (as a percentage of labour force).
d   Georgia officially left the Commonwealth of Independent States on 18 August 2009. However, its performance is discussed in the context of this group of countries for reasons of geographic proximity and similarities in economic structure.
e   New methodology starting in 2005.
f   Urban areas.
g   Break in series: new methodology starting in 2003.
h   Six main cities.
i   Break in series: new methodology starting in 2002.
j   Thirteen main cities.
k   Covers Quito, Guayaquil and Cuenca.
l   Metropolitan Lima.
m   Special Administrative Region of China.
n   Partly adopts the ILO definition; that is to say, it does not include one ILO criterion, namely, "currently available for work".
o   Break in series: new methodology starting in 2005.
p   Excluding Northern and Eastern provinces.

Table A.9
**Major developed economies: quarterly indicators of growth,
unemployment and inflation, 2010-2012**

Percentage	2010				2011				2012		
	I	II	III	IV	I	II	III	IV	I	II	III
	Growth of gross domestic product[a] *(percentage change in seasonally adjusted data from preceding quarter)*										
Canada	4.9	3.3	1.8	4.4	2.5	-0.8	5.8	2.1	1.7	1.7	0.6
France	1.2	2.6	1.6	1.6	3.5	0.2	0.8	0.1	-0.1	-0.2	0.9
Germany	2.7	9.1	2.8	2.4	5.0	1.8	1.5	-0.6	2.0	1.1	0.9
Italy	3.8	2.5	1.9	0.6	0.4	1.2	-0.6	-2.8	-3.1	-2.9	-0.7
Japan	5.1	5.1	4.7	-1.1	-8.0	-2.1	9.5	-1.2	5.2	0.3	-3.5
United Kingdom	2.4	2.9	2.5	-1.7	2.0	0.3	2.1	-1.4	-1.2	-1.5	3.9
United States	2.3	2.2	2.6	2.4	0.1	2.5	1.3	4.1	2.0	1.3	2.7
Major developed economies[b]	2.9	3.6	2.8	1.4	-0.2	1.1	2.7	1.4	1.7	0.5	1.1
Euro area	1.9	4.2	1.5	1.4	2.6	0.9	0.3	-1.3	0.0	-0.7	-0.2
	Unemployment rate[c] *(percentage of total labour force)*										
Canada	8.2	8.0	8.0	7.7	7.7	7.5	7.3	7.5	7.4	7.3	7.3
France	9.9	9.7	9.7	9.7	9.6	9.6	9.6	9.8	10.0	10.3	10.7
Germany	7.5	7.1	6.9	6.7	6.3	6.0	5.8	5.6	5.6	5.5	5.4
Italy	8.5	8.5	8.3	8.3	8.0	7.9	8.5	9.2	10.0	10.5	10.7
Japan	5.1	5.1	5.0	5.0	4.8	4.7	4.4	4.5	4.5	4.4	4.2
United Kingdom	7.9	7.8	7.7	7.8	7.7	7.9	8.3	8.3	8.1	7.9	..
United States	9.8	9.6	9.5	9.6	9.0	9.0	9.1	8.7	8.3	8.2	8.1
Major developed economies[b]	8.4	8.2	8.1	8.1	7.7	7.7	7.7	7.6	7.5	7.5	..
Euro area	10.1	10.2	10.1	10.1	10.0	9.9	10.2	10.6	10.9	11.3	11.5
	Change in consumer prices *(percentage change from the corresponding quarter of the previous year)*										
Canada	1.6	1.4	1.8	2.3	2.6	3.4	3.0	2.7	2.3	1.6	1.2
France	1.5	1.8	1.8	1.9	2.0	2.2	2.3	2.6	2.6	2.3	2.3
Germany	0.8	1.0	1.2	1.6	2.2	2.5	2.6	2.6	2.4	2.1	2.1
Italy	1.3	1.6	1.7	2.0	2.3	2.9	2.7	3.7	3.6	3.6	3.4
Japan	-0.9	-0.7	-1.0	-0.3	-0.5	-0.4	0.1	-0.3	0.3	0.2	-0.4
United Kingdom	3.3	3.4	3.1	3.4	4.1	4.4	4.7	4.7	3.5	2.7	2.4
United States	2.3	1.8	1.2	1.3	2.2	3.4	3.8	3.3	2.8	1.9	1.6
Major developed economies[b]	1.5	1.4	1.1	1.4	1.9	2.6	2.9	2.7	2.4	1.8	1.6
Euro area	1.1	1.6	1.7	2.0	2.5	2.8	2.7	2.9	2.7	2.5	2.5

Source: UN/DESA, based on Eurostat, OECD and national sources.

a Expressed as an annualized rate.
b Calculated as a weighted average, where weights are based on 2005 GDP in United States dollars.
c Seasonally adjusted data as standardized by OECD.

Table A.10
Selected economies in transition: quarterly indicators of growth and inflation, 2010-2012

Percentage	2010				2011				2012		
	I	II	III	IV	I	II	III	IV	I	II	III
	Rates of growth of gross domestic product[a]										
Armenia	3.4	8.2	-2.9	2.4	1.2	3.9	6.5	5.3	5.6	6.6	..
Azerbaijan	5.4	8.0	5.0	3.1	1.6	0.3	-0.1	-0.5	0.5	0.8	..
Belarus	4.3	9.2	7.0	10.2	10.4	11.0	1.5	0.0	3.1	2.6	..
Croatia	-2.7	-3.0	0.1	-0.2	-1.2	0.6	0.8	-0.4	-1.3	-2.2	..
Georgia	3.7	8.3	6.7	6.1	6.1	4.9	7.5	8.8	6.8	8.2	..
Kazakhstan	7.1	8.0	7.5	7.3	6.8	7.4	6.8	8.7	5.6	5.5	..
Kyrgyzstan	18.5	-2.2	-7.1	-1.8	0.6	8.1	11.4	1.0	-6.8	-4.6	..
Republic of Moldova	4.4	4.8	5.1	4.6	6.9	7.1	6.9	6.7	1.0	0.8	..
Russian Federation	3.5	4.9	3.8	4.9	4.0	3.4	5.0	4.8	4.9	4.0	..
The former Yugoslav Republic of Macedonia	0.0	2.5	4.5	4.0	6.4	3.7	1.2	0.9	-1.3	-0.9	..
Ukraine	4.5	5.4	3.3	3.7	5.4	3.9	6.5	4.7	2.0	3.0	..
	Change in consumer prices[a]										
Armenia	9.1	6.8	8.1	8.7	11.1	8.8	5.7	5.1	3.3	1.0	..
Azerbaijan	3.8	6.0	5.6	7.2	8.9	8.5	7.6	7.2	4.2	2.3	1.1
Belarus	6.1	6.8	7.7	10.0	12.6	31.7	63.1	102.4	107.8	82.4	52.3
Bosnia and Herzegovina	1.7	2.6	1.9	2.6	3.5	4.1	3.9	3.2	2.3	2.1	..
Croatia	0.9	0.7	1.1	1.5	2.2	2.3	2.1	2.4	1.5	3.5	..
Georgia	4.7	4.4	8.8	10.4	13.3	12.6	6.7	2.1	-1.3	-1.9	..
Kazakhstan	7.3	6.9	6.6	7.6	8.5	8.4	8.9	7.7	5.1	4.9	..
Kyrgyzstan	2.6	3.1	9.1	17.2	20.5	22.5	16.9	7.2	1.9	-0.3	..
Republic of Moldova	5.8	8.0	7.9	7.9	6.1	7.1	8.8	8.5	6.2	4.1	..
Russian Federation	7.2	5.9	6.2	8.2	9.5	9.5	8.1	6.6	3.8	3.8	6.0
The former Yugoslav Republic of Macedonia	0.3	0.9	2.1	3.1	3.9	4.7	3.7	3.3	2.4	2.2	..
Ukraine	11.2	8.3	8.5	9.5	7.7	10.8	8.5	5.0	2.9	0.4	..

Source: UN/DESA, based on data of the Economic Commission for Europe, European Bank for Reconstruction and Development and national sources.

a Percentage change from the corresponding period of the preceding year.

Table A.11
Major developing economies: quarterly indicators of growth, unemployment and inflation, 2010-2012

Percentage											
	2010				2011				2012		
	I	II	III	IV	I	II	III	IV	I	II	III
	Rates of growth of gross domestic product[a]										
Argentina	6.8	11.8	8.6	9.2	9.9	9.1	9.3	7.3	5.2	0.0	..
Brazil	9.3	8.8	6.9	5.3	4.2	3.3	2.1	1.4	0.8	0.5	0.9
Chile	2.8	7.1	7.7	6.7	9.9	6.3	3.7	4.5	5.2	5.7	5.7
China	11.9	10.3	9.6	9.8	9.7	9.5	9.1	8.9	8.1	7.8	7.7
Colombia	3.8	4.5	3.0	4.7	5.1	4.9	7.5	6.2	4.7	4.9	..
Ecuador	0.9	3.0	4.0	5.2	7.0	7.9	9.2	7.8	6.3	5.2	..
Hong Kong SAR[b]	7.9	6.4	6.6	6.4	7.8	5.1	4.3	2.8	0.7	1.2	1.3
India	13.0	9.5	8.9	10.0	9.7	9.0	6.9	6.2	5.6	3.9	2.8
Indonesia	5.9	6.3	5.8	6.8	6.4	6.5	6.5	6.5	6.3	6.4	6.2
Israel	2.2	6.0	5.3	6.4	6.9	3.5	5.2	3.0	3.3	3.5	3.4
Korea, Republic of	8.5	7.5	4.4	4.9	4.2	3.5	3.6	3.3	2.8	2.3	1.6
Malaysia	10.1	9.0	5.2	4.8	5.1	4.3	5.7	5.2	5.1	5.6	5.2
Mexico	4.4	7.5	5.1	4.2	4.3	2.9	4.4	3.9	4.9	4.4	3.3
Philippines	8.4	8.9	7.3	6.1	4.9	3.6	3.2	4.0	6.3	6.0	7.1
Singapore	16.5	19.8	10.6	12.5	9.1	1.2	6.0	3.6	1.5	2.3	1.3
South Africa	1.7	3.1	2.7	3.8	3.5	3.0	3.1	3.2	2.4	3.1	2.3
Taiwan Province of China	12.9	13.0	11.2	6.5	6.6	4.5	3.4	1.9	0.4	-0.2	1.0
Thailand	12.0	9.2	6.6	3.8	3.2	2.7	3.7	-8.9	0.4	4.4	3.0
Turkey	12.6	10.4	5.3	9.3	12.1	9.1	8.4	5.0	3.3	2.9	..
Venezuela, Bolivarian Republic of	-4.8	-1.7	-0.2	0.5	4.8	2.6	4.4	4.9	5.8	5.4	..
	Unemployment rate[c]										
Argentina	8.3	7.9	7.5	7.3	7.4	7.3	7.2	6.7	7.1	7.2	7.6
Brazil	7.4	7.3	6.6	5.7	6.3	6.3	6.0	5.2	5.8	5.9	5.4
Chile	9.3	8.6	8.2	7.3	7.3	7.1	7.4	7.0	6.5	6.6	6.4
Colombia	13.0	12.0	11.5	10.7	12.4	11.1	10.4	9.3	11.6	10.5	10.2
Ecuador	9.1	7.7	7.4	6.1	7.0	6.4	5.5	5.1	4.9	5.2	4.6
Hong Kong SAR[b]	4.4	4.8	4.4	3.7	3.4	3.7	3.4	3.1	3.3	3.3	3.5
Israel	7.0	5.9	7.2	6.5	5.7	5.2	6.1	6.8	6.8	6.9	6.7
Korea, Republic of	4.7	3.5	3.5	3.3	4.2	3.4	3.1	2.9	3.8	3.3	3.0
Malaysia	3.5	3.3	3.1	3.0	3.1	3.1	3.0	3.1	3.0	3.0	3.0
Mexico	5.3	5.2	5.6	5.3	5.2	5.2	5.6	4.9	4.9	4.8	5.2
Philippines	7.3	8.0	7.0	7.1	7.4	7.2	7.1	6.4	7.2	6.9	7.0
Singapore	2.2	2.2	2.1	2.2	1.9	2.1	2.0	2.0	2.1	2.0	1.9
South Africa	25.2	25.2	25.3	24.0	25.0	25.7	25.0	23.9	25.2	24.9	25.5
Taiwan Province of China	5.7	5.2	5.1	4.8	4.6	4.3	4.4	4.2	4.2	4.1	4.3
Thailand	1.1	1.3	0.9	0.8	0.8	0.6	0.6	0.6	0.7	0.9	0.6
Turkey	14.2	11.2	11.1	11.2	11.4	9.5	9.0	9.3	10.2	8.4	..
Uruguay	7.4	7.4	6.6	6.0	6.3	6.2	6.0	5.5	5.7	6.5	6.4
Venezuela, Bolivarian Republic of	9.2	8.2	9.3	8.1	9.0	8.6	8.3	7.3	9.3	8.3	7.7

Table A.11 (cont'd)

	2010				2011				2012		
	I	*II*	*III*	*IV*	*I*	*II*	*III*	*IV*	*I*	*II*	*III*
	Change in consumer prices[a]										
Argentina	9.0	10.6	11.1	11.1	10.1	9.7	9.8	9.5	9.7	9.9	10.0
Brazil	4.9	5.1	4.6	5.6	6.1	6.6	7.2	6.7	5.8	4.9	5.2
Chile	-0.3	1.2	2.3	2.5	2.9	3.3	3.1	4.0	4.1	3.1	2.6
China	2.0	2.8	3.2	4.7	5.1	5.9	6.4	4.6	3.8	2.8	1.9
Colombia	2.0	2.1	2.3	2.7	3.3	3.0	3.5	3.9	3.5	3.4	3.1
Ecuador	4.0	3.3	3.6	3.4	3.4	4.1	4.9	5.5	5.6	5.1	5.1
Hong Kong SAR[b]	1.9	2.6	2.3	2.7	3.8	5.1	6.5	5.7	5.2	4.2	3.0
India	15.3	13.6	10.3	9.2	9.0	8.9	9.2	8.4	7.2	10.1	9.8
Indonesia	3.7	4.4	6.2	6.3	6.8	5.9	4.7	4.1	3.7	4.6	4.5
Israel	3.5	2.8	2.0	2.5	4.0	4.1	3.3	2.5	1.8	1.6	1.8
Korea, Republic of	3.0	2.7	2.9	3.2	3.8	4.0	4.3	4.0	3.1	2.4	1.6
Malaysia	1.3	1.6	1.9	2.0	2.8	3.3	3.4	3.2	2.3	1.7	1.4
Mexico	4.8	4.0	3.7	4.3	3.5	3.3	3.4	3.5	3.9	3.9	4.6
Philippines	3.9	3.8	3.9	3.5	4.5	4.9	4.7	4.7	3.1	2.9	3.5
Singapore	0.9	3.1	3.3	4.0	5.1	4.7	5.5	5.6	4.9	5.3	4.2
South Africa	5.4	4.2	3.3	3.4	3.8	4.7	5.5	6.3	6.2	5.8	5.3
Taiwan Province of China	1.3	1.1	0.4	1.1	1.3	1.6	1.3	1.4	1.3	1.7	3.0
Thailand	3.7	3.2	3.3	2.9	3.0	4.1	4.1	4.0	3.4	2.5	2.9
Turkey	9.3	9.2	8.4	7.4	4.3	5.9	6.4	9.2	10.5	9.4	9.0
Venezuela, Bolivarian Republic of	25.1	31.0	29.3	27.2	28.2	23.1	25.8	27.4	25.3	22.6	18.5

Sources: IMF, *International Financial Statistics*, and national sources.

a   Percentage change from the corresponding quarter of the previous year.
b   Special Administrative Region of China.
c   Reflects national definitions and coverage. Not comparable across economies.

Table A.12
Major developed economies: financial indicators, 2003–2012

Percentage	2003	2004	2005	2006	2007	2008	2009	2010	2011	2012[a]
Short-term interest rates[b]										
Canada	3.0	2.3	2.8	4.2	4.6	3.3	0.7	0.8	1.2	1.2
France[c]	2.3	2.1	2.2	3.1	4.3	4.6	1.2	0.8	1.4	0.7
Germany[c]	2.3	2.1	2.2	3.1	4.3	4.6	1.2	0.8	1.4	0.7
Italy[c]	2.3	2.1	2.2	3.1	4.3	4.6	1.2	0.8	1.4	0.7
Japan	0.1	0.1	0.1	0.3	0.8	0.9	0.6	0.4	0.3	0.3
United Kingdom	3.7	4.6	4.7	4.8	6.0	5.5	1.2	0.7	0.9	0.9
United States	1.1	1.6	3.5	5.2	5.3	3.0	0.6	0.3	0.3	0.3
Long-term interest rates[d]										
Canada	4.8	4.6	4.1	4.2	4.3	3.6	3.2	3.2	2.8	1.9
France	4.1	4.1	3.4	3.8	4.3	4.2	3.7	3.1	3.3	2.7
Germany	4.1	4.0	3.3	3.8	4.2	4.0	3.2	2.7	2.6	1.5
Italy	4.3	4.3	3.6	4.1	4.5	4.7	4.3	4.0	5.4	5.7
Japan	1.0	1.5	1.4	1.7	1.7	1.5	1.3	1.1	1.1	0.9
United Kingdom	4.5	4.9	4.4	4.5	5.0	4.6	3.7	3.6	3.1	1.9
United States	4.0	4.3	4.3	4.8	4.6	3.7	3.3	3.2	2.8	1.8
General government financial balances[e]										
Canada	-0.1	0.8	1.5	1.6	1.4	-0.4	-4.8	-5.4	-4.5	-3.7
France	-4.1	-3.6	-3.0	-2.4	-2.8	-3.3	-7.5	-7.1	-5.2	-4.7
Germany	-4.2	-3.8	-3.3	-1.7	0.2	-0.1	-3.1	-4.1	-0.8	-0.7
Italy	-3.6	-3.6	-4.5	-3.4	-1.6	-2.7	-5.4	-4.5	-3.9	-2.7
Japan	-7.7	-5.9	-4.8	-1.3	-2.1	-1.9	-8.8	-8.4	-9.5	-9.9
United Kingdom	-3.4	-3.5	-3.4	-2.7	-2.8	-5.1	-11.5	-10.2	-7.8	-7.7
United States	-4.9	-4.4	-3.2	-2.0	-2.7	-6.4	-11.8	-11.2	-10.1	-8.6

Sources: UN/DESA, based on OECD, *Economic Outlook*; OECD, *Main Economic Indicators*; and Eurostat.

a   Average for the first nine months for short- and long-term interest rates.
b   Three-month Interbank Rate.
c   From January 1999 onwards, represents the three-month Euro Interbank Offered Rate (EURIBOR).
d   Yield on long-term government bonds.
e   Surplus (+) or deficit (-) as a percentage of nominal GDP. Estimates for 2012.

Table A.13
Selected economies: real effective exchange rates, broad measurement,[a] 2003–2012

Year 2000=100	2003	2004	2005	2006	2007	2008	2009	2010	2011	2012[b]
Developed economies										
Australia	111.8	121.2	128.1	133.8	142.8	141.0	130.6	146.1	157.3	157.7
Bulgaria	110.7	113.3	116.5	126.2	132.9	142.7	140.1	143.1	150.5	150.3
Canada	102.9	104.6	108.3	111.6	112.9	102.6	95.3	101.0	100.3	97.9
Czech Republic	117.4	121.7	129.1	134.0	139.4	156.5	148.8	149.5	155.7	150.4
Denmark	114.2	114.4	111.8	109.9	109.8	110.7	117.4	111.8	109.6	107.6
Euro area	117.3	121.0	119.5	121.3	126.1	131.1	125.4	117.5	120.5	114.8
Hungary	115.2	119.6	119.0	115.9	119.8	123.1	118.9	118.4	116.9	114.4
Japan	82.5	83.5	78.6	72.0	67.1	74.2	83.2	84.2	85.4	84.9
New Zealand	131.5	140.1	147.2	135.7	146.3	133.5	127.8	139.2	146.3	151.3
Norway	108.2	110.6	117.3	123.4	132.4	133.7	130.1	139.3	146.2	145.7
Poland	98.7	102.5	111.1	113.4	117.8	126.1	109.1	114.2	113.7	112.6
Romania	117.4	127.8	153.8	172.7	191.3	180.7	174.0	175.0	176.9	165.6
Slovakia	113.1	117.1	117.1	118.7	128.5	132.7	141.1	129.5	124.6	121.8
Sweden	97.3	96.2	93.1	94.4	97.4	91.5	89.4	92.3	92.4	90.8
Switzerland	112.3	110.0	105.7	101.2	96.2	98.9	107.0	110.1	117.7	113.8
United Kingdom	95.8	99.6	97.2	97.3	98.8	86.8	80.3	80.7	81.3	85.1
United States	97.8	91.6	89.3	86.5	82.4	79.7	88.0	83.5	78.5	82.0
Economies in transition										
Croatia	110.3	114.3	115.2	116.2	117.5	125.3	128.0	127.4	127.5	128.8
Russian Federation	131.2	140.7	155.3	170.5	180.3	191.5	182.1	198.6	204.3	206.5
Developing economies										
Argentina	62.1	60.6	59.9	58.3	57.6	58.7	56.8	57.5	55.8	59.2
Brazil	99.1	106.5	130.9	141.0	157.0	175.9	168.9	194.0	208.0	191.8
Chile	92.3	100.0	112.1	117.9	117.3	122.3	127.0	126.3	128.0	131.0
China	97.8	95.8	98.5	100.8	103.4	112.5	112.4	113.6	116.3	118.6
Colombia	88.1	95.2	105.0	102.6	110.2	113.3	106.4	124.1	123.3	126.2
Ecuador	114.1	114.3	121.9	130.5	126.2	135.3	112.4	128.9	141.6	142.2
Egypt	64.5	66.4	72.3	74.1	76.4	86.6	85.8	92.4	92.2	96.8
Hong Kong SAR[c]	94.9	89.6	86.4	83.9	79.8	75.6	80.6	77.5	74.2	76.7
India	98.3	99.3	101.3	98.8	106.4	98.6	94.1	100.8	97.2	92.0
Indonesia	123.4	112.5	114.5	142.1	149.2	162.3	163.9	183.9	183.5	181.1
Israel	87.8	85.2	86.3	86.8	88.0	98.7	97.8	102.9	102.8	98.9
Korea, Republic of	93.0	96.2	105.9	110.7	108.2	90.8	80.0	86.2	88.2	88.2
Kuwait	102.2	94.6	96.5	94.9	93.2	97.2	96.4	98.2	96.0	95.8
Malaysia	98.6	100.7	103.5	107.0	112.7	115.7	113.1	124.5	130.8	132.1
Mexico	99.6	98.0	103.4	105.9	105.9	105.6	91.0	98.9	100.8	98.4
Morocco	99.0	97.2	94.7	94.7	93.5	94.3	100.0	95.7	91.7	90.4
Nigeria	108.8	112.3	128.6	135.7	133.6	145.5	139.4	151.9	148.5	164.3
Pakistan	101.0	100.0	102.8	105.5	105.5	106.3	108.1	118.8	128.0	132.2
Peru	99.9	99.5	99.2	99.3	99.6	106.3	105.5	110.0	111.1	117.7
Philippines	107.3	100.4	107.9	129.4	135.8	130.5	128.6	118.1	110.2	111.9

Table A.13 (cont'd)	2003	2004	2005	2006	2007	2008	2009	2010	2011	2012[b]
Saudi Arabia	94.1	87.3	85.0	83.7	81.7	83.5	92.1	93.1	90.0	95.2
Singapore	95.4	102.5	106.9	112.4	119.6	125.8	114.0	116.6	118.8	121.9
South Africa	107.3	116.2	118.0	112.4	109.3	100.6	106.7	119.9	117.1	111.2
Taiwan Province of China	89.5	90.9	89.1	88.8	87.7	84.2	76.8	79.8	79.6	78.7
Thailand	100.3	100.0	102.6	111.7	125.3	120.0	112.6	123.0	125.4	124.8
Turkey	111.3	116.4	124.8	120.9	128.4	126.0	114.6	117.9	106.1	113.9
Venezuela, Bolivarian Republic of	94.5	98.9	99.7	108.2	120.0	140.4	191.0	116.0	134.2	152.3

Source: JPMorgan Chase.

a Indices based on a "broad" measure currency basket of 46 currencies (including the euro). The real effective exchange rate, which adjusts the nominal index for relative price changes, gauges the effect on international price competitiveness of the country's manufactures owing to currency changes and inflation differentials. A rise in the index implies a fall in competitiveness and vice versa. The relative price changes are based on indices most closely measuring the prices of domestically produced finished manufactured goods, excluding food and energy, at the first stage of manufacturing. The weights for currency indices are derived from 2000 bilateral trade patterns of the corresponding countries.

b Average for the first ten months.

c Special Administrative Region of China.

Table A.14
Indices of prices of primary commodities, 2003–2012

Year 2000=100											
	Non-fuel commodities					Combined index		Manufac-tured export prices	Real prices of non-fuel commo-dities[a]	Crude petroleum[b]
	Food	Tropical beverages	Vegetable oilseeds and oils	Agricul-tural raw materials	Minerals and metals	Dollar	SDR			
2003	104	94	137	111	98	105	99	108	97	101.8
2004	119	100	155	125	137	126	112	117	108	130.6
2005	127	126	141	129	173	140	126	120	117	183.5
2006	151	134	148	147	278	183	164	123	149	221.3
2007	164	148	226	164	313	207	178	133	155	250.4
2008	234	178	298	198	332	256	213	142	180	342.2
2009	220	181	213	163	232	213	182	134	159	221.2
2010	230	213	262	226	310	251	218	136	185	280.6
2011	265	270	333	289	349	295	247	148	199	389.3
2009 I	206	164	188	146	182	188	167	126	149	155.5
II	213	175	226	150	214	203	177	129	158	212.0
III	228	186	215	164	252	223	188	134	166	245.3
IV	233	201	224	193	278	237	197	137	173	269.3
2010 I	232	198	234	210	299	245	210	134	183	273.2
II	205	201	233	209	296	231	205	132	175	277.5
III	225	220	258	216	301	246	214	135	182	267.3
IV	257	233	322	268	344	284	242	141	201	303.5
2011 I	274	278	364	315	376	312	264	144	217	365.9
II	261	283	345	303	363	300	249	151	199	407.1
III	270	274	324	290	352	298	247	150	199	393.2
IV	255	247	299	248	304	270	228	146	185	391.0
2012 I	257	232	316	246	327	276	237	145	191	425.4
II	264	208	318	229	308	271	234	143	190	386.8
III	285	211	318	205	303	277	241	..	..	386.2

Sources: UNCTAD, *Monthly Commodity Price Bulletin*; United Nations, *Monthly Bulletin of Statistics*; and data from the Organization of the Petroleum Exporting Countries (OPEC) website, available from http://www.opec.org.

a   Combined index of non-fuel commodity prices in dollars, deflated by manufactured export price index.
b   The new OPEC reference basket, introduced on 16 June 2005, currently has 12 crudes.

Table A.15
World oil supply and demand, 2004–2013

	2004	*2005*	*2006*	*2007*	*2008*	*2009*	*2010*	*2011*	*2012*[a]	*2013*[b]
World oil supply[c, d] (millions of barrels per day)	**83.3**	**84.3**	**85.0**	**84.7**	**86.6**	**85.4**	**87.2**	**88.5**	**90.8**	**91.1**
Developed economies	17.4	16.5	16.3	16.0	16.8	17.0	17.3	17.3	18.1	18.6
Economies in transition	11.6	12.0	12.4	12.9	12.9	13.3	13.5	13.6	13.7	13.6
Developing economies	52.5	54.0	54.4	53.6	54.9	53.1	54.3	55.5	56.9	56.7
OPEC[e]	33.1	34.2	34.3	34.6	36.1	34.0	34.6	35.7	37.6	37.2
Non-OPEC	19.4	19.8	20.1	19.0	18.8	19.1	19.7	19.8	19.3	19.5
Processing gains[f]	1.9	1.9	1.9	2.2	2.0	2.0	2.1	2.1	2.1	2.2
World total demand[g]	**82.5**	**83.8**	**85.1**	**86.5**	**86.5**	**85.4**	**88.1**	**88.8**	**89.6**	**90.5**
Oil prices (dollars per barrel)										
OPEC basket[h]	36.1	50.6	61.1	69.1	94.5	61.1	77.5	107.5	109.9	102.0
Brent oil	38.3	54.4	65.4	72.7	97.6	61.9	79.6	110.9	110.0	105.0

Sources: United Nations, World Bank, International Energy Agency, U.S. Energy Information Administration, and OPEC.

a Partly estimated.
b Baseline scenario forecasts.
c Including global biofuels, crude oil, condensates, natural gas liquids (NGLs), oil from non-conventional sources and other sources of supply.
d Totals may not add up because of rounding.
e Includes Angola and Ecuador as of January 2007 and December 2007, respectively.
f Net volume gains and losses in the refining process (excluding net gain/loss in the economies in transition and China) and marine transportation losses.
g Including deliveries from refineries/primary stocks and marine bunkers, and refinery fuel and non-conventional oils.
h The new OPEC reference basket, introduced on 16 June 2005, currently has 12 crudes.

Table A.16
World trade:[a] changes in value and volume of exports and imports, by major country group, 2004–2014

Annual percentage change	2004	2005	2006	2007	2008	2009	2010	2011[b]	2012[c]	2013[c]	2014[c]
Dollar value of exports											
World	21.2	14.2	14.7	16.2	14.0	-19.9	19.7	17.6	5.0	6.9	8.1
Developed economies	18.4	9.4	12.5	15.4	11.5	-20.0	13.1	15.2	0.0	4.1	6.3
North America	13.9	11.5	10.9	11.9	10.2	-16.8	16.2	14.3	4.2	4.0	6.0
EU plus other Europe	19.4	9.0	13.6	17.2	11.2	-20.0	10.1	15.9	-1.0	5.0	6.9
Developed Asia	21.7	8.9	7.7	12.3	12.9	-23.7	32.2	10.4	-0.8	-1.6	3.2
Economies in transition	34.3	26.7	24.1	21.3	32.2	-32.6	26.7	30.9	-1.2	3.4	9.2
South-Eastern Europe	23.7	12.5	18.5	23.7	19.6	-21.1	7.8	15.4	-3.3	6.0	7.2
Commonwealth of Independent States	35.0	28.5	24.5	21.3	33.1	-33.5	28.6	32.0	-1.0	3.2	9.5
Developing economies	26.4	21.2	19.0	17.0	17.4	-18.6	28.1	20.7	11.2	9.9	10.8
Latin America and the Caribbean	22.9	20.1	18.7	12.8	15.7	-21.0	31.6	17.1	12.2	10.9	13.1
Africa	25.1	29.6	23.4	12.8	27.7	-26.5	25.9	18.0	24.5	5.5	4.0
Western Asia	31.8	30.9	18.7	15.8	29.3	-26.5	20.5	28.2	16.8	4.8	5.9
East and South Asia	26.3	18.7	18.6	18.4	14.0	-15.0	29.2	20.2	9.0	11.7	11.7
Dollar value of imports											
World	21.1	13.4	14.2	15.9	14.9	-20.2	18.8	18.0	4.6	6.6	8.3
Developed economies	18.7	11.3	12.8	13.1	12.0	-22.2	13.7	15.9	0.8	4.0	6.2
North America	15.7	13.1	10.3	6.4	8.1	-22.1	19.2	13.0	3.4	2.1	6.2
EU plus other Europe	19.8	10.3	14.2	16.9	11.8	-21.6	10.5	15.5	-1.4	4.9	7.1
Developed Asia	21.3	13.0	9.1	11.6	17.4	-23.8	24.1	23.6	9.2	2.8	1.4
Economies in transition	28.4	19.9	23.9	33.9	29.3	-29.9	20.5	27.5	2.5	7.0	12.3
South-Eastern Europe	24.4	8.5	15.1	30.9	23.1	-27.8	0.0	14.5	-2.8	6.7	7.8
Commonwealth of Independent States	29.9	21.7	25.7	34.1	30.3	-30.1	23.7	29.1	3.1	7.1	12.8
Developing economies	25.9	17.5	17.2	19.3	19.5	-15.8	27.2	20.7	10.0	11.5	10.7
Latin America and the Caribbean	20.4	18.5	18.0	19.2	20.7	-20.1	28.9	19.2	9.7	10.3	11.3
Africa	20.0	21.1	18.1	27.3	24.8	-11.6	10.7	17.9	17.7	12.5	12.8
Western Asia	30.9	21.0	19.7	29.1	22.6	-17.9	15.0	17.2	12.0	5.6	6.2
East and South Asia	27.3	16.0	16.5	16.6	17.7	-14.8	31.8	21.9	9.0	11.9	10.9
Volume of exports											
World	10.2	8.4	9.3	7.1	3.3	-9.6	12.8	6.9	3.5	4.0	4.9
Developed economies	8.0	5.8	8.9	6.3	2.0	-11.8	11.0	5.5	2.4	3.0	4.9
North America	7.9	6.1	6.3	7.6	4.0	-10.1	10.2	6.3	3.7	3.1	4.3
EU plus other Europe	7.5	5.8	9.6	5.7	1.6	-11.4	10.4	5.9	2.1	3.1	4.3
Developed Asia	11.5	5.3	8.6	7.6	1.3	-18.4	18.2	0.7	1.8	2.2	6.0
Economies in transition	12.9	4.1	7.5	7.4	1.6	-7.4	7.1	3.2	3.7	4.1	4.3
South-Eastern Europe	7.7	9.3	9.4	6.0	2.9	-12.9	12.3	4.6	1.2	4.1	4.6
Commonwealth of Independent States	13.2	4.0	7.1	7.6	1.5	-6.8	6.5	3.1	4.0	4.1	4.3
Developing economies	15.5	11.9	11.8	8.5	4.5	-5.5	17.2	9.2	4.1	5.3	6.2
Latin America and the Caribbean	12.4	7.4	7.2	5.3	1.6	-9.9	11.1	6.7	4.4	6.7	7.9
Africa	6.6	10.6	13.5	3.7	9.6	-14.4	10.2	0.2	9.2	6.6	6.2
Western Asia	14.0	9.9	7.4	5.7	4.3	-7.4	6.6	7.5	4.8	2.2	4.2
East and South Asia	17.9	14.3	13.3	10.8	4.3	-3.0	20.9	11.0	3.6	5.3	6.2

Table A.16 (cont'd)	2004	2005	2006	2007	2008	2009	2010	2011[b]	2012[c]	2013[c]	2014[c]
					Volume of imports						
World	11.4	8.5	9.4	7.9	2.0	-9.8	13.8	7.0	3.0	4.6	5.0
Developed economies	8.6	6.1	8.0	5.0	0.1	-11.9	10.5	4.6	1.8	3.2	3.9
North America	10.7	6.6	5.8	2.7	-1.9	-13.6	13.0	4.8	3.0	3.3	5.3
EU plus other Europe	7.6	6.3	9.5	5.9	1.1	-11.3	9.3	4.2	0.5	2.7	4.3
Developed Asia	8.9	4.8	5.4	5.2	-0.7	-10.7	11.0	7.6	8.0	2.5	-1.0
Economies in transition	18.7	11.1	15.7	22.2	11.8	-25.4	16.4	15.6	7.2	7.6	7.8
South-Eastern Europe	12.1	5.4	7.9	11.8	5.9	-19.7	4.6	3.5	1.6	4.5	5.5
Commonwealth of Independent States	20.2	12.0	17.1	24.1	12.5	-26.2	18.0	17.3	7.9	7.9	8.3
Developing economies	16.9	12.8	12.6	11.4	6.6	-5.4	18.9	10.1	5.1	6.1	7.0
Latin America and the Caribbean	13.8	11.2	14.1	13.0	8.0	-15.0	21.6	10.4	4.7	7.2	9.4
Africa	6.0	11.6	12.1	18.0	9.4	-6.3	7.9	8.7	14.8	10.3	9.0
Western Asia	21.2	15.4	13.6	19.9	8.2	-12.6	7.8	7.6	5.1	4.1	4.0
East and South Asia	18.4	12.9	11.8	9.2	5.5	-1.2	21.7	10.4	4.1	5.5	6.9

Source: UN/DESA.

a   Includes goods and non-factor services.
b   Partly estimated.
c   Baseline scenario forecasts, based in part on Project LINK.

Table A.17
Balance of payments on current accounts, by country or country group, summary table, 2003–2011

Billions of dollars									
	2003	*2004*	*2005*	*2006*	*2007*	*2008*	*2009*	*2010*	*2011*
Developed economies	**-316.8**	**-332.2**	**-502.4**	**-579.9**	**-532.6**	**-663.3**	**-226.8**	**-192.8**	**-262.3**
Japan	136.2	172.1	166.1	170.9	212.1	159.9	146.6	204.0	119.3
United States	-519.1	-628.5	-745.8	-800.6	-710.3	-677.1	-381.9	-442.0	-465.9
Europe[a]	87.3	146.8	106.6	82.1	22.9	-93.0	92.6	135.1	173.4
EU-15	45.4	112.5	48.0	33.2	40.9	-57.7	34.3	44.8	72.1
New EU member States	-28.5	-45.7	-40.1	-60.7	-102.6	-113.9	-34.5	-39.1	-37.6
Economies in transition[b]	**30.1**	**56.4**	**80.1**	**87.4**	**55.8**	**83.8**	**31.3**	**65.9**	**105.5**
South-Eastern Europe	-5.7	-7.1	-7.4	-8.7	-15.4	-24.6	-10.7	-6.9	-9.1
Commonwealth of Independent States[c]	36.2	63.9	88.2	97.2	73.2	111.2	43.2	74.0	116.2
Developing economies	**223.0**	**275.0**	**458.8**	**709.5**	**791.4**	**776.0**	**420.9**	**446.8**	**548.4**
Net fuel exporters	78.7	119.5	268.1	390.6	351.6	448.9	85.8	231.0	462.0
Net fuel importers	144.3	155.4	190.7	318.9	439.8	327.1	335.2	215.8	86.4
Latin America and the Caribbean	10.6	23.0	37.7	51.1	15.3	-30.0	-19.9	-55.8	-71.8
Net fuel exporters	11.5	16.1	28.3	34.5	22.6	42.8	6.1	9.2	19.1
Net fuel importers	-0.9	6.9	9.4	16.6	-7.3	-72.8	-26.0	-65.0	-90.9
Africa	1.0	12.0	37.7	85.2	69.4	62.1	-34.3	1.4	-21.8
Net fuel exporters	6.1	24.6	55.2	106.9	102.8	113.6	4.9	40.0	33.9
Net fuel importers	-5.1	-12.5	-17.5	-21.7	-33.4	-51.5	-39.2	-38.6	-55.7
Western Asia	40.0	58.3	142.6	184.6	145.6	228.0	43.8	104.2	254.8
Net fuel exporters[d]	51.2	74.7	165.0	212.2	184.2	273.2	56.4	150.1	338.9
Net fuel importers	-11.3	-16.4	-22.4	-27.7	-38.6	-45.2	-12.6	-45.8	-84.2
East and South Asia	171.4	181.6	240.8	388.7	561.1	515.8	431.3	397.0	387.2
Net fuel exporters	9.9	4.2	19.6	37.0	42.0	19.2	18.3	31.8	70.0
Net fuel importers	161.5	177.4	221.2	351.6	519.1	496.5	413.0	365.2	317.2
World residual[e]	**-63.8**	**-0.8**	**36.5**	**217.0**	**314.6**	**196.4**	**225.5**	**319.9**	**391.6**

Source: International Monetary Fund (IMF), *World Economic Outlook*, October 2012; and IMF, *Balance of Payments Statistics*.

a Europe consists of the EU-15, the new EU member States and Iceland, Norway and Switzerland.
b Includes Georgia.
c Excludes Georgia, which left the Commonwealth of Independent States on 18 August 2009.
d Data for Iraq not available prior to 2005.
e Statistical discrepancy.

Table A.18
Balance of payments on current accounts, by country or country group, 2003–2011

Billions of dollars	2003	2004	2005	2006	2007	2008	2009	2010	2011
Developed economies									
Trade balance	-307.7	-421.8	-637.3	-781.1	-782.6	-912.8	-475.1	-586.9	-773.1
Services, net	108.0	162.2	214.6	279.4	386.4	426.8	382.1	435.9	524.1
Income, net	53.0	132.3	165.5	164.0	160.6	152.8	190.2	305.4	345.5
Current transfers, net	-170.1	-204.9	-245.2	-242.2	-297.0	-330.1	-323.9	-347.1	-358.7
Current-account balance	-316.8	-332.2	-502.4	-579.9	-532.6	-663.3	-226.8	-192.8	-262.3
Japan									
Trade balance	104.0	128.5	93.9	81.1	105.1	38.5	43.3	91.0	-20.6
Services, net	-31.4	-34.3	-24.1	-18.2	-21.2	-20.8	-20.4	-16.1	-22.2
Income, net	71.2	85.7	103.9	118.7	139.8	155.3	135.9	141.5	176.0
Current transfers, net	-7.5	-7.9	-7.6	-10.7	-11.5	-13.1	-12.3	-12.4	-13.8
Current-account balance	136.2	172.1	166.1	170.9	212.1	159.9	146.6	204.0	119.3
United States									
Trade balance	-540.4	-663.5	-780.7	-835.7	-818.9	-830.1	-505.8	-645.1	-738.4
Services, net	49.4	58.2	72.1	82.4	122.2	131.8	126.6	150.4	178.5
Income, net	43.7	65.1	68.6	44.2	101.5	147.1	119.7	183.9	227.0
Current transfers, net	-71.8	-88.2	-105.7	-91.5	-115.1	-125.9	-122.5	-131.1	-133.1
Current-account balance	-519.1	-628.5	-745.8	-800.6	-710.3	-677.1	-381.9	-442.0	-465.9
Europe[a]									
Trade balance	103.9	81.9	14.3	-58.7	-93.4	-157.9	-7.6	-43.7	-46.7
Services, net	95.9	145.8	176.0	226.4	301.9	340.5	295.7	327.4	402.6
Income, net	-21.4	27.5	46.8	53.2	-16.6	-84.9	-9.1	51.6	25.0
Current transfers, net	-91.1	-108.5	-130.5	-138.7	-168.9	-190.7	-186.5	-200.2	-207.4
Current-account balance	87.3	146.8	106.6	82.1	22.9	-93.0	92.6	135.1	173.4
EU-15									
Trade balance	102.7	79.0	2.8	-64.4	-73.9	-148.7	-39.1	-78.1	-103.0
Services, net	64.7	110.0	133.9	177.4	241.4	267.6	228.7	253.6	318.6
Income, net	-31.4	30.5	37.1	57.1	40.7	9.9	25.8	66.4	62.1
Current transfers, net	-90.6	-107.0	-125.8	-136.9	-167.4	-186.5	-181.1	-197.1	-205.6
Current-account balance	45.4	112.5	48.0	33.2	40.9	-57.7	34.3	44.8	72.1
New EU member States									
Trade balance	-29.1	-34.7	-36.3	-52.1	-79.4	-101.3	-25.9	-30.2	-27.1
Services, net	8.0	9.5	13.2	15.8	22.9	26.7	23.4	25.7	31.7
Income, net	-15.4	-28.2	-25.9	-34.9	-57.6	-51.9	-43.1	-48.6	-58.5
Current transfers, net	8.0	7.7	8.9	10.5	11.5	12.6	11.1	13.9	16.3
Current-account balance	-28.5	-45.7	-40.1	-60.7	-102.6	-113.9	-34.5	-39.1	-37.6
Economies in transition[b]									
Trade balance	43.1	71.2	106.4	128.3	109.7	163.6	93.8	152.6	220.2
Services, net	-7.0	-10.5	-12.2	-11.9	-18.4	-22.1	-18.9	-27.0	-32.7
Income, net	-16.4	-17.0	-28.4	-44.3	-51.0	-77.4	-61.7	-77.3	-100.8
Current transfers, net	10.5	12.7	14.2	15.1	15.6	19.6	18.1	17.6	18.7
Current-account balance	30.1	56.4	80.1	87.4	55.8	83.8	31.3	65.9	105.5

Table A.18 (cont'd)	2003	2004	2005	2006	2007	2008	2009	2010	2011
South-Eastern Europe									
Trade balance	-18.6	-22.6	-23.1	-25.6	-34.4	-44.6	-29.3	-24.9	-28.9
Services, net	6.2	6.7	7.3	8.0	9.8	11.7	9.7	9.6	10.9
Income, net	-0.6	-0.3	-1.1	-1.2	-1.9	-2.9	-2.8	-2.9	-3.2
Current transfers, net	7.3	9.1	9.5	10.2	11.0	11.2	11.8	11.4	12.0
Current-account balance	-5.7	-7.1	-7.4	-8.7	-15.4	-24.6	-10.7	-6.9	-9.1
Commonwealth of Independent States[c]									
Trade balance	62.3	94.7	130.8	156.0	147.0	212.1	125.6	180.1	252.5
Services, net	-13.3	-17.2	-19.5	-20.0	-28.4	-33.8	-28.9	-37.1	-44.4
Income, net	-15.8	-16.8	-27.3	-43.2	-49.2	-74.4	-58.9	-74.1	-97.3
Current transfers, net	2.9	3.1	4.3	4.5	3.9	7.4	5.4	5.2	5.4
Current-account balance	36.2	63.9	88.2	97.2	73.2	111.2	43.2	74.0	116.2
Developing economies									
Trade balance	303.7	365.3	578.7	774.7	842.2	861.4	543.9	663.2	830.5
Services, net	-59.2	-60.0	-78.7	-87.7	-98.0	-144.2	-150.1	-169.3	-201.7
Income, net	-123.9	-149.1	-190.8	-164.9	-163.0	-183.2	-180.2	-270.8	-300.9
Current transfers, net	102.3	118.7	149.5	187.6	210.1	241.3	207.0	223.6	220.7
Current-account balance	223.0	275.0	458.8	709.5	791.4	776.0	420.9	446.8	548.4
Net fuel exporters									
Trade balance	185.9	254.2	409.8	526.2	533.4	712.5	340.3	532.0	827.2
Services, net	-63.6	-75.6	-88.6	-113.3	-149.9	-207.3	-190.4	-204.9	-233.1
Income, net	-34.5	-52.4	-56.6	-34.3	-36.6	-57.8	-53.5	-84.9	-112.8
Current transfers, net	-8.2	-5.2	4.7	13.5	6.5	3.6	-9.5	-9.3	-16.8
Current-account balance	78.7	119.5	268.1	390.6	351.6	448.9	85.8	231.0	462.0
Net fuel importers									
Trade balance	117.9	111.1	168.9	248.5	308.9	148.9	203.5	131.1	3.2
Services, net	4.4	15.6	9.9	25.7	51.9	63.1	40.3	35.6	31.4
Income, net	-89.4	-96.7	-134.2	-130.7	-126.4	-125.4	-126.7	-186.0	-188.1
Current transfers, net	110.5	124.0	144.8	174.1	203.6	237.7	216.5	232.9	237.5
Current-account balance	144.3	155.4	190.7	318.9	439.8	327.1	335.2	215.8	86.4
Latin America and the Caribbean									
Trade balance	43.8	59.7	83.0	101.7	72.5	44.8	55.7	49.0	72.8
Services, net	-12.9	-13.6	-17.1	-18.1	-23.9	-32.2	-33.0	-49.7	-63.7
Income, net	-58.2	-67.9	-81.3	-96.5	-100.6	-109.9	-100.5	-116.5	-143.7
Current transfers, net	37.9	44.8	53.1	64.0	67.3	67.4	57.8	61.4	62.8
Current-account balance	10.6	23.0	37.7	51.1	15.3	-30.0	-19.9	-55.8	-71.8
Africa									
Trade balance	16.2	33.7	67.7	95.3	97.2	115.7	0.5	52.9	47.0
Services, net	-8.4	-11.1	-15.3	-22.1	-33.7	-54.5	-48.2	-53.4	-66.1
Income, net	-27.8	-35.5	-45.4	-38.0	-51.4	-65.2	-48.7	-65.9	-81.0
Current transfers, net	21.0	24.9	30.6	50.2	57.2	65.5	61.8	67.7	78.6
Current-account balance	1.0	12.0	37.7	85.2	69.4	62.1	-34.3	1.4	-21.8

Table A.18 (cont'd)

	2003	2004	2005	2006	2007	2008	2009	2010	2011
Western Asia[d]									
Trade balance	83.6	110.9	186.9	237.8	223.3	343.7	168.1	246.7	427.7
Services, net	-18.2	-25.7	-27.5	-44.9	-63.1	-88.1	-80.4	-89.0	-102.2
Income, net	-14.1	-17.5	-7.2	6.8	12.4	4.1	-2.9	-9.0	-9.9
Current transfers, net	-11.3	-9.4	-9.5	-15.2	-27.0	-31.7	-41.0	-44.4	-60.8
Current-account balance	40.0	58.3	142.6	184.6	145.6	228.0	43.8	104.2	254.8
East Asia									
Trade balance	175.6	191.2	278.6	391.4	507.5	479.7	430.9	437.8	414.1
Services, net	-21.7	-16.3	-29.0	-20.6	-2.8	-2.4	-13.3	-5.4	-16.3
Income, net	-16.1	-20.9	-46.2	-27.0	-12.8	-2.0	-14.6	-59.5	-46.2
Current transfers, net	19.6	24.7	34.4	39.1	52.4	64.8	51.0	54.7	42.7
Current-account balance	157.5	178.8	237.7	382.9	544.2	540.1	454.0	427.6	394.3
South Asia									
Trade balance	-15.5	-30.3	-37.4	-51.4	-58.2	-122.4	-111.3	-123.3	-131.1
Services, net	1.9	6.6	10.3	18.0	25.4	33.0	24.8	28.3	46.5
Income, net	-7.7	-7.2	-10.6	-10.2	-10.6	-10.2	-13.6	-19.9	-20.0
Current transfers, net	35.2	33.7	40.8	49.4	60.2	75.3	77.4	84.3	97.5
Current-account balance	13.9	2.9	3.1	5.8	16.8	-24.4	-22.7	-30.6	-7.1
World residual[e]									
Trade balance	39.1	14.7	47.9	121.9	169.4	112.3	162.6	228.8	277.6
Services, net	41.7	91.7	123.8	179.9	269.9	260.5	213.1	239.6	289.8
Income, net	-87.3	-33.7	-53.8	-45.2	-53.5	-107.8	-51.8	-42.7	-56.2
Current transfers, net	-57.3	-73.5	-81.5	-39.5	-71.3	-69.2	-98.8	-105.9	-119.3
Current-account balance	-63.8	-0.8	36.5	217.0	314.6	196.4	225.5	319.9	391.6

Source: International Monetary Fund (IMF), *World Economic Outlook*, October 2012; and IMF, *Balance of Payments Statistics*.

a   Europe consists of EU-15, new EU member States plus Iceland, Norway and Switzerland.

b   Includes Georgia.

c   Excludes Georgia, which left the Commonwealth of Independent States on 18 August 2009.

d   Data for Iraq not available prior to 2005.

e   Statistical discrepancy.

Table A.19
Net ODA from major sources, by type, 1990-2011

Donor group or country	Growth rate of ODA (2010 prices and exchange rates)					ODA as a percentage of GNI	Total ODA (millions of dollars)	Percentage distribution of ODA by type, 2011			
								Bilateral	Multilateral		
	1990-2000	2000-2008	2009	2010	2011	2011	2011	Total	Total (United Nations and Other)	United Nations	Other
Total DAC countries	**-0.5**	**5.2**	**1.1**	**6.3**	**-2.7**	**0.31**	**133 526**	**69.4**	**30.6**	**4.8**	**25.8**
Total EU	-0.3	5.8	-0.2	6.1	-2.7	0.45	72 315	60.5	39.5	5.1	34.4
Austria	4.9	11.7	-31.6	9.5	-14.3	0.27	1 107	43.4	56.6	3.0	53.6
Belgium	-0.1	6.4	12.0	18.9	-13.3	0.53	2 800	57.2	42.8	6.1	36.7
Denmark	4.2	-0.8	3.3	3.9	-2.4	0.86	2 981	73.9	26.1	09.4	16.7
Finland	-4.6	7.0	12.7	8.2	-4.3	0.52	1 409	60.6	39.4	11.7	27.7
France[a]	-2.5	3.7	19.1	6.9	-5.6	0.46	12 994	65.4	34.6	1.8	32.8
Germany	-0.8	6.2	-11.5	12.4	5.9	0.40	14 533	61.4	38.6	2.3	36.3
Greece	...	6.2	-13.0	-13.6	-39.3	0.11	331	18.1	81.9	3.7	78.2
Ireland	13.2	14.6	-18.2	-4.1	-3.1	0.52	904	67.8	32.2	10.0	22.2
Italy	-6.7	4.7	-31.2	-4.8	33.0	0.19	4 241	37.4	62.6	3.8	58.8
Luxembourg	17.1	7.2	3.4	-2.7	-5.4	0.99	413	68.7	31.3	12.6	18.7
Netherlands	1.9	2.6	-4.4	2.7	-6.4	0.75	6 324	66.3	33.7	10.6	23.1
Portugal	5.5	1.1	-14.8	31.6	-3.0	0.29	669	66.6	33.4	0.5	32.9
Spain	8.1	10.5	-0.8	-5.4	-32.7	0.29	4 264	54.6	45.4	5.4	40.1
Sweden	-0.5	8.1	7.9	-7.3	10.5	1.02	5606	65.4	34.6	12.1	22.5
United Kingdom	1.5	9.3	11.8	13.8	-0.8	0.56	13 739	58.4	41.6	4.1	37.6
Australia	0.1	5.1	-0.4	12.0	5.7	0.35	4 799	85.1	14.9	4.7	10.2
Canada	-2.8	4.7	-9.7	14.2	-5.3	0.31	5 291	76.5	23.5	5.4	18.1
Japan	0.8	-2.2	-10.8	12.0	-10.8	0.18	10 604	59.1	40.9	4.7	36.2
New Zealand	3.1	4.7	-2.3	-6.4	10.7	0.28	429	76.1	23.9	10.7	13.2
Norway	1.9	3.6	18.7	1.2	-8.3	1.00	4 936	76.0	24.0	13.0	11.0
Switzerland	2.4	3.9	11.9	-4.3	13.2	0.46	3 086	76.5	23.5	6.3	17.2
United States	-2.7	9.8	7.9	4.1	-0.9	0.20	30 745	88.2	11.8	2.6	9.2

Source: UN/DESA, based on OECD/DAC online database, available from http://www.oecd-ilibrary.org/statistics.

a Excluding flows from France to the Overseas Departments, namely Guadeloupe, French Guiana, Martinique and Réunion.

Table A.20

Total net ODA flows from OECD Development Assistance Committee countries, by type, 2002–2011

	2002	2003	2004	2005	2006	2007	2008	2009	2010	2011
	Net disbursements at current prices and exchange rates *(billions of dollars)*									
Official Development Assistance	58.6	69.4	79.9	107.8	104.8	104.2	122.0	119.8	128.5	133.5
Bilateral official development assistance	41.0	50.0	54.6	82.9	77.3	73.4	86.8	83.7	91.0	92.9
of which:										
Technical cooperation	15.5	18.4	18.7	20.8	22.4	15.0	17.2	17.5	19.0	0.9
Humanitarian aid	2.8	4.4	5.2	7.1	6.7	6.5	8.8	8.6	9.3	9.7
Debt forgiveness	5.4	9.8	8.0	26.2	18.9	9.7	11.1	1.9	4.2	0.1
Bilateral loans	1.1	-1.1	-2.8	-0.9	-2.4	-2.3	-1.2	2.5	3.3	..
Contributions to multilateral institutions[a]	17.6	19.5	25.2	24.9	27.5	30.8	35.1	36.1	37.5	40.7

Source: UN/DESA, based on OECD/DAC online database, available at http://www.oecd.org/dac/stats/idsonline.

a Grants and capital subscriptions. Does not include concessional lending to multilateral agencies.

Table A.21

Commitments and net flows of financial resources, by selected multilateral institutions, 2002–2011

Billions of dollars										
	2002	*2003*	*2004*	*2005*	*2006*	*2007*	*2008*	*2009*	*2010*	*2011*
Resource commitments[a]	**95.3**	**67.6**	**55.9**	**71.7**	**64.7**	**74.5**	**135.2**	**193.7**	**245.4**	**163.8**
Financial institutions, excluding International Monetary Fund (IMF)	38.5	43.1	45.7	51.4	55.7	66.6	76.1	114.5	119.6	106.8
Regional development banks[b]	16.8	20.4	21.5	23.0	23.1	31.3	36.1	54.4	45.4	45.9
World Bank Group[c]	21.4	22.2	23.7	27.7	31.9	34.7	39.4	59.4	73.4	59.9
International Bank for Reconstruction and Development	10.2	10.6	10.8	13.6	14.2	12.8	13.5	32.9	44.2	26.7
International Development Association	8.0	7.6	8.4	8.7	9.5	11.9	11.2	14.0	14.6	16.3
International Financial Corporation	3.2	4.1	4.6	5.4	8.2	10.0	14.6	12.4	14.6	16.9
International Fund for Agricultural Development	0.4	0.4	0.5	0.7	0.7	0.6	0.6	0.7	0.8	1.0
International Monetary Fund	52.2	17.8	2.6	12.6	1.0	2.0	48.7	68.2	114.1	45.7
United Nations operational agencies[d]	4.6	6.7	7.6	7.7	8.3	6.3	10.5	11.0	11.6	11.3
Net flows	**2.0**	**-11.7**	**-20.2**	**-39.6**	**-25.9**	**-6.8**	**40.7**	**52.3**	**62.5**	**77.2**
Financial institutions, excluding IMF	-11.2	-14.8	-10.2	0.8	5.2	-11.4	21.8	20.4	25.1	36.5
Regional development banks[b]	-3.9	-8.0	-6.6	-1.7	3.0	5.9	21.2	15.5	9.8	10.2
World Bank Group[c]	-7.3	-6.7	-3.7	2.5	2.2	5.5	0.7	4.9	15.4	26.3
International Bank for Reconstruction and Development	-12.1	-11.2	-8.9	-2.9	-5.1	-1.8	-6.2	-2.1	8.3	17.2
International Development Association	4.8	4.5	5.3	5.4	7.3	7.2	6.8	7.0	7.0	9.1
International Monetary Fund	13.2	3.1	-10.0	-40.4	-31.0	-18.0	18.9	32.0	37.4	40.7
Memorandum item (in units of 2000 purchasing power)[e]										
Resource commitments	97.2	62.6	47.8	59.8	54.9	56.0	97.3	146.7	183.1	242.5
Net flows	2.0	-10.8	-17.3	-33.0	-21.9	-5.1	29.3	39.6	46.6	114.3

Sources: Annual reports of the relevant multilateral institutions, various issues.

a Loans, grants, technical assistance and equity participation, as appropriate; all data are on a calendar year basis.

b African Development Bank (AfDB), Asian Development Bank (ADB), Caribbean Development Bank (CDB), European Bank for Reconstruction and Development (EBRD), Inter-American Development Bank (IaDB) (including Inter-American Investment Corporation (IaIC)).

c Data is for fiscal year.

d United Nations Development Program (UNDP), United Nations Population Fund (UNFPA), United Nations Children's Fund (UNICEF) and the World Food Programme (WFP).

e Totals deflated by the United Nations index of manufactured export prices (in dollars) of developed economies: 2000=100.

Table A.22
Greenhouse gas emissions[a] of Annex I Parties to the United Nations Framework Convention on Climate Change, 1990–2014

Teragram CO_2 equivalent

	1990	2000	2009	2010	2011[b]	2012[b]	2013[c]	2014[c]	Annual growth rate 1990-2014	Cumulative change between 1990 and 2014	Reached reduction commitments in 2012[d]
Australia	418	494	547	543	548	556	558	562	1.2	34.6	No
Austria	78	80	80	85	85	87	86	86	0.4	10.6	No
Belarus	139	79	88	89	89	82	75	68	-3.0	-51.4	-
Belgium	143	146	125	132	123	121	111	108	-1.2	-24.5	Yes
Bulgaria	114	63	59	61	55	47	43	39	-4.3	-65.6	Yes
Canada	589	718	690	692	691	685	677	677	0.6	14.9	No
Croatia	31	26	29	29	28	27	27	27	-0.7	-15.1	Yes
Czech Republic	196	146	135	139	135	124	117	111	-2.4	-43.5	Yes
Denmark	70	70	62	63	55	53	51	49	-1.5	-30.2	Yes
Estonia	41	17	16	21	23	20	15	14	-4.4	-66.2	Yes
Finland	70	69	66	75	73	63	61	59	-0.7	-15.6	Yes
France	562	569	520	528	503	490	477	467	-0.8	-16.9	Yes
Germany	1 246	1 039	912	937	915	876	848	832	-1.7	-33.2	Yes
Greece	105	127	125	118	111	102	98	97	-0.3	-7.5	No
Hungary	97	77	67	68	61	58	53	51	-2.6	-47.4	Yes
Iceland	4	4	5	5	5	5	5	5	1.3	36.4	No
Ireland	55	68	62	61	55	50	46	44	-0.9	-20.2	Yes
Italy	519	552	492	501	486	466	453	452	-0.6	-13.0	Yes
Japan	1 267	1 342	1 207	1 258	1 221	1 219	1 194	1 191	-0.2	-4.6	No
Latvia	27	10	11	12	10	12	14	15	-2.4	-43.8	Yes
Liechtenstein	–	–	–	–	–	–	–	–	-0.5	-13.8	No
Lithuania	49	19	20	21	15	12	10	8	-7.3	-83.6	Yes
Luxembourg	13	10	12	12	13	13	14	13	0.1	2.6	No
Malta	2	3	3	3	3	3	3	3	1.6	45.2	-
Monaco	–	–	–	–	–	–	–	–	-1.2	-26.9	Yes
Netherlands	212	213	199	210	212	215	210	207	-0.1	-2.2	No
New Zealand	60	69	71	72	71	70	70	70	0.6	16.7	No
Norway	50	53	51	54	48	46	45	44	-0.6	-12.5	Yes
Poland	457	385	382	401	384	398	367	337	-1.2	-25.8	Yes
Portugal	60	82	74	71	66	64	59	58	-0.2	-3.7	No
Romania	253	141	123	121	113	102	95	88	-4.3	-65.4	Yes
Russian Federation	3 349	2 040	2 112	2 202	2 347	2 499	2 668	2 873	-0.6	-14.2	Yes
Slovakia	72	49	44	46	41	40	35	32	-3.3	-54.9	Yes
Slovenia	18	19	19	20	20	20	20	21	0.5	13.7	No
Spain	283	381	366	356	331	298	265	236	-0.7	-16.4	No
Sweden	73	69	60	66	63	64	55	51	-1.5	-29.8	Yes
Switzerland	53	52	52	54	53	52	52	51	-0.1	-3.2	No

Table A.22 (cont'd)											
	1990	*2000*	*2009*	*2010*	*2011*[b]	*2012*[b]	*2013*[c]	*2014*[c]	*Annual growth rate 1990-2014*	*Cumulative change between 1990 and 2014*	*Reached reduction commitments in 2012*[d]
Turkey	187	297	370	402	435	449	464	484	4.0	158.7	-
Ukraine	930	396	365	383	381	374	378	377	-3.7	-59.4	Yes
United Kingdom	767	674	576	594	561	541	499	475	-2.0	-38.1	Yes
United States	6 161	7 072	6 588	6 802	6 460	6 132	5 813	5 658	-0.4	-8.2	No
All Annex I Parties	**18 822**	**17 720**	**16 785**	**17 305**	**16 891**	**16 534**	**16 131**	**16 043**	**-0.7**	**-14.7**	

Source: UN/DESA, based on data of the United Nations Framework Convention on Climate Change (UNFCCC) online database, available from http://unfccc.int/ghg_data/ghg_data_unfccc/data_sources/items/3816.php (accessed on 8 November 2012).

Note: Based on the historical data provided by the UNFCCC for the GHG emissions of the Annex 1 Parties up to 2010, DESA/DPAD extrapolated the data to 2013. The extrapolation is based on the following procedure:

- GHG/GDP intensity for each country is modelled using time-series regression techniques, to reflect the historical trend of GHG/GDP. While the trend for each individual country would usually be a complex function of such factors as change in structure of the economy, technology change, emission mitigation measures, as well as other economic and environmental policies, the time-series modelling could be considered a reduced form of a more complex structural modelling for the relations between economic output and GHG emissions.
- GHG/GDP intensity for each country is extrapolated for the out-of-sample period (2011-2014), using parameters derived from the time-series regression model.
- In some cases, the extrapolated GHG/GDP intensity for individual countries was adjusted to take account of announced emission control measures taken by Governments.
- The projected GHG emissions were arrived at using GDP estimates in accordance with the *World Economic Situation and Prospects 2013* baseline forecast and the extrapolated GHG/GDP intensity.

a   Without land use, land-use change and forestry.
b   Estimated.
c   Baseline scenario forecasts.
d   Based on UN/DESA estimates of emission levels for 2012. There was no established commitments for Belarus, Malta and Turkey.

United Nations publication
Sales No. E.13.II.C.2
ISBN 978-92-1-109166-3